THE BLACK ATLANTIC

Modernity and Double Consciousness

PAUL GILROY

The Black Atlantic

The Black Atlantic

Modernity and Double Consciousness

Paul Gilroy

Harvard University Press
Cambridge, Massachusetts

James Weldon Johnson, "O Black and Unknown Bards," copyright 1917 by James Weldon
Johnson, from *Saint Peter Relates an Incident* by James Weldon Johnson. Used by permission of Viking Penguin, a division of Penguin Books USA Inc.

Percy Mayfield, "The River's Invitation," on *The Incredible Percy Mayfield,* Specialty
Records, SNTF 5010, 1972. Used by permission of MCA Music Limited.

Richard Wright, quotations from manuscript "Melody Limited," Yale Collection of American Literature, Beinecke Rare Book and Manuscript Library, Yale University. Reprinted by
permission of Ellen Wright for the estate of Richard Wright.

Richard Wright, excerpts from *The Outsider* copyright 1953 by Richard Wright. Reprinted
by permission of HarperCollins Publishers.

This book is printed on acid-free paper, and its binding materials
have been chosen for strength and durability.

Library of Congress Cataloging-in-Publication Data

Gilroy, Paul.
    The black Atlantic : modernity and double consciousness / Paul
Gilroy.
        p.   cm.
    Includes bibliographical references (p.) and index.
    ISBN 0–674–07605–2 (acid-free paper) (cloth)
    ISBN 0-674-07606-0 (pbk.)
    1. Blacks—Intellectual life. 2. Afro-Americans—Intellectual
life. 3. Afrocentrism. I. Title.
    CB235.G55 1993
    305.896'073—dc20
    93–16042
        CIP

For Cora Hatshepsut
and my mother

Contents

Preface

THIS BOOK WAS FIRST CONCEIVED while I was working at South Bank Polytechnic in London's Elephant and Castle. It grew from a difficult period when I was lecturing on the history of sociology to a large group of second-year students who had opted not to study that subject as a major part of their degree. The flight from sociology was, for many of them, a deliberate sign of their disengagement from the life of the mind. To make things worse, these lectures were very early in the morning. With the help of writers like Michel Foucault, Marshall Berman, Richard Sennett, Fredric Jameson, Jurgen Habermas, Stuart Hall, Cornel West, Jane Flax, bell hooks, Donna Haraway, Nancy Hartsock, Sandra Harding, Janet Wolff, Seyla Benhabib, and Zygmunt Bauman, as well as a good dose of the classics, I would try to persuade them that the history and the legacy of the Enlightenment were worth understanding and arguing about. I worked hard to punctuate the flow of the Europe-centred material with observations drawn from the dissonant contributions of black writers to Enlightenment and counter-Enlightenment concerns.

The Black Atlantic developed from my uneven attempts to show these students that the experiences of black people were part of the abstract modernity they found so puzzling and to produce as evidence some of the things that black intellectuals had said—sometimes as defenders of the West, sometimes as its sharpest critics—about their sense of embeddedness in the modern world.

Chapter 1 sets out the dimensions of the polemical arguments that are developed in more detail later. It shows how different nationalist paradigms for thinking about cultural history fail when confronted by the intercultural and transnational formation that I call the black Atlantic. It makes some political and philosophical claims for black vernacular culture and casts a fresh eye on the history of black nationalist thought that has had to repress its own ambivalence about exile from Africa.

Chapter 2 was prompted by the absence of a concern with "race" or ethnicity from most contemporary writings about modernity. It argues that racial slavery was integral to western civilisation and looks in detail at the master/mistress/slave relationship which is foundational to both black critiques and affirmations of modernity. It argues that the literary and philosophical modernisms of the black Atlantic have their origins in a well-developed sense of the complicity of racialised reason and white supremacist terror.

Chapter 3 pursues these themes in conjunction with a historical commentary on aspects of black music. It offers an inventory of queries about the ideas of ethnic authenticity that are routinely constructed through discussions of that music, the gender identities it celebrates, and the images of "race" as family that have become an important part of both producing and interpreting it. The chapter tries to demonstrate why the polarisation between essentialist and anti-essentialist theories of black identity has become unhelpful. It proposes that analyzing the history of black Atlantic music might play a useful role in constructing a more satisfactory set of anti-anti-essentialist arguments.

Chapter 4 examines a small part of the work of W. E. B. Du Bois, whose stimulating theory of "double consciousness" provides one of the central organising themes of my own work. It questions the location of his work in the emergent canon of African-American cultural history and explores the impact of his Pan-Africanism and anti-imperialism on the elements of his thinking that were configured by a belief in African-American exceptionalism. This chapter is intended to show how black Atlantic political culture changed as it moved out of the early phases that had been dominated by the need to escape slavery and various attempts to acquire meaningful citizenship in post-emancipation societies. I suggest that Du Bois's travels and studentship in Europe transformed his understanding of "race" and its place in the modern world.

Chapter 5 continues this line of argument with a parallel discussion of Richard Wright's work and critical responses to it. In his case, black Atlantic politics is re-examined against the backgrounds of European fascism and the construction of post-colonial, independent nation states in Africa and elsewhere. Wright is defended against those tendencies in African-American literary criticism which argue that the work he produced while living in Europe was worthless when compared to his supposedly authentic earlier writings. He is applauded for his attempts to link the plight of black Americans with the experiences of other colonised peoples and to build a theory of racial subordination that included a psychology.

The book concludes with a critical discussion of Africentrism and the way it has understood the idea of tradition as invariant repetition rather than a stimulus toward innovation and change. This chapter includes a meditation on the diaspora concept which was imported into Pan-African politics and black history from unacknowledged Jewish sources. I suggest that this concept should be cherished for its ability to pose the relationship between ethnic sameness and differentiation: a *changing* same. I also argue that exchanges between blacks and Jews are important for the future of black Atlantic cultural politics as well as for its history.

It is essential to emphasise that there is nothing definitive here. Black Atlantic culture is so massive and its history so little known that I have done scarcely more than put down some preliminary markers for more detailed future investigations. My concerns are heuristic and my conclusions are strictly provisional. There are also many obvious omissions. I have said virtually nothing about the lives, theories, and political activities of Frantz Fanon and C. L. R. James, the two best-known black Atlantic thinkers. Their lives fit readily into the pattern of movement, transformation, and relocation that I have described. But they are already well known if not as widely read as they should be, and other people have begun the labour of introducing their writings into contemporary critical theory.

There are two aspirations that I would like to share with readers before they embark on the sea voyage that I would like reading this book to represent. Neither aspiration is restricted by the racialised examples I have used to give them substance. The first is my hope that the contents of this book are unified by a concern to repudiate the dangerous obsessions with "racial" purity which are circulating inside and outside black politics. It is, after all, essentially an essay about the inescapable hybridity and intermixture of ideas. The second is my desire that the book's heartfelt plea against the closure of the categories with which we conduct our political lives will not go unheard. The history of the black Atlantic yields a course of lessons as to the instability and mutability of identities which are always unfinished, always being remade.

What matters for the dialectician is having the wind of world history in his sails. Thinking for him means: to set the sails. It is the way they are set that matters. Words are his sails. The way they are set turns them into concepts.

Walter Benjamin

We have left the land and have embarked. We have burned our bridges behind us— indeed, we have gone farther and destroyed the land behind us. Now, little ship, look out! Beside you is the ocean: to be sure, it does not always roar, and at times it lies spread out like silk and gold and reveries of graciousness. But hours will come when you realize that it is infinite and that there is nothing more awesome than infinity. Oh, the poor bird that felt free now strikes the walls of this cage! Woe, when you feel homesick for the land as if it had offered more *freedom*—and there is no longer any "land."

Nietzsche

In my clothing I was rigged out in sailor style. I had on a red shirt and a tarpaulin hat and black cravat, tied in sailor fashion, carelessly and loosely about my neck. My knowledge of ships and sailors' talk came much to my assistance, for I knew a ship from stem to stern, and from keelson to crosstrees, and could talk sailor like an "old salt."

Frederick Douglass

1

The Black Atlantic as a Counterculture of Modernity

We who are homeless,—Among Europeans today there is no lack of those who are entitled to call themselves homeless in a distinctive and honourable sense . . . We children of the future, how could we be at home in this today? We feel disfavour for all ideals that might lead one to feel at home even in this fragile, broken time of transition; as for "realities," we do not believe that they will last. The ice that still supports people today has become very thin; the wind that brings the thaw is blowing; we ourselves who are homeless constitute a force that breaks open ice and other all too thin "realities."

> *Nietzsche*

On the notion of modernity. It is a vexed question. Is not every era "modern" in relation to the preceding one? It seems that at least one of the components of "our" modernity is the spread of the awareness we have of it. The awareness of our awareness (the double, the second degree) is our source of strength and our torment.

> *Edouard Glissant*

STRIVING TO BE both European and black requires some specific forms of double consciousness. By saying this I do not mean to suggest that taking on either or both of these unfinished identities necessarily exhausts the subjective resources of any particular individual. However, where racist, nationalist, or ethnically absolutist discourses orchestrate political relationships so that these identities appear to be mutually exclusive, occupying the space between them or trying to demonstrate their continuity has been viewed as a provocative and even oppositional act of political insubordination.

The contemporary black English, like the Anglo-Africans of earlier generations and perhaps, like all blacks in the West, stand between (at least) two great cultural assemblages, both of which have mutated through the course of the modern world that formed them and assumed new configurations. At present, they remain locked symbiotically in an antagonistic relationship marked out by the symbolism of colours which adds to the conspicuous cultural power of their central Manichean dynamic—black and white. These colours support a special rhetoric that has grown to be associated with a language of nationality and national belonging as well as the languages of "race" and ethnic identity.

Though largely ignored by recent debates over modernity and its discontents, these ideas about nationality, ethnicity, authenticity, and cultural integrity are characteristically modern phenomena that have profound implications for cultural criticism and cultural history. They crystallised with the revolutionary transformations of the West at the end of the eighteenth and the beginning of the nineteenth centuries and involved novel typologies and modes of identification. Any shift towards a postmodern condition should not, however, mean that the conspicuous power of these modern subjectivities and the movements they articulated has been left behind. Their power has, if anything, grown, and their ubiquity as a means to make political sense of the world is currently unparalleled by the languages of class and socialism by which they once appeared to have been surpassed. My concern here is less with explaining their longevity and enduring appeal than with exploring some of the special political problems that arise from the fatal junction of the concept of nationality with the concept of culture and the affinities and affiliations which link the blacks of the West to one of their adoptive, parental cultures: the intellectual heritage of the West since the Enlightenment. I have become fascinated with how successive generations of black intellectuals have understood this connection and how they have projected it in their writing and speaking in pursuit of freedom, citizenship, and social and political autonomy.

If this appears to be little more than a roundabout way of saying that the reflexive cultures and consciousness of the European settlers and those of the Africans they enslaved, the "Indians" they slaughtered, and the Asians they indentured were not, even in situations of the most extreme brutality, sealed off hermetically from each other, then so be it. This seems as though it ought to be an obvious and self-evident observation, but its stark character has been systematically obscured by commentators from all sides of political opinion. Regardless of their affiliation to the right, left, or centre, groups have fallen back on the idea of cultural nationalism, on the overintegrated conceptions of culture which present immutable, ethnic differences as an absolute break in the histories and experiences of "black" and "white" people. Against this choice stands another, more difficult option: the theorisation of creolisation, métissage, mestizaje, and hybridity. From the viewpoint of ethnic absolutism, this would be a litany of pollution and impurity. These terms are rather unsatisfactory ways of naming the processes of cultural mutation and restless (dis)continuity that exceed racial discourse and avoid capture by its agents.

This book addresses one small area in the grand consequence of this historical conjunction—the stereophonic, bilingual, or bifocal cultural forms originated by, but no longer the exclusive property of, blacks dispersed within the structures of feeling, producing, communicating, and remembering that I have heuristically called the black Atlantic world. This chapter is therefore rooted in and routed through the special stress that grows with the effort involved in trying to face (at least) two ways at once.

My concerns at this stage are primarily conceptual: I have tried to address the continuing lure of ethnic absolutisms in cultural criticism produced both by blacks and by whites. In particular, this chapter seeks to explore the special relationships between "race," culture, nationality, and ethnicity which have a bearing on the histories and political cultures of Britain's black citizens. I have argued elsewhere that the cultures of this group have been produced in a syncretic pattern in which the styles and forms of the Caribbean, the United States, and Africa have been reworked and reinscribed in the novel context of modern Britain's own untidy ensemble of regional and class-oriented conflicts. Rather than make the invigorating flux of those mongrel cultural forms my focal concern here, I want instead to look at broader questions of ethnic identity that have contributed to the scholarship and the political strategies that Britain's black settlers have generated and to the underlying sense of England as a cohesive cultural community against which their self-conception has so often been defined. Here the ideas of nation, nationality, national belonging, and nationalism are paramount. They are extensively supported by a clutch of rhetorical strategies that can be named "cultural insiderism."[1] The essential trademark of cultural insiderism which also supplies the key to its popularity is an absolute sense of ethnic difference. This is maximised so that it distinguishes people from one another and at the same time acquires an incontestable priority over all other dimensions of their social and historical experience, cultures, and identities. Characteristically, these claims are associated with the idea of national belonging or the aspiration to nationality and other more local but equivalent forms of cultural kinship. The range and complexity of these ideas in English cultural life defies simple summary or exposition. However, the forms of cultural insiderism they sanction typically construct the nation as an ethnically homogeneous object and invoke ethnicity a second time in the hermeneutic procedures deployed to make sense of its distinctive cultural content.

The intellectual seam in which English cultural studies has positioned itself—through innovative work in the fields of social history and literary criticism—can be indicted here. The statist modalities of Marxist analysis that view modes of material production and political domination as exclusively *national* entities are only one source of this problem. Another factor, more evasive but nonetheless potent for its intangible ubiquity, is a quiet cultural nationalism which pervades the work of some radical thinkers. This crypto-nationalism means that they are often disinclined to consider the cross catalytic or transverse dynamics of racial politics as a significant element in the formation and reproduction of English national identities. These formations are treated as if they spring, fully formed, from their own special viscera.

My search for resources with which to comprehend the doubleness and cultural intermixture that distinguish the experience of black Britons in contemporary Europe required me to seek inspiration from other sources and, in effect, to make an intellectual journey across the Atlantic. In black America's histories of cultural and political debate and organisation I found another, second perspective with which to orient my own position. Here too the lure of ethnic particularism and nationalism has provided an ever-present danger. But that narrowness of vision which is content with the merely national has also been challenged from within that black community by thinkers who were prepared to renounce the easy claims of African-American exceptionalism in favour of a global, coalitional politics in which anti-imperialism and anti-racism might be seen to interact if not to fuse. The work of some of those thinkers will be examined in subsequent chapters.

This chapter also proposes some new chronotopes[2] that might fit with a theory that was less intimidated by and respectful of the boundaries and integrity of modern nation states than either English or African-American cultural studies have so far been. I have settled on the image of ships in motion across the spaces between Europe, America, Africa, and the Caribbean as a central organising symbol for this enterprise and as my starting point. The image of the ship—a living, micro-cultural, micro-political system in motion—is especially important for historical and theoretical reasons that I hope will become clearer below. Ships immediately focus attention on the middle passage, on the various projects for redemptive return to an African homeland, on the circulation of ideas and activists as well as the movement of key cultural and political artefacts: tracts, books, gramophone records, and choirs.

The rest of this chapter falls into three sections. The first part addresses some conceptual problems common to English and African-American versions of cultural studies which, I argue, share a nationalistic focus that is antithetical to the rhizomorphic, fractal structure of the transcultural, international formation I call the black Atlantic. The second section uses the life and writings of Martin Robison Delany, an early architect of black nationalism whose influence still registers in contemporary political movements, to bring the black Atlantic to life and to extend the general arguments by introducing a number of key themes that will be used to map the responses to modernity's promises and failures produced by later thinkers. The final section explores the specific counterculture of modernity produced by black intellectuals and makes some preliminary points about the internality of blacks to the West. It initiates a polemic which runs through the rest of the book against the ethnic absolutism that currently dominates black political culture.

Cultural Studies in Black and White

Any satisfaction to be experienced from the recent spectacular growth of cultural studies as an academic project should not obscure its conspicuous problems with ethnocentrism and nationalism. Understanding these difficulties might commence with a critical evaluation of the ways in which notions of ethnicity have been mobilised, often by default rather than design, as part of the distinctive hermeneutics of cultural studies or with the unthinking assumption that cultures always flow into patterns congruent with the borders of essentially homogeneous nation states. The marketing and inevitable reification of cultural studies as a discrete academic subject also has what might be called a secondary ethnic aspect. The project of cultural studies is a more or less attractive candidate for institutionalisation according to the ethnic garb in which it appears. The question of whose cultures are being studied is therefore an important one, as is the issue of where the instruments which will make that study possible are going to come from. In these circumstances it is hard not to wonder how much of the recent international enthusiasm for cultural studies is generated by its profound associations with England and ideas of Englishness. This possibility can be used as a point of entry into consideration of the ethnohistorical specificity of the discourse of cultural studies itself.

Looking at cultural studies from an ethnohistorical perspective requires more than just noting its association with English literature, history, and New Left politics. It necessitates constructing an account of the borrowings made by these English initiatives from wider, modern, European traditions of thinking about culture, and at every stage examining the place which these cultural perspectives provide for the images of their racialised[3] others as objects of knowledge, power, and cultural criticism. It is imperative, though very hard, to combine thinking about these issues with consideration of the pressing need to get black cultural expressions, analyses, and histories taken seriously in academic circles rather than assigned via the idea of "race relations" to sociology and thence abandoned to the elephants' graveyard to which intractable policy issues go to await their expiry. These two important conversations pull in different directions and sometimes threaten to cancel each other out, but it is the struggle to have blacks perceived as agents, as people with cognitive capacities and even with an intellectual history—attributes denied by modern racism—that is for me the primary reason for writing this book. It provides a valuable warrant for questioning some of the ways in which ethnicity is appealed to in the English idioms of cultural theory and history, and in the scholarly productions of black America. Understanding the political culture of blacks in Britain demands close attention to both these traditions. This book is situated on their cusp.

Histories of cultural studies seldom acknowledge how the politically radical and openly interventionist aspirations found in the best of its scholarship are already articulated to black cultural history and theory. These links are rarely seen or accorded any significance. In England, the work of figures like C. L. R. James and Stuart Hall offers a wealth of both symbols and concrete evidence for the practical links between these critical political projects. In the United States the work of interventionist scholars like bell hooks and Cornel West as well as that of more orthodox academics like Henry Louis Gates, Jr., Houston A. Baker, Jr., Anthony Appiah, and Hazel Carby, points to similar convergences. The position of these thinkers in the contested "contact zones"[4] between cultures and histories is not, however, as exceptional as it might appear at first. We shall see below that successive generations of black intellectuals (especially those whose lives, like James's, crisscrossed the Atlantic Ocean) noted this intercultural positionality and accorded it a special significance before launching their distinct modes of cultural and political critique. They were often urged on in their labour by the brutal absurdity of racial classification that derives from and also celebrates racially exclusive conceptions of national identity from which blacks were excluded as either non-humans or non-citizens. I shall try to show that their marginal endeavours point to some new analytic possibilities with a general significance far beyond the well-policed borders of black particularity. For example, this body of work offers intermediate concepts, lodged between the local and the global, which have a wider applicability in cultural history and politics precisely because they offer an alternative to the nationalist focus which dominates cultural criticism. These intermediate concepts, especially the undertheorised idea of diaspora examined in Chapter 6, are exemplary precisely because they break the dogmatic focus on discrete *national* dynamics which has characterised so much modern Euro-American cultural thought.

Getting beyond these national and nationalistic perspectives has become essential for two additional reasons. The first arises from the urgent obligation to reevaluate the significance of the modern nation state as a political, economic, and cultural unit. Neither political nor economic structures of domination are still simply co-extensive with national borders. This has a special significance in contemporary Europe, where new political and economic relations are being created seemingly day by day, but it is a worldwide phenomenon with significant consequences for the relationship between the politics of information and the practices of capital accumulation. Its effects underpin more recognisably political changes like the growing centrality of transnational ecological movements which, through their insistence on the association of sustainability and justice, do so much to shift the moral and scientific precepts on which the modern separation of politics and ethics was built. The second reason relates to the tragic popularity of ideas about the integrity and purity of cultures. In particular, it concerns the relationship between nationality and ethnicity. This too currently has a special force in Europe, but it is also reflected directly in the post-colonial histories and complex, transcultural, political trajectories of Britain's black settlers.

What might be called the peculiarity of the black English requires attention to the intermixture of a variety of distinct cultural forms. Previously separated political and intellectual traditions converged and, in their coming together, overdetermined the process of black Britain's social and historical formation. This blending is misunderstood if it is conceived in simple ethnic terms, but right and left, racist and anti-racist, black and white tacitly share a view of it as little more than a collision between fully formed and mutually exclusive cultural communities. This has become the dominant view where black history and culture are perceived, like black settlers themselves, as an illegitimate intrusion into a vision of authentic British national life that, prior to their arrival, was as stable and as peaceful as it was ethnically undifferentiated. Considering this history points to issues of power and knowledge that are beyond the scope of this book. However, though it arises from present rather than past conditions, contemporary British racism bears the imprint of the past in many ways. The especially crude and reductive notions of culture that form the substance of racial politics today are clearly associated with an older discourse of racial and ethnic difference which is everywhere entangled in the history of the idea of culture in the modern West. This history has itself become hotly contested since debates about multiculturalism, cultural pluralism, and the responses to them that are sometimes dismissively called "political correctness" arrived to query the ease and speed with which European particularisms are still being translated into absolute, universal standards for human achievement, norms, and aspirations.

It is significant that prior to the consolidation of scientific racism in the nineteenth century,[5] the term "race" was used very much in the way that the word "culture" is used today. But in the attempts to differentiate the true, the good, and the beautiful which characterise the junction point of capitalism, industrialisation, and political democracy and give substance to the discourse of western modernity, it is important to appreciate that scientists did not monopolise either the image of the black or the emergent concept of biologically based racial difference. As far as the future of cultural studies is concerned, it should be equally important that both were centrally employed in those European attempts to think through beauty, taste, and aesthetic judgement that are the precursors of contemporary cultural criticism.

Tracing the racial signs from which the discourse of cultural value was constructed and their conditions of existence in relation to European aesthetics and philosophy as well as European science can contribute much to an ethnohistorical reading of the aspirations of western modernity as a whole and to the critique of Enlightenment assumptions in particular. It is certainly the case that ideas about "race," ethnicity, and nationality form an important seam of continuity linking English cultural studies with one of its sources of inspiration—the doctrines of modern European aesthetics that are consistently configured by the appeal to national and often racial particularity.[6]

This is not the place to go deeply into the broader dimensions of this intellectual inheritance. Valuable work has already been done by Sander Gilman,[7] Henry Louis Gates, Jr.,[8] and others on the history and role of the image of the black in the discussions which found modern cultural axiology. Gilman points out usefully that the figure of the black appears in different forms in the aesthetics of Hegel, Schopenhauer, and Nietzsche (among others) as a marker for moments of cultural relativism and to support the production of aesthetic judgements of a supposedly universal character to differentiate, for example, between authentic music and, as Hegel puts it, "the most detestable noise." Gates emphasises a complex genealogy in which ambiguities in Montesquieu's discussion of slavery prompt responses in Hume that can be related, in turn, to philosophical debates over the nature of beauty and sublimity found in the work of Burke and Kant. Critical evaluation of these representations of blackness might also be connected to the controversies over the place of racism and anti-Semitism in the work of Enlightenment figures like Kant and Voltaire.[9] These issues deserve an extended treatment that cannot be provided here. What is essential for the purposes of this opening chapter is that debates of this sort should not be brought to an end simply by denouncing those who raise awkward or embarrassing issues as totalitarian forces working to legitimate their own political line. Nor should important enquiries into the contiguity of racialised reason and unreasonable racism be dismissed as trivial matters. These issues go to the heart of contemporary debates about what constitutes the canon of western civilisation and how this precious legacy should be taught.

In these embattled circumstances, it is regrettable that questions of "race" and representation have been so regularly banished from orthodox histories of western aesthetic judgement, taste, and cultural value.[10] There is a plea here that further enquiries should be made into precisely how discussions of "race," beauty, ethnicity, and culture have contributed to the critical thinking that eventually gave rise to cultural studies. The use of the concept of fetishism in Marxism and psychoanalytic studies is one obvious means to open up this problem.[11] The emphatically national character ascribed to the concept of modes of production (cultural and otherwise) is another fundamental question which demonstrates the ethnohistorical specificity of dominant approaches to cultural politics, social movements, and oppositional consciousnesses.

These general issues appear in a specific form in the distinctive English idioms of cultural reflection. Here too, the moral and political problem of slavery loomed large not least because it was once recognised as *internal* to the structure of western civilisation and appeared as a central political and philosophical concept in the emergent discourse of modern English cultural uniqueness.[12] Notions of the primitive and the civilised which had been integral to pre-modern understanding of "ethnic" differences became fundamental cognitive and aesthetic markers in the processes which generated a constellation of subject positions in which Englishness, Christianity, and other ethnic and racialised attributes would finally give way to the dislocating dazzle of "whiteness."[13] A small but telling insight into this can be found in Edmund Burke's discussion of the sublime, which has achieved a certain currency lately. He makes elaborate use of the association of darkness with blackness, linking them to the skin of a real, live black woman. Seeing her produces a sublime feeling of terror in a boy whose sight has been restored to him by a surgical operation.

> Perhaps it may appear on enquiry, that blackness and darkness are in some degree painful by their natural operation, independent of any associations whatever. I must observe that the ideas of blackness and darkness are much the same; and they differ only in this, that blackness is a more confined idea.
>
> Mr Cheselden has given us a very curious story of a boy who had

been born blind, and continued so until he was thirteen or fourteen years old; he was then couched for a cataract, by which operation he received his sight . . . Cheselden tells us that the first time the boy saw a black object, it gave him great uneasiness; and that some time after, upon accidentally seeing a negro woman, he was struck with great horror at the sight.[14]

Burke, who opposed slavery and argued for its gradual abolition, stands at the doorway of the tradition of enquiry mapped by Raymond Williams which is also the infrastructure on which much of English cultural studies came to be founded. This origin is part of the explanation of how some of the contemporary manifestations of this tradition lapse into what can only be called a morbid celebration of England and Englishness. These modes of subjectivity and identification acquire a renewed political charge in the post-imperial history that saw black settlers from Britain's colonies take up their citizenship rights as subjects in the United Kingdom. The entry of blacks into national life was itself a powerful factor contributing to the circumstances in which the formation of both cultural studies and New Left politics became possible. It indexes the profound transformations of British social and cultural life in the 1950s and stands, again usually unacknowledged, at the heart of laments for a more human scale of social living that seemed no longer practicable after the 1939–45 war.

The convoluted history of black settlement need not be recapitulated here. One recent fragment from it, the struggle over Salman Rushdie's book *The Satanic Verses,* is sufficient to demonstrate that racialised conflict over the meaning of English culture is still very much alive and to show that these antagonisms have become enmeshed in a second series of struggles in which Enlightenment assumptions about culture, cultural value, and aesthetics go on being tested by those who do not accept them as universal moral standards. These conflicts are, in a sense, the outcome of a distinct historical period in which a new, ethnically absolute and culturalist racism was produced. It would explain the burning of books on English streets as manifestations of irreducible cultural differences that signposted the path to domestic racial catastrophe. This new racism was generated in part by the move towards a political discourse which aligned "race" closely with the idea of national belonging and which stressed complex cultural difference rather than simple biological hierarchy. These strange conflicts emerged in circumstances where blackness and Englishness appeared suddenly to be mutually exclusive attributes and where the conspicuous antagonism between them proceeded on the terrain of culture, not that of politics. Whatever view of Rushdie one holds, his fate offers another small, but significant, omen of the extent to which the almost metaphysical values of England and Englishness are currently being contested through their connection to "race" and ethnicity. His experiences are also a reminder of the difficulties involved in attempts to construct a more pluralistic, post-colonial sense of British culture and national identity. In this context, locating and answering the nationalism if not the racism and ethnocentrism of English cultural studies has itself become a directly political issue.

Returning to the imperial figures who supplied Raymond Williams with the raw material for his own brilliant critical reconstruction of English intellectual life is instructive. Apart from Burke, Thomas Carlyle, John Ruskin, Charles Kingsley, and the rest of Williams's cast of worthy characters can become valuable not simply in attempts to purge cultural studies of its doggedly ethnocentric focus but in the more ambitious and more useful task of actively reshaping contemporary England by reinterpreting the cultural core of its supposedly authentic national life. In the work of reinterpretation and reconstruction, reinscription and relocation required to transform England and Englishness, discussion of the cleavage in the Victorian intelligentsia around the response to Governor Eyre's handling of the Morant Bay Rebellion in Jamaica in 1865 is likely to be prominent.[15] Like the English responses to the 1857 uprising in India examined by Jenny Sharpe,[16] it may well turn out to be a much more formative moment than has so far been appreciated. Morant Bay is doubly significant because it represents an instance of metropolitan, internal conflict that emanates directly from an external colonial experience. These crises in imperial power demonstrate their continuity. It is part of my argument that this inside/outside relationship should be recognised as a more powerful, more complex, and more contested element in the historical, social, and cultural memory of our glorious nation than has previously been supposed.

I am suggesting that even the laudable, radical varieties of English cultural sensibility examined by Williams and celebrated by Edward Thompson and others were not produced spontaneously from their own internal and intrinsic dynamics. The fact that some of the most potent conceptions of Englishness have been constructed by alien outsiders like Carlyle, Swift, Scott, or Eliot should augment the note of caution sounded here. The most heroic, subaltern English nationalisms and countercultural patriotisms are perhaps better understood as having been generated in a complex pattern of antagonistic relationships with the supra-national and imperial world for which the ideas of "race," nationality, and national culture provide the primary (though not the only) indices. This approach would obviously bring William Blake's work into a rather different focus from that supplied by orthodox cultural history, and, as Peter Linebaugh has suggested, this overdue reassessment can be readily complemented by charting the long-neglected involvement of black slaves and their descendants in the radical history of our country in general and its working-class movements in particular.[17] Oluadah Equiano, whose involvement in the beginnings of organised working-class politics is now being widely recognised; the anarchist, Jacobin, ultra-radical, and Methodist heretic Robert Wedderburn; William Davidson, son of Jamaica's attorney general, hanged for his role in the Cato Street conspiracy to blow up the British cabinet in 1819;[18] and the Chartist William Cuffay are only the most urgent, obvious candidates for rehabilitation. Their lives offer invaluable means of seeing how thinking with and through the discourses and the imagery of "race" appears in the core rather than at the fringes of English political life. Davidson's speech from the scaffold before being subject to the last public decapitation in England is, for example, one moving appropriation of the rights of dissident freeborn Englishmen that is not widely read today.

Of this infamous trio, Wedderburn is perhaps the best known, thanks to the efforts of Peter Linebaugh and Iain McCalman.[19] The child of a slave dealer, James Wedderburn, and a slave woman, Robert was brought up by a Kingston conjure woman who acted as an agent for smugglers. He migrated to London at the age of seventeen in 1778. There, having published a number of disreputable ultra-radical tracts as part of his subversive political labours, he presented himself as a living embodiment of the horrors of slavery in a debating chapel in Hopkins Street near the Haymarket, where he preached a version of chiliastic anarchism based on the teachings of Thomas Spence and infused with deliberate blasphemy. In one of the debates held in his "ruinous hayloft with 200 persons of the lowest description," Wedderburn defended the inherent rights of the Caribbean slave to slay his master, promising to write home and "tell them to murder their masters as soon as they please." After this occasion he was tried and acquitted on a charge of blasphemy after persuading the jury that he had not been uttering sedition but merely practising the "true and infallible genius of prophetic skill."[20]

It is particularly significant for the direction of my overall argument that both Wedderburn and his sometime associate Davidson had been sailors, moving to and fro between nations, crossing borders in modern machines that were themselves micro-systems of linguistic and political hybridity. Their relationship to the sea may turn out to be especially important for both the early politics and poetics of the black Atlantic world that I wish to counterpose against the narrow nationalism of so much English historiography. Wedderburn served in the Royal Navy and as a privateer, while

Davidson, who ran away to sea instead of studying law, was pressed into naval service on two subsequent occasions. Davidson inhabited the same ultra-radical subculture as Wedderburn and was an active participant in the Marylebone Reading Society, a radical body formed in 1819 after the Peterloo massacre. He is known to have acted as the custodian of their black flag, which significantly bore a skull and crossbones with the legend "Let us die like men and not be sold as slaves," at an open air meeting in Smithfield later that year.[21] The precise details of how radical ideologies articulated the culture of the London poor before the institution of the factory system to the insubordinate maritime culture of pirates and other pre-industrial workers of the world will have to await the innovative labours of Peter Linebaugh and Marcus Rediker.[22] However, it has been estimated that at the end of the eighteenth century a quarter of the British navy was composed of Africans for whom the experience of slavery was a powerful orientation to the ideologies of liberty and justice. Looking for similar patterns on the other side of the Atlantic network we can locate Crispus Attucks at the head of his "motley rabble of saucy boys, negroes, mulattoes, Irish teagues and outlandish jack tars"[23] and can track Denmark Vesey sailing the Caribbean and picking up inspirational stories of the Haitian revolution (one of his co-conspirators testified that he had said they would "not spare one white skin alive for this was the plan they pursued in San Domingo").[24] There is also the shining example of Frederick Douglass, whose autobiographies reveal that he learnt of freedom in the North from Irish sailors while working as a ship's caulker in Baltimore. He had less to say about the embarrassing fact that the vessels he readied for the ocean—Baltimore Clippers—were slavers, the fastest ships in the world and the only craft capable of outrunning the British blockade. Douglass, who played a neglected role in English anti-slavery activity, escaped from bondage disguised as a sailor and put this success down to his ability to "talk sailor like an old salt."[25] These are only a few of the nineteenth-century examples. The involvement of Marcus Garvey, George Padmore, Claude McKay, and Langston Hughes with ships and sailors lends additional support to Linebaugh's prescient suggestion that "the ship remained perhaps the most important conduit of Pan-African communication before the appearance of the long-playing record."[26]

Ships and other maritime scenes have a special place in the work of J. M. W. Turner, an artist whose pictures represent, in the view of many contemporary critics, the pinnacle of achievement in the English school in painting. Any visitor to London will testify to the importance of the Clore Gallery as a national institution and of the place of Turner's art as an enduring expression of the very essence of English civilisation. Turner was secured on the summit of critical appreciation by John Ruskin, who, as we have seen, occupies a special place in Williams's constellation of great Englishmen. Turner's celebrated picture of a slave ship[27] throwing overboard its dead and dying as a storm comes on was exhibited at the Royal Academy to coincide with the world anti-slavery convention held in London in 1840. The picture, owned by Ruskin for some twenty-eight years, was rather more than an answer to the absentee Caribbean landlords who had commissioned its creator to record the tainted splendour of their country houses, which, as Patrick Wright has eloquently demonstrated, became an important signifier of the contemporary, ruralist distillate of national life.[28] It offered a powerful protest against the direction and moral tone of English politics. This was made explicit in an epigraph Turner took from his own poetry and which has itself retained a political inflection: "Hope, hope, fallacious hope where is thy market now?" Three years after his extensive involvement in the campaign to defend Governor Eyre,[29] Ruskin put the slave ship painting up for sale at Christie's. It is said that he had begun to find it too painful to live with. No buyer was found at that time, and he sold the picture to an American three years later. The painting has remained in the United States ever since. Its exile in Boston is yet another pointer towards the shape of the Atlantic as a system of cultural exchanges. It is more important, though, to draw attention to Ruskin's inability to discuss the picture except in terms of what it revealed about the aesthetics of painting water. He relegated the information that the vessel was a slave ship to a footnote in the first volume of *Modern Painters*.[30]

In spite of lapses like this, the New Left heirs to the aesthetic and cultural tradition in which Turner and Ruskin stand compounded and reproduced its nationalism and its ethnocentrism by denying imaginary, invented Englishness any external referents whatsoever. England ceaselessly gives birth to itself, seemingly from Britannia's head. The political affiliations and cultural preferences of this New Left group amplified these problems. They are most visible and most intense in the radical historiography that supplied a counterpart to Williams's subtle literary reflections. For all their enthusiasm for the work of C. L. R. James, the influential British Communist Party's historians' group[31] is culpable here. Their predilections for the image of the freeborn Englishman and the dream of socialism in one country that framed their work are both to be found wanting when it comes to nationalism. This uncomfortable pairing can be traced through the work of Edward Thompson and Eric Hobsbawm, visionary writers who contributed so much to the strong foundations of English cultural studies and who share a non-reductive Marxian approach to economic, social, and cultural history in which the nation—understood as a stable receptacle for counter-hegemonic class struggle—is the primary focus. These problems within English cultural studies form at its junction point with practical politics and instantiate wider difficulties with nationalism and with the discursive slippage or connotative resonance between "race," ethnicity, and nation.

Similar problems appear in rather different form in African-American letters where an equally volkish popular cultural nationalism is featured in the work of several generations of radical scholars and an equal number of not so radical ones. We will see below that absolutist conceptions of cultural difference allied to a culturalist understanding of "race" and ethnicity can be found in this location too.

In opposition to both of these nationalist or ethnically absolute approaches, I want to develop the suggestion that cultural historians could take the Atlantic as one single, complex unit of analysis in their discussions of the modern world and use it to produce an explicitly transnational and intercultural perspective.[32] Apart from the confrontation with English historiography and literary history this entails a challenge to the ways in which black American cultural and political histories have so far been conceived. I want to suggest that much of the precious intellectual legacy claimed by African-American intellectuals as the substance of their particularity is in fact only partly their absolute ethnic property. No less than in the case of the English New Left, the idea of the black Atlantic can be used to show that there are other claims to it which can be based on the structure of the African diaspora into the western hemisphere. A concern with the Atlantic as a cultural and political system has been forced on black historiography and intellectual history by the economic and historical matrix in which plantation slavery—"capitalism with its clothes off"—was one special moment. The fractal patterns of cultural and political exchange and transformation that we try and specify through manifestly inadequate theoretical terms like creolisation and syncretism indicate how both ethnicities and political cultures have been made anew in ways that are significant not simply for the peoples of the Caribbean but for Europe, for Africa, especially Liberia and Sierra Leone, and of course, for black America.

It bears repetition that Britain's black settler communities have forged a compound culture from disparate sources. Elements of political sensibility and cultural expression transmitted from black America over a long period of time have been reaccentuated in Britain. They are central, though no longer dominant, within the increasingly novel configurations that characterise another newer black vernacular culture. This is not content to be either dependent upon or simply imitative of the African diaspora cultures of America and the Caribbean. The rise and rise of Jazzie B and Soul II

Soul at the turn of the last decade constituted one valuable sign of this new assertive mood. North London's Funki Dreds, whose name itself projects a newly hybridised identity, have projected the distinct culture and rhythm of life of black Britain outwards into the world. Their song "Keep On Moving" was notable for having been produced in England by the children of Caribbean settlers and then re-mixed in a (Jamaican) dub format in the United States by Teddy Riley, an African-American. It included segments or samples of music taken from American and Jamaican records by the JBs and Mikey Dread respectively. This formal unity of diverse cultural elements was more than just a powerful symbol. It encapsulated the playful diasporic intimacy that has been a marked feature of transnational black Atlantic creativity. The record and its extraordinary popularity enacted the ties of affiliation and affect which articulated the discontinuous histories of black settlers in the new world. The fundamental injunction to "Keep On Moving" also expressed the restlessness of spirit which makes that diaspora culture vital. The contemporary black arts movement in film, visual arts, and theatre as well as music, which provided the background to this musical release, have created a new topography of loyalty and identity in which the structures and presuppositions of the nation state have been left behind because they are seen to be outmoded. It is important to remember that these recent black Atlantic phenomena may not be as novel as their digital encoding via the transnational force of north London's Soul II Soul suggests. Columbus's pilot, Pedro Nino, was also an African. The history of the black Atlantic since then, continually crisscrossed by the movements of black people—not only as commodities but engaged in various struggles towards emancipation, autonomy, and citizenship—provides a means to reexamine the problems of nationality, location, identity, and historical memory. They all emerge from it with special clarity if we contrast the national, nationalistic, and ethnically absolute paradigms of cultural criticism to be found in England and America with those hidden expressions, both residual and emergent, that attempt to be global or outer-national in nature. These traditions have supported countercultures of modernity that touched the workers' movement but are not reducible to it. They supplied important foundations on which it could build.

Turner's extraordinary painting of the slave ship remains a useful image not only for its self-conscious moral power and the striking way that it aims directly for the sublime in its invocation of racial terror, commerce, and England's ethico-political degeneration. It should be emphasised that ships were the living means by which the points within that Atlantic world were joined. They were mobile elements that stood for the shifting spaces in between the fixed places that they connected.[33] Accordingly they need

to be thought of as cultural and political units rather than abstract embodi-
ments of the triangular trade. They were something more—a means to
conduct political dissent and possibly a distinct mode of cultural production. The ship provides a chance to explore the articulations between the
discontinuous histories of England's ports, its interfaces with the wider
world.[34] Ships also refer us back to the middle passage, to the half-
remembered micro-politics of the slave trade and its relationship to both
industrialisation and modernisation. As it were, getting on board promises
a means to reconceptualise the orthodox relationship between modernity
and what passes for its prehistory. It provides a different sense of where
modernity might itself be thought to begin in the constitutive relationships
with outsiders that both found and temper a self-conscious sense of western civilisation.[35] For all these reasons, the ship is the first of the novel
chronotopes presupposed by my attempts to rethink modernity via the history of the black Atlantic and the African diaspora into the western hemisphere.

In the venturesome spirit proposed by James Clifford in his influential
work on travelling culture,[36] I want to consider the impact that this outer-
national, transcultural reconceptualisation might have on the political and
cultural history of black Americans and that of blacks in Europe. In recent
history, this will certainly mean reevaluating Garvey and Garveyism, pan-
Africanism, and Black Power as hemispheric if not global phenomena. In
periodising modern black politics it will require fresh thinking about the
importance of Haiti and its revolution for the development of African-
American political thought and movements of resistance. From the European side, it will no doubt be necessary to reconsider Frederick Douglass's
relationship to English and Scottish radicalisms and to meditate on the
significance of William Wells Brown's five years in Europe as a fugitive slave,
on Alexander Crummell's living and studying in Cambridge, and upon
Martin Delany's experiences at the London congress of the International
Statistical Congress in 1860.[37] It will require comprehension of such difficult and complex questions as W. E. B. Du Bois's childhood interest in
Bismarck, his investment in modelling his dress and moustache on that of
Kaiser Wilhelm II, his likely thoughts while sitting in Heinrich Von
Treitschke's seminars,[38] and the use his tragic heroes make of European
culture.

Notable black American travellers, from the poet Phyllis Wheatley onwards, went to Europe and had their perceptions of America and racial
domination shifted as a result of their experiences there. This had important consequences for their understanding of racial identities. The radical journalist and political organiser Ida B. Wells is typical, describing her

productive times in England as like "being born again in a new condition."[39] Lucy Parsons is a more problematic figure in the political history of black America,[40] but how might her encounters with William Morris, Annie Besant, and Peter Kropotkin impact upon a rewriting of the history of English radicalism? What of Nella Larsen's relationship to Denmark, where George Padmore was held in jail during the early 1930s and which was also the home base of his banned paper the *Negro Worker,* circulated across the world by its supporters in the Colonial Seamen's Association?[41] What of Sarah Parker Remond's work as a medical practitioner in Italy and the life of Edmonia Lewis,[42] the sculptor, who made her home in Rome? What effects did living in Paris have upon Anna Cooper, Jessie Fauset, Gwendolyn Bennett,[43] and Lois Maillou Jones?

It would appear that there are large questions raised about the direction and character of black culture and art if we take the powerful effects of even temporary experiences of exile, relocation, and displacement into account. How, for example, was the course of the black vernacular art of jazz changed by what happened to Quincy Jones in Sweden and Donald Byrd in Paris? This is especially interesting because both men played powerful roles in the remaking of jazz as a popular form in the early 1970s. Byrd describes his sense of Europe's appeal as something that grew out of the view of Canada he developed as a young man growing up in Detroit:

> That's why Europe was so important to me. Living across the river from Canada as a kid, I used to go down and sit and look at Windsor, Ontario. Windsor represented Europe to me. That was the rest of the world that was foreign to me. So I always had a feeling for the foreign, the European thing, because Canada was right there. We used to go to Canada. For black people, you see, Canada was a place that treated you better than America, the North. For my father Detroit was better than the South, to me born in the North, Canada was better. At least that was what I thought. Later on I found out otherwise, but anyway, Canada represented for me something foreign, exotic, that was not the United States.[44]

Richard Wright's life in exile, which has been written off as a betrayal of his authenticity and as a process of seduction by philosophical traditions supposedly outside his narrow ethnic compass,[45] will be explored below as an exemplary instance of how the politics of location and the politics of identity get inscribed in analyses of black culture. Many of the figures listed here will be dealt with in later chapters. They are all potential candidates for inclusion in the latest African-American cultural canon, a canon that is conditional on and possibly required by the academic packaging of black cultural studies.[46] Chapter 4 will discuss what version of the politics and philosophy of W. E. B. Du Bois will be constructed for that canon from the rich transnational textures of his long and nomadic life. Du Bois's travel experiences raise in the sharpest possible form a question common to the lives of almost all these figures who begin as African-Americans or Caribbean people and are then changed into something else which evades those specific labels and with them all fixed notions of nationality and national identity. Whether their experience of exile is enforced or chosen, temporary or permanent, these intellectuals and activists, writers, speakers, poets, and artists repeatedly articulate a desire to escape the restrictive bonds of ethnicity, national identification, and sometimes even "race" itself. Some speak, like Wells and Wright, in terms of the rebirth that Europe offered them. Whether they dissolved their African-American sensibility into an explicitly pan-Africanist discourse or political commitment, their relationship to the land of their birth and their ethnic political constituency was absolutely transformed. The specificity of the modern political and cultural formation I want to call the black Atlantic can be defined, on one level, through this desire to transcend both the structures of the nation state and the constraints of ethnicity and national particularity. These desires are relevant to understanding political organising and cultural criticism. They have always sat uneasily alongside the strategic choices forced on black movements and individuals embedded in national political cultures and nation states in America, the Caribbean, and Europe.

Martin Delany and the Institution of the Fatherland

The powerful and important figure of Martin Robison Delany—journalist, editor, doctor, scientist, judge, soldier, inventor, customs inspector, orator, politician, and novelist—provides an opportunity to examine the distinctive effects produced where the black Atlantic politics of location frames the doorway of double consciousness. His life also offers an invaluable opportunity to consider some of the issues raised within the histories of black culture and politics by travel and voluntary relocation. Marked by its European origins, modern black political culture has always been more interested in the relationship of identity to roots and rootedness than in seeing identity as a process of movement and mediation that is more appropriately approached via the homonym routes. Focusing on a figure like Delany demands careful attention to the interplay between these two dimensions of racial ontology. His life reveals a confrontation between his nationalism and the experiences of travel that have been largely ignored by historians except where they can be read as Ethiopianist or emigrationist gestures against American racism. This is no longer sufficient.

Delany is vital to the concerns of this book for several other reasons. He is still regularly hailed as the principal progenitor of black nationalism in America. Though he introduced his 1879 *Principia of Ethnology* with a fawning dedication to the Earl of Shaftesbury which would not find favour among Africentrists these days, his arguments in this final publication do prefigure the tone and content of contemporary Africalogical thought in an uncanny manner. Delany has been identified by Molefi Kete Asante as a pioneer in this field[47] and makes an attractive ancestor for Africentrists thanks to endearing traits like his willingness to don his dashiki while delivering lectures on Africa in the Town Hall, the Baptist church, and "the colored school" in Chatham, Ontario, where he made his home in exile. Apart from his sartorial and ideological proclivities, the proximity to Africa in Delany's family history has the effect of making his political choices look stark and vivid. They are far less ambiguous, for example, than those of his sometime associate Frederick Douglass, who had been sired by a white man, taught to read by a white woman, and had his freedom bought by two more. This much is clear from the closing passage of Delany's first book, *The Condition, Elevation, Emigration and Destiny of the Colored People of the United States Politically Considered* (1852). Though its assertive Christianity strikes a somewhat discordant note, the work ends movingly with a recognisably pan-African flourish that places the forces of science, Enlightenment, and progress in concert with the project of racial regeneration in the period after slavery:

> "Princes shall come forth out of Egypt; Ethiopia shall soon stretch forth her hands unto God" Ps.lxviii.31. With faith in this blessed promise, thank God; in this our grand advent into Africa, we want "No kettle drums nor flageolets, Bag pipes, trombones, nor bayonets" but with an abiding trust in God our heavenly king, we shall boldly advance, singing sweet songs of redemption, in the regeneration of our race and restoration of our father-land from the gloom and darkness of our superstition and ignorance, to the glorious light of a more pristine brightness—the light of the highest godly civilization.[48]

Delany is a figure of extraordinary complexity whose political trajectory through abolitionisms and emigrationisms, from Republicans to Democrats,[49] dissolves any simple attempts to fix him as consistently either conservative or radical. Thirdly, Delany's life is valuable because of his seven-month spell in England,[50] his exile in Chatham, his travels in the South and in Africa, as well as his dreams of autonomous black settlement in Central and South America. He is justly renowned for having organised and led the first scientific expedition to Africa from the western hemisphere:

the 1859 Niger Valley Exploring Party marshalled by Delany in conjunction with Robert Campbell, a Jamaican naturalist who had been head of the science department at the Institute for Colored Youth in Philadelphia. These peregrinations are re-coded in the wanderings of Henrico Blacus/ Henry Holland, the eponymous hero of Delany's novel *Blake; or, the Huts of America,* his single venture into fiction, serialised in the *Anglo African Magazine* during 1859 and the *Weekly Anglo-African* in 1861. Delany is also interesting because he thought of himself as a man of science.[51] His idea of himself as a polymath aspired to and indeed expressed a competence across disciplines that distinguishes him as an exceptional intellect. He modelled his career on standards of appropriately manly achievement set in the eighteenth century by savants and philosophes whose legacy, as we shall see, was readily appropriated for his theories of racial integrity and citizenship. He was, like William Wells Brown, Sarah Parker Remond, and others, a black person studying and practising medicine in a period when slaves' desires to run away from bondage were still sometimes being rationalised by medical opinion as an illness—drapetomania or dysaesthesia Aetheopis[52]—and when J. Marion Sims was perfecting the procedures of gynaecological surgery on the women he held in bondage.[53] Quite apart from his more practically oriented medical studies, Delany is known to have taken up phrenology in pursuit of answers to the arguments of racist ethnology. His work in this area could be used to initiate some interesting inquiries into the relationship between scientific reason and racial domination. We will see below that his aspirations as a cultivated man of science were intertwined with his political radicalisation in complex ways. Both were given an additional spur by Delany's bitter reaction to being denied the right to patent his 1852 invention for transporting locomotives over mountainous terrain because, though free, he was not formally a citizen of the United States.[54]

Delany was born in Charlestown, Virginia, in May 1812. He was the son of a slave father and a free mother who had both apparently enjoyed the benefits of African blood which was not only pure but royal too. Delany's Mandingo grandfather had returned to Africa after being manumitted and his father, Samuel, had purchased his own freedom in the early 1820s. The family made their home in Chambersburg, Pennsylvania. Active in abolitionist circles as a speaker, journalist, and writer, Delany published the *Mystery* in 1843 and became co-editor with Douglass of the *North Star* (1847). He came under the spell of Garrisonian abolitionism[55] at an early age and complemented his work in the anti-slavery cause with his medical activities as a cupper, leecher, and bleeder.[56] In 1850, having studied medicine under a number of different practitioners, he applied to Harvard to train in medicine there and was accepted along with two other black students, Isaac Snowden and Daniel Hunt, on the condition that they were sponsored by the American Colonisation Society and would only practice their medical skills outside the United States in Liberia after graduation.⁵⁷ A white female student, Harriot K. Hunt, who had been admitted at the same time as the three black men, was persuaded to withdraw after private meetings with members of the faculty. Delany, Snowden, and David Hunt began to attend lectures in November of that year but were asked to withdraw from the college by the Dean—Oliver Wendell Holmes, a celebrated admirer of Samuel Morton's *Crania Americana*—at the end of the winter term after protests from angry white students who felt that their presence would lower educational standards. The bitterness and righteous anger that had been compounded in Delany by a fruitless legal battle to claim his wife's inheritance were elaborated further as a result of this additional humiliation at the hands of Harvard. He returned to Philadelphia eager to make the clarion call for American citizenship *and* in favour of a plan for black emigration to Central or South America that would be announced by his first book.

Published on Delany's fortieth birthday, *The Condition* tempered its emigrationist proposals with a polemic against the American Colonisation Society and its plans for Liberian settlement. The book is notable for the elaborate theories of nationality and citizenship it derived from a reading of European history and perhaps most of all for its outspoken advocacy of a strong state that could focus the zionist aspirations of American blacks and aid in building their political counter-power against the white supremacist state. It began by comparing the lot of blacks in America to that of the disenfranchised minority nations found in Europe.

> That there have [*sic*] in all ages, in almost every nation, existed a nation within a nation—a people who although forming a part and parcel of the population, yet were from force of circumstances, known by the peculiar position they occupied, forming in fact, by deprivation of political equality with others, no part, and if any, but a restricted part of the body politics of such nations, is also true. Such then are the Poles in Russia, the Hungarians in Austria, the Scotch, Irish and Welsh in the United Kingdom, *and such also are the Jews scattered throughout not only the length and breadth of Europe but almost the habitable globe, maintaining their national characteristics, and looking forward in high hopes of seeing the day when they may return to their former national position of self-government and independence let that be in whatever part of the habitable world it may* . . . Such then is the condition of various classes in Europe; yes, nations, for centuries within

nations, even without the hope of redemption among those who op-
press them. And however unfavourable their condition, there is none
more so than that of the coloured people of the United States.[58] (emphasis added)

From the point of view of the history of the diaspora concept explored in
Chapter 6, it is especially interesting that though he does not use that pivotal term Delany looks immediately to Jewish experiences of dispersal as a
model for comprehending the history of black Americans and, more significantly still, cites this history as a means to focus his own zionist proposals for black American colonisation of Nicaragua[59] and elsewhere. The acquisition of a powerful fatherland that could guarantee and champion the
rights of slaves was, for Delany, far more significant than petty details like
a geographical location within what his collaborator, Robert Campbell,
called in his own report of their Niger Expedition the African *mother* land.
Delany's primary concern was not with Africa as such but rather with the
forms of citizenship and belonging that arose from the (re)generation of
modern nationality in the form of an autonomous, black nation state. Liberia was rejected in this role because it was not an adequate or sufficiently
serious vehicle for the hopes and dreams of black soldier citizens and their
families. Its geography was one factor in its disfavour, but its centrality to
the "deep laid scheme" of American slaveholders proved to be a more substantial disadvantage.[60] With his appeals to gain American citizenship looking increasingly fruitless, Delany left America in 1856. However, he went
north not east, not to Africa but to Canada.[61] It was from this new location
that he planned his trip to Africa and to Europe. He left the new world for
the old in 1859, arriving in Monrovia, the Liberian capital, on July 12th.
There he met with Alexander Crummell and other dignitaries.

Delany's 1859 report of his trip, the *Official Report of the Niger Valley
Exploring Party*,[62] is an interesting document that outlines his vision of a
dynamic alliance, both commercial and civilising, between English capital,
black American intellect, and African labour power. These disparate forces
were to collaborate to their mutual benefit in the export of African cotton
to England for processing. The *Report* is more interesting in the context of
this chapter for the insights it provides into those structures of feeling that
might be termed the inner dialectics of diaspora identification. Delany, ever
the doctor and rationalist, described in detail the sequence of clinical
symptoms he experienced as his initial elation at arriving in Africa gave way
to a special and characteristic form of melancholy:

The first sight and impressions of the coast of Africa are always inspiring, producing the most pleasant emotions. These pleasing sensations
continue for several days, more or less until they merge into feelings

of almost intense excitement . . . a hilarity of feeling almost akin to approaching intoxication . . . like the sensation produced by the beverage of champagne wine . . . The first symptoms are succeeded by a relaxity of feelings in which there is a disposition to stretch, gape and yawn with fatigue. The second may or may not be succeeded by actual febrile attacks . . . but whether or not such symptoms ensue, there is one most remarkable . . . A feeling of regret that you left your native country for a strange one; an almost frantic desire to see friends and nativity; a despondency and loss of the hope of ever seeing those you love at home again. These feelings, of course, must be resisted and regarded as a mere morbid affection [*sic*] of the mind . . . When an entire recovery takes place, the love of the country is most ardent and abiding.[63]

The ambivalence over exile and homecoming conveyed by these remarks has a history that is probably as long as the presence of African slaves in the west. At this point, it is necessary to appreciate that any discomfort at the prospect of fissures and fault lines in the topography of affiliation that made pan-Africanism such a powerful discourse was not eased by references to some African essence that could magically connect all blacks together. Nowadays, this potent idea is frequently wheeled in when it is necessary to appreciate the things that (potentially) connect black people to one another rather than think seriously about divisions in the imagined community of the race and the means to comprehend or overcome them, if indeed that is possible. Delany's African tour confirmed the dissimilarities between African-American ideologues and the Africans with whom they treated. Thus it is not surprising that though at the end of his account of his adventures in Africa Delany promised to return to Africa with his family, he never did so.

More than anything produced by Edward Wilmot Blyden, Alexander Crummell, and his other proto-nationalist peers, Delany's writings registered contradictory responses toward Africa. The ancient, ancestral home simply would not do as it was. He was acutely aware that it needed to be remade wholesale. In part, this was to be accomplished through grandiose modernisation schemes like the trans-African commercial railway link he had first proposed in an extraordinary appendix to *The Condition*. Africa's superstition and its heathen culture were to be swept away. These plans revealed that the proposed mission to elevate the black American racial self was inseparable from a second mission to elevate and enlighten the uncultured Africans by offering them the benefits of civilised life: cesspools, furniture, cutlery, missionaries, and "Some sort of a garment to cover the entire person above the knees, should it be but a single shirt or chemise, instead of a loose native cloth thrown around them, to be dropped at pleasure, at any moment exposing the entire upper part of the person as in Liberia, where that part of the person is entirely uncovered— I am certain that it would go far towards impressing them with some of the habits of civilised life."[64] If this statement can be read as a small sign of Delany's practical commitment to the fruits of Euro-American modernity, it is less surprising that his political positions could shift once more in later life and blend his nationalism anew with a decidedly America-centric brand of patriotism. The civil war was the catalyst for this process. It rekindled his enthusiasm for an American future for American blacks. Delany was commissioned as a major in the Union army, proudly assuming the regalia of the first black field officer in the history of the United States. The publication that had serialised *Blake* now offered its readers glorious photographic postcards of Delany in his dark blue uniform for twenty-five cents.

His decision to remain inside the shell of that patriotism after the war was over was facilitated by the same resolutely elitist version of black nationalism that had animated his earlier projects. It stressed the obligation of blacks to better themselves through the universal values of thrift, temperance, and hard work. This brand of black nationalism had also proved extremely popular with English anti-slavery audiences whose movement Delany's visit had helped to revitalise. He arrived in London from Africa during the spring of 1860 in search of backing for the enterprising colonial schemes: "fearless, bold and adventurous deeds of daring"[65] which were integral to realising the special respect that followed from the possession of national status.

I have already pointed out that the contrasting accounts that Delany and Campbell provided of the Niger Valley experiences are at variance over the gendering of their African homeland. Campbell saw Africa as his motherland while Delany, even when he refered to Africa with the female pronoun, persisted in calling the continent the fatherland. I want to suggest that this obstinacy expresses something profound and characteristic about Delany's sense of the necessary relationship between nationality, citizenship, and masculinity. He was probably the first black thinker to make the argument that the integrity of the race is primarily the integrity of its male heads of household and secondarily the integrity of the families over which they preside. The model he proposed aligned the power of the male head of household in the private sphere with the noble status of the soldier-citizen which complemented it in the public realm. Delany's appeal today is that of a supreme patriarch. He sought a variety of power for the black man in the white world that could only be built on the foundations which the roles of husband and father provided. There is something of the same attitude conveyed in the way that he named his seven children after famous figures of African descent: Alexandre Dumas, Toussaint L'Ouverture, Rameses Placido, St. Cyprian, Faustin Soulouque, Charles Lenox Remond, Ethiopia Halle. In a section on the education of girls in *The Condition* Delany made his views on the proper relationship between the sexes clearer still.

> Let our young women have an education; let their minds be well informed; well stored with useful information and practical proficiency, rather than the light, superficial acquirements, popularly and fashionably called accomplishments. We desire accomplishments, but they must be useful.
>
> Our females must be qualified, because they are to be the mothers of our children. As mothers are the first nurses and instructors of children; from them children consequently get their first impressions, which being always the most lasting should be the most correct.[66]

Women were to be educated but only for motherhood. The public sphere was to be the sole province of an enlightened male citizenry who seem to have taken their cues from Rousseau's conception of civic life in Sparta. Delany can now be recognised as the progenitor of black Atlantic patriarchy.

With the fundamental question of gender roles and relations still in mind, I want briefly to examine his novel *Blake; or, The Huts of America* as a narrative of familial reconstruction. The momentum of the book is supplied by the zeal with which its hero strives to reconstruct and regenerate his family life. This struggle is presented as absolutely homologous with both the liberation of slaves and the regeneration of Africa which Delany had described thus in the Niger Valley report:

> Africa is our fatherland and we its legitimate descendants . . . I have outgrown, long since, the boundaries of North America, and with them have also outgrown the boundaries of their claims . . . Africa, to be regenerated must have a national character, and her position among the existing nations of the earth will depend mainly upon the high standard she may gain compared with them in all her relations, morally, religiously, socially, politically and commercially.
>
> I have determined to leave to my children the inheritance of a country, the possession of territorial domain, the blessings of a national education, and the indisputable right of self-government; that they may not succeed to the servility and degradation bequeathed to us by

our fathers. If we have not been born to fortunes, we should impart the seeds which shall germinate and give birth to fortunes for them.[67]

Blake was the fourth novel written by a black American and certainly a more radical work than the other comparable early attempts at fiction. The book took its epigraph from Harriet Beecher Stowe's *Uncle Tom's Cabin* and was, as Delany's domiciliary title implies, an explicit, intertextual response to that work. Both the structure of the book and its geographical compass confirm Delany's claim to have outgrown the boundaries of North America. *Blake* was written in Canada and concerns a Cuban who, after travelling to Africa as a sailor on a slave ship, is himself enslaved in the United States. He escapes to Canada, but then returns to the United States in order to find the wife who has been unjustly parted from him by an evil slave master and to lead slave resistance there. He discovers her in Cuba and secures her freedom. He then visits Africa again, this time as a senior crewman on a second slaver. This journey, across the Atlantic from west to east—a middle passage in reverse—is undertaken as part of a grand plan to lead a revolutionary slave revolt in Cuba which is at that moment in danger of being annexed by the southern American states. The topography of the black Atlantic world is directly incorporated into Delany's tale. His travelling hero, Blake, assumes various names in the different locations he visits, but his English appellation is surely significant in that it offers an echo of an earlier, explicitly Atlanticist radicalism.

Ships occupy a primary symbolic and political place in the work. One chapter is called "Transatlantic" and another, chapter 52, is entitled "The Middle Passage" and includes a harrowing scene of a slaver throwing overboard the dead and dying just as Turner had depicted it: amidst the rage of nature itself. Delany's use of music is complex and bold and has been understood as further evidence of his deeply contradictory relationship to America and its culture. The sharp parodies of patriotic songs and popular material by Stephen Foster that he has his characters sing can be interpreted as illustrations of the dense cultural syncretisms that double consciousness can generate.[68]

Blake includes some strikingly sympathetic portraits of black women and offers one of the few presentations of the middle passage and life in the barracoons to be found in nineteenth-century black writing. It makes African-American experience visible within a hemispheric order of racial domination. The version of black solidarity *Blake* advances is explicitly anti-ethnic and opposes narrow African-American exceptionalism in the name of a truly pan-African, diaspora sensibility. This makes blackness a matter of politics rather than a common cultural condition. The terror of slavery

is powerfully invoked, only partly from within the conventions of an abolitionist literary genre that exhibits an intense fascination with the image of
divided families. Slavery is seen in an ethical light but is primarily presented
as an exploitative economic system of an international nature. Delany was
a member of the African Methodist Episcopal church, but he used his hero
Blake to convey criticisms of religion in general and Christianity in particular. It is this representation of religious belief which supplies the key to the
book's anti-ethnic, pan-African stance. Blake refused to "stand still and see
salvation" wherever it was offered to him: by the rituals of the white church
on the plantation, in the Catholic church or in the superstitions of the
conjurers he interacts with during a visit to the Dismal Swamp. His
scepticism and strictly instrumental orientation towards religion, which he
saw as a valuable tool for the political project he sought to advance, are
important because African-American religion is so often the central sign
for the folk-cultural, narrowly ethnic definition of racial authenticity that
is being challenged here in the name of rhizomorphic,[69] routed, diaspora
cultures.

Both Delany and his hero boast of their rational principles. Stealing
from the master was rationalised in terms derived from a labour theory of
value and, from this rationalist stance, blacks were rebuked for confusing
spiritual means with moral ends. Black Americans were not uniquely oppressed, and if they were to be free, they must contribute to the establishment of the strong and completely synthetic supra-ethnic nation state that
Delany saw as indispensable to the ongoing struggle to defeat racial oppression everywhere in the new world and to the longer-term project of
African regeneration. This anti-mystical racial rationalism required that
blacks of all shades, classes, and ethnic groups give up the merely accidental
differences that served only to mask the deeper unity waiting to be constructed not so much from their African heritage as from the common
orientation to the future produced by their militant struggles against slavery. Ethnic and religious differences symbolise intraracial divisions in the
book. Black survival depends upon forging a new means to build alliances
above and beyond petty issues like language, religion, skin colour, and to
a lesser extent gender. The best way to create the new metacultural identity
which the new black citizenship demands was provided by the abject condition of the slaves and ironically facilitated by the transnational structure
of the slave trade itself. Abyssa, a Soudanese slave and former textile mer-
chant, brought from Africa on Blake's second transatlantic trip; Placido, a
Cuban revolutionary poet who is also Blake's cousin; Gofer Gondolier, a
West Indian cook who has attended a Spanish grandee in Genoa; the
wealthy quadroons and octoroons of Cuba; Blake himself; and indeed their

white revolutionary supporters constitute something like a rainbow army for the emancipation of the oppressed men and women of the new world. Because religion marks these petty ethnic differences with special clarity, its overcoming signifies the utopian move beyond ethnicity and the establishment of a new basis for community, mutuality and reciprocity:

> I first a catholic and my wife bred as such are both Baptists; Abyssa Soudan once a pagan was in her own native land converted to the Methodist or Wesleyan belief; Madame Sabastina and family are Episcopalians; Camina from long residence in the colony a Presbyterian and Placide is a believer in the Swedenborgian doctrines. We have all agreed to know no sects, no denomination and but one religion for the sake of our redemption from Bondage and degradation . . . No religion but that which brings us liberty will we know; no God but he who owns us as his children will we serve. The whites accept nothing but that which promotes their interests and happiness, socially politically and religiously. They would discard a religion, tear down a church, overthrow a government or desert a country which did not enhance their freedom. In God's great and righteous name are we not willing to do the same?[70]

Blake is useful to this chapter's argument against ethnic absolutisms because its affirmation of the intercultural and transnational is more than enough to move discussion of black political culture beyond the binary opposition between national and diaspora perspectives. The suggestive way that it locates the black Atlantic world in a webbed network, between the local and the global, challenges the coherence of all narrow nationalist perspectives and points to the spurious invocation of ethnic particularity to enforce them and to ensure the tidy flow of cultural output into neat, symmetrical units. I should add that this applies whether this impulse comes from the oppressors or the oppressed.

Black Politics and Modernity

Rereading *Blake* in this way and looking at the routes of its nationalist author leads us back to the question of whether nationalist perspectives are an adequate means to understand the forms of resistance and accommodation intrinsic to modern black political culture. The recent history of blacks, as people in but not necessarily of the modern, western world, a history which involves processes of political organisation that are explicitly transnational and international in nature, demands that this question is considered very carefully. What, after all, is being opposed by the move-

ments of slaves and their descendants: slavery? capitalism? coerced industrialisation? racial terror? or the ethnocentrism and European solipsism that
these processes help to reproduce? How are the discontinuous histories of
diaspora resistance raised in fictional form by *Blake* and lived by figures like
its creator to be *thought*? How have they been theorised by those who have
experienced the consequences of racial domination?

In the final part of this chapter, I want to look more specifically at the
positions of the nation state, and the idea of nationality in accounts of
black opposition and expressive culture, particularly music. I will also use
a brief discussion of black music that anticipates a more extensive treatment of these themes in Chapter 3 to ask implicit questions about the
tendencies towards ethnocentrism and ethnic absolutism of black cultural
theory.

The problem of weighing the claims of national identity against other
contrasting varieties of subjectivity and identification has a special place in
the intellectual history of blacks in the west. Du Bois's concept of double
consciousness has been referred to already and will be explored in greater
detail in Chapter 4. It is only the best-known resolution of a familiar problem which points towards the core dynamic of racial oppression as well as
the fundamental antinomy of diaspora blacks. How has this doubleness,
what Richard Wright calls the dreadful objectivity[71] which follows from
being both inside and outside the West, affected the conduct of political
movements against racial oppression and towards black autonomy? Are the
inescapable pluralities involved in the movements of black peoples, in Africa and in exile, ever to be synchronised? How would these struggles be
periodised in relation to modernity: the fatal intermediation of capitalism,
industrialisation, and a new conception of political democracy? Does posing these questions in this way signify anything more than the reluctant
intellectual affiliation of diaspora blacks to an approach which mistakenly
attempts a premature totalisation of infinite struggles, an approach which
itself has deep and problematic roots within the ambiguous intellectual
traditions of the European Enlightenment which have, at different moments, been both a lifeline and a fetter?

Delany's work has provided some powerful evidence to show that the
intellectual heritage of Euro-American modernity determined and possibly
still determines the manner in which nationality is understood within black
political discourse. In particular, this legacy conditions the continuing aspiration to acquire a supposedly authentic, natural, and stable "rooted"
identity. This invariant identity is in turn the premise of a thinking "racial"
self that is both socialised and unified by its connection with other kindred
souls encountered usually, though not always, within the fortified frontiers

of those discrete ethnic cultures which also happen to coincide with the contours of a sovereign nation state that guarantees their continuity.

Consider for a moment the looseness with which the term "black nationalism" is used both by its advocates and by sceptics. Why is a more refined political language for dealing with these crucial issues of identity, kinship, generation, affect, and affiliation such a long time coming? A small but telling example can be drawn from the case of Edouard Glissant, who has contributed so much to the emergence of a creole counter-discourse that can answer the alchemy of nationalisms. Discussion of these problems suffers when his translator excises Glissant's references to the work of Deleuze and Guattari from the English edition of his 1981 book *Le discours antillais*,[72] presumably because to acknowledge this exchange would somehow violate the aura of Caribbean authenticity that is a desirable frame around the work. This typical refusal to accept the complicity and syncretic interdependency of black and white thinkers has recently become associated with a second difficulty: the overintegrated conceptions of pure and homogeneous culture which mean that black political struggles are construed as somehow automatically *expressive* of the national or ethnic differences with which they are associated.

This overintegrated sense of cultural and ethnic particularity is very popular today, and blacks do not monopolise it. It masks the arbitrariness of its own political choices in the morally charged language of ethnic absolutism and this poses additional dangers because it overlooks the development and change of black political ideologies and ignores the restless, recombinant qualities of the black Atlantic's affirmative political cultures. The political project forged by thinkers like Delany in the difficult journey from slave ship to citizenship is in danger of being wrecked by the seemingly insoluble conflict between two distinct but currently symbiotic perspectives. They can be loosely identified as the essentialist and the pluralist standpoints though they are in fact two different varieties of essentialism: one ontological, the other strategic. The antagonistic relationship between these two outlooks has been especially intense in discussions of black art and cultural criticism. The ontological essentialist view has often been characterised by a brute pan-Africanism. It has proved unable to specify precisely where the highly prized but doggedly evasive essence of black artistic and political sensibility is currently located, but that is no obstacle to its popular circulation. This perspective sees the black intellectual and artist as a leader. Where it pronounces on cultural matters, it is often allied to a realist approach to aesthetic value that minimises the substantive political and philosophical issues involved in the processes of artistic representation. Its absolutist conception of ethnic cultures can be identified by the way in which it registers incomprehending disappointment with the actual cultural choices and patterns of the mass of black people. It has little to say about the profane, contaminated world of black popular culture and looks instead for an artistic practice that can disabuse the mass of black people of the illusions into which they have been seduced by their condition of exile and unthinking consumption of inappropriate cultural objects like the wrong hair care products, pop music, and western clothing. The community is felt to be on the wrong road, and it is the intellectual's job to give them a new direction, firstly by recovering and then by donating the racial awareness that the masses seem to lack.

This perspective currently confronts a pluralistic position which affirms blackness as an open signifier and seeks to celebrate complex representations of a black particularity that is *internally* divided: by class, sexuality, gender, age, ethnicity, economics, and political consciousness. There is no unitary idea of black community here, and the authoritarian tendencies of those who would police black cultural expression in the name of their own particular history or priorities are rightly repudiated. The ontologically grounded essentialism is replaced by a libertarian, strategic alternative: the cultural saturnalia which attends the end of innocent notions of the essential black subject.[73] Here, the polyphonic qualities of black cultural expression form the main aesthetic consideration and there is often an uneasy but exhilarating fusion of modernist and populist techniques and styles. From this perspective, the achievements of popular black cultural forms like music are a constant source of inspiration. They are prized for their implicit warning against the pitfalls of artistic conceit. The difficulty with this second tendency is that in leaving racial essentialism behind by viewing "race" itself as a social and cultural construction, it has been insufficiently alive to the lingering power of specifically racialised forms of power and subordination.

Each outlook compensates for the obvious weaknesses in the other camp, but so far there has been little open and explicit debate between them. Their conflict, initially formulated in debates over black aesthetics and cultural production,[74] is valuable as a preliminary guide to some of the dilemmas faced by cultural and intellectual *historians* of the modern, western, African diaspora. The problems it raises become acute, particularly for those who seek to comprehend cultural developments and political resistances which have had scant regard for either modern borders or premodern frontiers. At its worst, the lazy, casual invocation of cultural insiderism which frequently characterises the ontological essentialist view is nothing more than a symptom of the growing cleavages *within* the black communities. There, uneasy spokespeople of the black elite—some of them professional cultural commentators, artists, writers, painters, and film makers as well as political leaders—have fabricated a volkish outlook as an expression of their own contradictory position. This neo-nationalism seems out of tune with the spirit of the novel Africentric garb in which it appears before us today. It incorporates commentary on the special needs and desires of the relatively privileged castes within black communities, but its most consistent trademark is the persistent mystification of that group's increasingly problematic relationships with the black poor, who, after all, supply the elite with a dubious entitlement to speak on behalf of the phantom constituency of black people in general. The idea of blacks as a national or proto-national group with its own hermetically enclosed culture plays a key role in this mystification, and, though seldom overtly named, the misplaced idea of a national interest gets invoked as a means to silence dissent and censor political debate when the incoherences and inconsistencies of Africalogical discourse are put on display.

These problems take on a specific aspect in Britain, which currently lacks anything that can be credibly called a black bourgeoisie. However, they are not confined to this country and they cannot be overlooked. The idea of nationality and the assumptions of cultural absolutism come together in other ways.[75] It should be emphasised that, where the archaeology of black critical knowledges enters the academy, it currently involves the construction of canons which seems to be proceeding on an exclusively *national* basis—African-American, Anglophone Caribbean, and so on. This is not an oblique plea for the legitimacy of an equally distinctive black English or British cultural inventory. If it seems indelicate to ask who the formation of such canons might serve, then the related question of where the impulse to formalise and codify elements of our cultural heritage in this particular pattern comes from may be a better one to pursue. Is this impulse towards cultural protectionism the most cruel trick which the west can play upon its dissident affiliates? The same problem of the status enjoyed by national boundaries in the writing of cultural history is evident in recent debates over hip hop culture, the powerful expressive medium of America's urban black poor which has created a global youth movement of considerable significance. The musical components of hip hop are a hybrid form nurtured by the social relations of the South Bronx where Jamaican sound system culture was transplanted during the 1970s and put down new roots. In conjunction with specific technological innovations, this routed and re-rooted Caribbean culture set in train a process that was to transform black America's sense of itself and a large portion of the popular music industry as well. Here we have to ask how a form which flaunts and glories in its own malleability as well as its transnational character becomes interpreted as an expression of some authentic African-American essence? How can rap be discussed as if it sprang intact from the entrails of the blues?[76] Another way of approaching this would be to ask what is it about black America's writing elite which means that they need to claim this diasporic cultural form in such an assertively nationalist way?[77]

An additional, and possibly more profound, area of political difficulty comes into view when the voguish language of absolute cultural difference associated with the ontological essentialist standpoint provides an embarrassing link between the practice of blacks who comprehend racial politics through it and the activities of their foresworn opponents—the ethnic absolutists of the racist right—who approach the complex dynamics of race, nationality, and ethnicity through a similar set of pseudo-precise, culturalist equations. This unlikely convergence is part of the history of hip hop because black music is so often the principal symbol of racial authenticity. Analysing it leads rapidly and directly back to the status of nationality and national cultures in a post-modern world where nation states are being eclipsed by a new economy of power that accords national citizenship and national boundaries a new significance. In seeking to account for the controversy over hip hop's origins we also have to explore how the absolutist and exclusivist approach to the relationship between "race," ethnicity, and culture places those who claim to be able to resolve the relationship between the supposedly incommensurable discourses characteristic of different racial groups, in command of the cultural resources of their own group as a whole. Intellectuals can claim this vanguard position by virtue of an ability to translate from one culture to another, mediating decisive oppositions along the way. It matters little whether the the black communities involved are conceived as entire and self-sustaining nations or as proto-national collectivities.

No less than their predecessor Martin Delany, today's black intellectuals have persistently succumbed to the lure of those romantic conceptions of "race," "people," and "nation" which place themselves, rather than the people they supposedly represent, in charge of the strategies for nation building, state formation, and racial uplift. This point underscores the fact that the status of nationality and the precise weight we should attach to the conspicuous differences of language, culture, and identity which divide the blacks of the diaspora from one another, let alone from Africans, are unresolved within the political culture that promises to bring the disparate peoples of the black Atlantic world together one day. Furthermore, the dependence of those black intellectuals who have tried to deal with these matters on theoretical reflections derived from the canon of occidental modernity—from Herder to Von Trietschke and beyond—is surely salient.

W. E. B. Du Bois's work will be explored below as a site of this affiliation. The case of his 1888 Fisk graduation address on Bismarck provides a preliminary example. Reflecting on it some years later in *Dusk of Dawn* he wrote, "Bismarck was my hero. He made a nation out of a mass of bickering peoples. He had dominated the whole development with his strength until he crowned an emperor at Versailles. This foreshadowed in my mind the kind of thing that American Negroes must do, marching forward with strength and determination under trained leadership."[78] This model of national development has a special appeal to the bickering peoples of the black Atlantic diaspora. It is an integral component of their responses to modern racism and directly inspired their efforts to construct nation states on African soil and elsewhere. The idea of nationality occupies a central, if shifting place in the work of Alexander Crummell, Edward Blyden, Martin Delany, and Frederick Douglass. This important group of post-Enlightenment men, whose lives and political sensibilities can ironically be defined through the persistent crisscrossing of national boundaries, often seem to share the decidedly Hegelian belief that the combination of Christianity and a nation state represents the overcoming of all antinomies.

The themes of nationality, exile, and cultural affiliation accentuate the inescapable fragmentation and differentiation of the black subject. This fragmentation has recently been compounded further by the questions of gender, sexuality, and male domination which have been made unavoidable by the struggles of black women and the voices of black gay men and lesbians. I cannot attempt to resolve these tensions here, but the dimension of social and political differentiation to which they refer provides a frame for what follows. As indices of differentiation, they are especially important because the intracommunal antagonisms which appear between the local and immediate levels of our struggles and their hemispheric and global dynamics can only grow. Black voices from within the overdeveloped countries may be able to go on resonating in harmony with those produced from inside Africa or they may, with varying degrees of reluctance, turn away from the global project of black advancement once the symbolic and political, if not the material and economic, liberation of Southern Africa is completed.

I want to make these abstract and difficult points more concrete and more accessible by constructing a conclusion for this chapter out of some of the lessons waiting to be learned from considering elements of the musical output of blacks in the West which will be explored in more detail in Chapter 3. The history and significance of these musics are consistently overlooked by black writers for two reasons: because they exceed the frameworks of national or ethnocentric analysis with which we have been too easily satisfied, and because talking seriously about the politics and aesthetics of black vernacular cultures demands an embarrassing confrontation with substantive intraracial differences that make the easy essentialism from which most critical judgements are constructed simply untenable. As these internal divisions have grown, the price of that embarrassment has been an aching silence.

To break that silence, I want to argue that black musical expression has played a role in reproducing what Zygmunt Bauman has called a distinctive counterculture of modernity.[79] I will use a brief consideration of black musical development to move beyond an understanding of cultural processes which, as I have already suggested, is currently torn between seeing them either as the expression of an essential, unchanging, sovereign racial self or as the effluent from a constituted subjectivity that emerges contingently from the endless play of racial signification. This is usually conceived solely in terms of the inappropriate model which *textuality* provides. The vitality and complexity of this musical culture offers a means to get beyond the related oppositions between essentialists and pseudo-pluralists on the one hand and between totalising conceptions of tradition, modernity, and postmodernity on the other. It also provides a model of performance which can supplement and partially displace concern with textuality.

Black music's obstinate and consistent commitment to the idea of a better future is a puzzle to which the enforced separation of slaves from literacy and their compensatory refinement of musical art supplies less than half an answer. The power of music in developing black struggles by communicating information, organising consciousness, and testing out or deploying the forms of subjectivity which are required by political agency, whether individual or collective, defensive or transformational, demands attention to both the formal attributes of this expressive culture and its distinctive *moral* basis. The formal qualities of this music are becoming better known,[80] and I want to concentrate instead on the moral aspects and in particular on the disjunction between the ethical value of the music and its status as an ethnic sign.

In the simplest possible terms, by posing the world as it is against the world as the racially subordinated would like it to be, this musical culture supplies a great deal of the courage required to go on living in the present. It is both produced by and expressive of that "transvaluation of all values" precipitated by the history of racial terror in the new world. It contains a theodicy but moves beyond it because the profane dimensions of that racial terror made theodicy impossible.[81] I have considered its distinctive critique of capitalist social relations elsewhere.[82] Here, because I want to show that its critical edge includes but also surpasses anti-capitalism, it is necessary to draw out some of the inner philosophical dynamics of this counterculture and to explore the connection between its normative character and its utopian aspirations. These are interrelated and even inseparable from each other and from the critique of racial capitalism[83] that these expressive cultures construct but also surpass. Comprehending them necessitates an analysis of the lyrical content and the forms of musical expression as well as the often hidden social relations in which these deeply encoded oppositional practices are created and consumed. The issue of normative content focuses attention on what might be called the politics of fulfilment:[84] the notion that a future society will be able to realise the social and political promise that present society has left unaccomplished. Reflecting the foundational semantic position of the Bible, this is a discursive mode of communication. Though by no means literal, it can be grasped through what is said, shouted, screamed, or sung. The politics of fulfilment practised by the descendants of slaves demands, as Delany did, that bourgeois civil society live up to the promises of its own rhetoric. It creates a medium in which demands for goals like non-racialised justice and rational organisation of the productive processes can be expressed. It is immanent within modernity and is no less a valuable element of modernity's counter-discourse for being consistently ignored.

The issue of how utopias are conceived is more complex not least because they strive continually to move beyond the grasp of the merely linguistic, textual, and discursive. The invocation of utopia references what, following Seyla Benhabib's suggestive lead, I propose to call the politics of transfiguration. This emphasises the emergence of qualitatively new desires, social relations, and modes of association within the racial community of interpretation and resistance *and* between that group and its erstwhile oppressors. It points specifically to the formation of a community of needs and solidarity which is magically made audible in the music itself and palpable in the social relations of its cultural utility and reproduction. Created under the very nose of the overseers, the utopian desires which fuel the complementary politics of transfiguration must be invoked by other, more deliberately opaque means. This politics exists on a lower frequency where it is played, danced, and acted, as well as sung and sung about, because words, even words stretched by melisma and supplemented or mutated by the screams which still index the conspicuous power of the slave sublime, will never be enough to communicate its unsayable claims to truth. The wilfully damaged signs which betray the resolutely utopian politics of transfiguration therefore partially transcend modernity, constructing both an imaginary anti-modern past and a postmodern yet-to-come. This is not a counter-discourse but a counterculture that defiantly reconstructs its own critical, intellectual, and moral genealogy in a partially hidden public sphere of its own. The politics of transfiguration therefore reveals the hidden internal fissures in the concept of modernity. The bounds of politics are extended precisely because this tradition of expression refuses to accept that the political is a readily separable domain. Its basic desire is to conjure up and enact the new modes of friendship, happiness, and solidarity that are consequent on the overcoming of the racial oppression on which modernity and its antinomy of rational, western progress as excessive barbarity relied. Thus the vernacular arts of the children of slaves give rise to a verdict on the role of art which is strikingly in harmony with Adorno's reflections on the dynamics of European artistic expression in the wake of Auschwitz: "Art's Utopia, the counterfactual yet-to-come, is draped in black. It goes on being a recollection of the possible with a critical edge against the real; it is a kind of imaginary restitution of that catastrophe, which is world history; it is a freedom which did not pass under the spell of necessity and which may well not come to pass ever at all."[85] These sibling dimensions of black sensibility, the politics of fulfilment and the politics of transfiguration, are not co-extensive. There are significant tensions between them but they are closely associated in the vernacular cultures of the black Atlantic diaspora. They can also be used to reflect the idea of doubleness with which this chapter began and which is often argued to be the constitutive force giving rise to black experience in the modern world. The politics of fulfilment is mostly content to play occidental rationality at its own game. It necessitates a hermeneutic orientation that can assimilate the semiotic, verbal, and textual. The politics of transfiguration strives in pursuit of the sublime, struggling to repeat the unrepeatable, to present the unpresentable. Its rather different hermeneutic focus pushes towards the mimetic, dramatic, and performative.

It seems especially significant that the cultural expressions which these musics allow us to map out do not seek to exclude problems of inequality or to make the achievement of racial justice an exclusively abstract matter. Their grounded ethics offers, among other things, a continuous commentary on the systematic and pervasive relations of domination that supply its conditions of existence. Their grounded aesthetics is never separated off into an autonomous realm where familiar political rules cannot be applied and where, as Salman Rushdie memorably puts it, "the little room of literature"[86] can continue to enjoy its special privileges as a heroic resource for the well-heeled adversaries of liberal capitalism.

I am proposing, then, that we reread and rethink this expressive counterculture not simply as a succession of literary tropes and genres but as a philosophical discourse which refuses the modern, occidental separation of ethics and aesthetics, culture and politics. The traditional teaching of ethics and politics—practical philosophy—came to an end some time ago, even if its death agonies were prolonged. This tradition had maintained the idea that a good life for the individual and the problem of the best social and political order for the collectivity could be discerned by rational means. Though it is seldom acknowledged even now, this tradition lost its exclusive claim to rationality partly through the way that slavery became internal to western civilisation and through the obvious complicity which both plantation slavery and colonial regimes revealed between rationality and the practice of racial terror. Not perceiving its residual condition, blacks in the west eavesdropped on and then took over a fundamental question from the intellectual obsessions of their enlightened rulers. Their progress from the status of slaves to the status of citizens led them to enquire into what the best possible forms of social and political existence might be. The memory of slavery, actively preserved as a living intellectual resource in their expressive political culture, helped them to generate a new set of answers to this enquiry. They had to fight—often through their spirituality—to hold on to the unity of ethics and politics sundered from each other by modernity's insistence that the true, the good, and the beautiful had distinct origins and belong to different domains of knowledge. First slavery itself and then their memory of it induced many of them to query the foundational moves of modern philosophy and social thought, whether they came from the natural rights theorists who sought to distinguish between the spheres of morality and legality, the idealists who wanted to emancipate politics from morals so that it could become a sphere of strategic action, or the political economists of the bourgeoisie who first formulated the separation of economic activity from both ethics and politics. The brutal excesses of the slave plantation supplied a set of moral and political responses to each of these attempts. The history and utility of black music discussed in Chapter 3 enable us to trace something of the means through which the unity of ethics and politics has been reproduced as a form of folk knowledge. This subculture often appears to be the intuitive expression of some racial essence but is in fact an elementary historical acquisition produced from the viscera of an alternative body of cultural and political expression that considers the world critically from the point of view of its emancipatory transformation. In the future, it will become a place which is capable of satisfying the (redefined) needs of human beings that will emerge once the violence—epistemic and concrete—of racial typology is at an end. Reason is thus reunited with the happiness and freedom of individuals and the reign of justice within the collectivity.

I have already implied that there is a degree of convergence here with other projects towards a critical theory of society, particularly Marxism. However, where lived crisis and systemic crisis come together, Marxism allocates priority to the latter while the memory of slavery insists on the priority of the former. Their convergence is also undercut by the simple fact that in the critical thought of blacks in the West, social self-creation through labour is not the centre-piece of emancipatory hopes. For the descendants of slaves, work signifies only servitude, misery, and subordination. Artistic expression, expanded beyond recognition from the grudging gifts offered by the masters as a token substitute for freedom from bondage, therefore becomes the means towards both individual self-fashioning and communal liberation. Poiesis and poetics begin to coexist in novel forms—autobiographical writing, special and uniquely creative ways of manipulating spoken language, and, above all, the music. All three have overflowed from the containers that the modern nation state provides for them.

2

Masters, Mistresses, Slaves, and the Antinomies of Modernity

Every Idea thrown into the mind of the Negro is caught up and realised with the whole energy of his will; but this realisation involves a wholesale destruction . . . it is manifest that want of self-control distinguishes the character of the Negroes. This condition is capable of no development or Culture, and as we see them at this day, such they have always been. The only essential connection between the Negroes and the Europeans is slavery . . . we may conclude slavery to have been the occasion of the increase in human feeling among the Negroes.

> *Hegel*

How man deals with man is seen, for example in Negro slavery, the ultimate object of which is sugar and coffee.

> *Schopenhauer*

You had better all die—die immediately, than live slaves and entail your wretchedness upon your prosperity. If you would be free in this generation, here is your only hope.

> *Henry Highland Garnet*

. . . the free hills of old Scotland, where the ancient "Black Douglass" once met his foes . . . almost every hill, river, mountain and lake of which has been made classic by the heroic deeds of her noble sons. Scarcely a stream but has been poured into song, or a hill that is not associated with some fierce and bloody conflict between liberty and slavery.

> *Frederick Douglass*

FOR SOME YEARS now, Euro-American social theory, philosophy, and cultural criticism have hosted bitter and politically charged debates into the scope and status of the concept of modernity and the related ideas of modernism and modernisation. These debates have not always been conducted explicitly, and their key concepts have been nuanced in a variety of ways according to the particular disciplinary context in which they have arisen, yet despite some lack of consistency in their application a surprisingly coherent series of exchanges has taken shape. These exchanges have been dominated by a constellation of formally opposed yet mutually reinforcing theoretical positions from many of the leading theorists of the

Euro-American academic establishment. Jurgen Habermas, Jean François Lyotard, Fredric Jameson, and a host of other women and men have applied themselves to the task of examining these ideas and the distinctiveness of contemporary life in the West to which they point. Sometimes writers have been concerned to identify and account for recent decisive shifts in the cultural climate of the overdeveloped countries and in their relationship to the rest of the world. Many participants have constructed intellectual detours through modernity as a way of demarcating what is novel or historically original in the contemporary postmodern condition. Others have analysed the postmodern as if it had simply effaced or replaced the modern and, like Lyotard, have not delved deeply into the history of the postmodern, its emergence from modernity, or its relationship to the processes of modernisation.[1]

However they approach their task, these authors share a preoccupation with the impact of post-war changes on the cognitive and technological bases of social and cultural life in the overdeveloped world where they have been able to detect "a sort of sorrow in the Zeitgeist."[2] The concept of postmodernism is often introduced to emphasise the radical or even catastrophic nature of the break between contemporary conditions and the epoch of modernism. Thus there is little attention given to the possibility that much of what is identified as postmodern may have been foreshadowed, or prefigured, in the lineaments of modernity itself. Defenders and critics of modernity seem to be equally unconcerned that the history and expressive culture of the African diaspora, the practice of racial slavery, or the narratives of European imperial conquest may require all simple periodisations of the modern and the postmodern to be drastically rethought.[3]

The pivotal relationship between the modern and the postmodern raises a number of further issues not least because it constitutes a small part of wider enquiries into the continuing viability of what Habermas has called the Enlightenment project.[4] These discussions profess to be more than merely scholastic contributions to the intellectual history of the West. They have certainly acquired a broader political currency, particularly where they have pronounced upon the idea of progress and the view of civilisation guided steadily towards perfection by secular, rational principles that sustains that idea. Habermas and others have, for example, focused attention on the relationship between freedom and reason, which has been a fundamental feature of western political discourses since the end of the eighteenth century. This has gained a special resonance during a period in which technological transformations and political upheavals appear to jeopardise both freedom and reason in equal measure. The contemporary restructuring of political and economic relations in the overdeveloped countries has called many of the historic assumptions of western rational-ism into question. Arguing against the defenders of modern rationalism, incredulous voices have drawn critical attention to the bold, universalist claims of occidental modernity and its hubristic confidence in its own infal-libility. It is disappointing that the position of the sceptics has sometimes been undersold by a chorus of rhetorical commentary which draws its en-thusiasm from the excesses of anti-political post-structuralism in general and deconstructive literary criticism in particular.

I will not attempt to reconstruct the whole complexity of these ex-changes here. A number of authors have already provided a valuable sec-ondary literature on the principal positions involved.[5] I am, however, keen to emphasise that this extensive and unusual international debate is clearly tied both to the fate of the intellectual as a discrete, authoritative caste and to the future of the universities in which so many of its learned protagonists have acquired secure perches. In Europe at least, these institutions of higher learning are being ventilated by the chill breeze of downward mo-bility at a time when the autonomous cultural power and preeminence of their mandarin inhabitants as public intellectuals are also being severely reduced. This is only one of several reasons why it may be possible to argue that what is increasingly perceived as the crisis of modernity and modern values is perhaps better understood as the crisis of the intellectuals whose self-consciousness was once served by these terms.[6] Focusing on the role of intellectuals within modernity is an important way of drawing out the particularity that lurks beneath the universalist claims of the Enlighten-ment project which was, in theory, valid for humanity as a whole even if humanity was to be rather restrictively defined. The meaning of being an intellectual in settings that have denied access to literacy and encouraged other forms of communication in its place is a recurring question in what follows.

Recent discussions of modernity and its possible eclipse are also insepa-rable from the currently bleak fortunes of expressly socialistic forces in the overdeveloped countries. It would therefore be wrong to suppose that the political importance of this debate is entirely diminished by its academic origins and special appeal to those dissident affiliates of the bourgeoisie who once, joyfully or regretfully, placed their weapons of criticism in align-ment with the proletariat's criticism of weapons. Reformist and revolution-ary leftist alike are now being challenged to defend the protocols of secular reason and the ideal of human and social perfectibility irrespective of whether it is carried out under the banner of working class self-eman-cipation or the standard of more modest and avowedly realist political phi-losophies.

Though it may not contain the final verdict on the grand narrative of Euro-American progress and the infinite expansion of productive forces that is often seen by left and right alike as an essential precondition for the enhancement of social and political freedoms, this debate is important for several reasons which have not, so far, been noted from within it. It can be argued that much of the supposed novelty of the postmodern evaporates when it is viewed in the unforgiving historical light of the brutal encounters between Europeans and those they conquered, slaughtered, and enslaved. The periodisation of the modern and the postmodern is thus of the most profound importance for the history of blacks in the West and for chronicling the shifting relations of domination and subordination between Europeans and the rest of the world. It is essential for our understanding of the category of "race" itself and of the genesis and development of successive forms of racist ideology. It is relevant, above all, in elaborating an interpretation of the origins and evolution of black politics. This task requires careful attention to the complex intermixture of African and European philosophical and cultural systems and ideas. A concept of modernity that is worth its salt ought, for example, to have something to contribute to an analysis of how the particular varieties of radicalism articulated through the revolts of enslaved people made selective use of the ideologies of the western Age of Revolution and then flowed into social movements of an anti-colonial and decidedly anti-capitalist type. Lastly, the overcoming of scientific racism (one of modernity's more durable intellectual products) and its post-war transmutation into newer, cultural forms that stress complex difference rather than simple biological hierarchy may provide a telling, concrete example of what scepticism towards the grand narratives of scientific reason adds up to.

To note the potential of this debate around modernity to address these pressing issues of race and racism is not to say that all the elements of its successful resolution are already in evidence. In what seems to be a step backwards from what we can call the high modern era, interest in the social and political subordination of blacks and other non-European peoples does not generally feature in contemporary debates around the philosophical, ideological, or cultural content and consequences of modernity. Instead, an innocent modernity emerges from the apparently happy social relations that graced post-Enlightenment life in Paris, Berlin, and London. These European locations are readily purged of any traces of the people without history whose degraded lives might raise awkward questions about the limits of bourgeois humanism. Montesquieu's famous question "how can one be Persian?"[7] remains stubbornly and wilfully unanswered. What might be labelled an easy postmodernism attacks both rationality and universality through an obvious and banal relativism, but such a position holds no promise for those who retreat from the suggestion that all modes of life are irreconcilable and the related idea that any ethical or political position is as valid as any other. The work of a number of black thinkers will be examined below as part of a general argument that there are other bases for ethics and aesthetics than those which appear immanent within the versions of modernity that these myopically Eurocentric theories construct. This chapter will examine some omissions and absences in these debates as well as some of the unacknowledged and frequently ethnocentric premises from which they have been conducted.

I want also to offer a critique of and a corrective to these exchanges, and my fundamental concern with the history of the African diaspora necessitates the specific starting point—the black Atlantic—that I set down in Chapter 1. The distinctive historical experiences of this diaspora's populations have created a unique body of reflections on modernity and its discontents which is an enduring presence in the cultural and political struggles of their descendants today. I want to bring to the fore elements of this alternative sequence of enquiries into the politics of life in the West. This discontinuous "tradition" has been occluded by the dominance of European and American writing elites whose loud modernist voices have dominated the clamour of philosophical and political discourses that reaches out from the eighteenth century to haunt us now. However, I am suggesting something more than the corrective inclusion of those black commentaries on the modern which have so far been overlooked by western intellectual history. I intend not only to question the credibility of a tidy, holistic conception of modernity but also to argue for the inversion of the relationship between margin and centre as it has appeared within the master discourses of the master race. In other words, I am seeking to contribute to some *re*constructive intellectual labour which, through looking at the modern cultural history of blacks in the modern world, has a great bearing on ideas of what the West was and is today. This initially requires a return to and a rethinking of the characteristically modern relationship between the master and the slave. I see this work as complementing and extending the work of feminist philosophers who have opposed the figuration of woman as a sign for the repressed or irrational other of rationality identified as male. Their exposure of what Rosi Braidotti calls the "unacknowledged and camouflaged sexual distinction at the very heart of philosophy"[8] can be paralleled by an archaeology of the icons of the blacks that appear as signs of irrational disorder or as a means to celebrate the power of human nature uncorrupted by the decadence of the civilising process. In either guise, blacks enjoy a subordinate position in the dualistic system that reproduces the dominance of bonded whiteness, masculinity, and rationality.

Slavery and the Enlightenment Project

If popular writers like Jurgen Habermas and Marshall Berman are to be believed, the unfulfilled promise of modernity's Enlightenment project remains a beleaguered but nonetheless vibrant resource which may even now be able to guide the practice of contemporary social and political struggles. In opposition to this view, I propose that the history of the African diaspora and a reassessment of the relationship between modernity and slavery may require a more complete revision of the terms in which the modernity debates have been constructed than any of its academic participants may be willing to concede.

Despite the many positive qualities of Berman's work, the persuasive generality of his argument leads him to speak rather hastily of the "intimate unity of the modern self and the modern environment." This is conveyed in an instinctive manner by "the first great wave of writers and thinkers about modernity—Goethe, Hegel, Marx, Stendhal and Baudelaire, Carlyle and Dickens, Herzen and Dostoevsky."[9] Their conspicuous European-centredness aside, remarks like this would seem not only to endorse the view of modernity as an absolute break with its past but also to deny the possibility that the distinctiveness of the modern self might reside in its being a necessarily fractured or compound entity. From Berman's perspective, the powerful impact of issues like "race" and gender on the formation and reproduction of modern selves can too easily be set aside. The possibility that the modern subject may be located in historically specific and unavoidably complex configurations of individualisation and embodiment—black and white, male and female, lord and bondsman—is not entertained. Berman compounds these difficulties by arguing that "modern environments and experiences cut across *all* boundaries of geography and ethnicity, of class and nationality, of religion and ideology: in this sense modernity can be said to unite all mankind"[10] (emphasis added). This could be read as a suggestion that an all-encompassing modernity effects everyone in a uniform and essentially similar way. This approach therefore runs contrary to my own concern with the variations and discontinuities in modern experience and with the decentred and inescapably plural nature of modern subjectivity and identity.

Like Habermas, Berman makes some very bold claims for the Enlightenment's ideological and political bequest: "these images and ideas provide a rich legacy for modern political thought and form a sort of agenda for nearly all the radical movements of the past two centuries."[11] He notes perceptively, but rather ruefully, that Montesquieu and Rousseau "have given us an agenda, *but no utopia*"[12] (emphasis added). We shall see below that the expressions of black Atlantic radicalism which are explored in subsequent chapters have consistently acquired and sometimes even refined their utopian tones. One of my aims is to defend this choice and illuminate the occasional strengths with which it has endowed diaspora politics and aesthetics.

Elsewhere, in an interesting exchange with Perry Anderson,[13] Berman goes so far as to suggest that his own entirely laudable desire to remain as close as possible to the insinuating rhythms of everyday life, and his admirable belief that left intellectuals should cultivate the capacity to read the signs in the street in defiance of contemporary pressures to retreat into a contemplative state, are both valuable products of this special modernist perspective. Though not immune to the lure of the esoteric, for a variety of reasons black intellectuals, most of whom have not held academic positions, have tended to find it easier to remain in contact with the level of culture which Berman so rightly finds invigorating.

The same set of issues emerges in even sharper focus when, in another article, Berman describes a return to the area of the South Bronx where he spent his boyhood.[14] The breakdancers and graffitists that he observes moving across the shadows of that desolate urban landscape are not so easily to be claimed for the overarching modernism he seeks to affirm. Their history, which for all its appeal does not enter directly into Berman's accounts of the dizzying allure and the democratic potential of modern society, originates in distinctively modern institutions of the western hemisphere like the sugar plantation.[15] It constitutes the lineage of a variety of social thought—a movement or sequence of movements in cultural politics and political culture—which is an extremely ambiguous component of his modernist vision and has little to do with the innocent, European modernity that appears in the wider debates in which he is participating.

Later on we shall see in detail how specific groups of black intellectuals—again not simply writers—have analysed and sought to come to terms with their inherently ambivalent relationship to the West and its dubious political legacies. Here it is only necessary to note that the contemporary descendants and the protective cultural forms of black radicalism also raise queries about the assumption of symmetrical intersubjectivity which features in so much of this discourse on the nature of modernity and modernisation. In view of this, it is unsurprising that Berman speaks of those who make it out of the ruins of the South Bronx simply as "working-class heroes,"[16] as if their membership of or affiliation to an identifiable and cohesive working class is a self-evident fact that somehow confirms his sense of the centripetal effects of modernity.

I should emphasise that Berman is not being singled out for attack here, and that I have a great deal of sympathy with his persuasive and stimulating account of modernity and its attendant political choices. Pointing to some of the lapses in his narrative of the modern should not lead one to overlook the fact that he, unlike many of his theoretical peers, does at least notice the black and Hispanic presence in the ruins of the modern city. He may not be concerned with the impact of racial categories and meanings in the work of "intuitive" modernists like Hegel, but he does recognise the contemporary cultural products of modern black history and seek to portray their positive value. Berman even appreciates that "not much of [their] art is produced in commodity form for sale."[17] However, none of these important insights interrupts his haste to annexe the cultural forms of the black Atlantic for an image of the working class. In a small way, Berman's inability to give due weight to the plurality that I believe is integral to the modern raises further profound problems about his presentation of the continuity of modern identity and the totalising wholeness with which he invests his conception of modern experience.

Pointing out aspects of the particularity of modern black experiences should not be understood as an occasion for staging the confrontation between the regional values of a distinct sector or community and the supposed universalism of occidental rationality. I am not suggesting that the contemporary traces of black intellectual history comprise or even refer to a lifeworld that is incommensurable with that of the former slaveholders. That would be the easy way out, for in focusing on racial slavery and its aftermath we are required to consider a historical relationship in which dependency and antagonism are intimately associated and in which black critiques of modernity may also be, in some significant senses, its affirmation. The key to comprehending this lies not in the overhasty separation of the cultural forms particular to both groups into some ethnic typology but in a detailed and comprehensive grasp of their complex interpenetration.[18] The intellectual and cultural achievements of the black Atlantic populations exist partly inside and not always against the grand narrative of Enlightenment and its operational principles. Their stems have grown strong, supported by a lattice of western politics and letters. Though African linguistic tropes and political and philosophical themes are still visible for those who wish to see them, they have often been transformed and adapted by their New World locations to a new point where the dangerous issues of purified essences and simple origins lose all meaning. These modern black political formations stand simultaneously both inside and outside the western culture which has been their peculiar step-parent. This complex relationship points once again to the need to engage critically with the way in which modernity has been theorised and periodised by its most enthusiastic defenders and critics. Regrettably, both groups have been equally slow in perceiving the centrality of ideas of race and culture to their ongoing investigations.

Like Berman, whose work bears his influence, Jurgen Habermas's writings convey a deep faith in the democratic potential of modernity. Modernity is understood as a distinct configuration with its own spatial and temporal characteristics defined above all through the consciousness of novelty that surrounds the emergence of civil society, the modern state, and industrial capitalism. Neither writer would accept that the normative potential of this new era has been exhausted, but theirs is not a positivistic or naive enthusiasm. Modernity is apprehended through its counter-discourses and often defended solely through its counterfactual elements, yet their analyses remain substantially unaffected by the histories of barbarity which appear to be such a prominent feature of the widening gap between modern experience and modern expectation. There is a scant sense, for example, that the universality and rationality of enlightened Europe and America were used to sustain and relocate rather than eradicate an order of racial difference inherited from the premodern era. The figure of Columbus does not appear to complement the standard pairing of Luther and Copernicus that is implicitly used to mark the limits of this particular understanding of modernity. Locke's colonial interests and the effect of the conquest of the Americas on Descartes and Rousseau are simply non-issues. In this setting, it is hardly surprising that if it is perceived to be relevant at all, the history of slavery is somehow assigned to blacks. It becomes our special property rather than a part of the ethical and intellectual heritage of the West as a whole.[19] This is only just preferable to the conventional alternative response which views plantation slavery as a premodern residue that disappears once it is revealed to be fundamentally incompatible with enlightened rationality and capitalist industrial production.

Like a good many ex-slaves and abolitionists, Habermas is tenaciously committed to the course of making bourgeois civil society live up to its political and philosophical promises. Drawing his theory of modernity from the work of Kant and Hegel, he notes its contemporary crises but says that they can be resolved only from within modernity itself by the completion of the Enlightenment project. There is perhaps an irony in seeing the affiliates of historical materialism defending the very humanistic rationality which for many years was one of their major intellectual foes.

Habermas recognises the intimate ties between the idea of modernity and the development of European art which is able to act as a reconciler of the fragmented moments of reason. Using Weber and Nietzsche, he also defines modernity through its supercession of religious world views and the process of cultural rationalisation whereby science, morality, and art are separated into autonomous spheres, each governed by its own epistemological rules and procedures of validation. The differentiation of these spheres of value is characterised by an emphasis on decentration and reflexivity. Thus the modernisation of the lifeworld sees the concepts of authenticity, aesthetics, and ethics sharply differentiated while the modern is identified in the rift between secular and sacred spheres of action opened up by the death of God and the consequent hole at the centre of the lifeworld. This divergence proceeds closely articulated with the reification of consciousness that can be apprehended in the severing of expert cultures from the lifeworld and the latter's "colonisation" by debased forms of pseudo-reason which serve only to integrate and functionalise the social system. Under these conditions, everyday consciousness becomes a "fragmented consciousness" divorced from the opportunity to engage in reflexive, self-critical practice or the chance to analyse experience in terms of distinct, cognitive, practical, and aesthetic standards.

Habermas does not follow Hegel in arguing that slavery is itself a modernising force in that it leads both master and servant first to self-consciousness and then to disillusion, forcing both to confront the unhappy realisation that the true, the good, and the beautiful do not have a single shared origin. This is probably because though Habermas's theory of modernity draws heavily on Hegel, its Kantian focus absolves it from exploring the dialectic of master and slave in which Hegel's allegory of consciousness and freedom is rooted. I will return to this point later on. It is interesting that when Habermas does finally touch on the master/slave relationship he is exclusively concerned with the psychological dimensions of the allegory. He cites Hegel's observation that it is only the "Wild Moguls" who have their Lords outside themselves whereas the authentic offspring of European modernity remain enslaved even as they carry their Lord inside themselves.[20] It is particularly disappointing that he has not found the modern demand that European masters take their enslaved other seriously worthy of more detailed comment. Habermas is acute in appreciating that Hegel's account of the master/slave relationship is secreted inside many of the writings of contemporary theorists of modernity. He gives this account of the special significance of Hegel's work in initiating the debates over modernity which prefigure contemporary discussions: "Hegel is not the first philosopher to belong to the modern age but he is the first for whom modernity became a problem. In his theory the constellation among modernity, time consciousness and rationality becomes visible for the first time. Hegel himself explodes this constellation, because rationality puffed up into absolute spirit neutralizes the conditions under which modernity attained a consciousness of itself."[21] These words endorse the idea that a journey back to Hegel may be worth making. Struggling to specify the value of the same difficult passages, the historian David Brion Davis describes them thus:

> It was Hegel's genius to endow lordship and bondage with such a rich resonance of meanings that the model could be applied to every form of physical and psychological domination . . . Above all, Hegel bequeathed a message that would have a profound impact on future thought . . . we can expect nothing from the mercy of God or from the mercy of those who exercise worldly lordship in His or other names; that man's true emancipation, whether physical or spiritual, must always depend on those who have endured and overcome some form of slavery.[22]

Brion Davis is not alone in seeking to defend a more directly social reading of Hegel's text than Habermas's own more strictly delimited and essentially psychological concerns would sanction. The writings of Alexander Kojève have been particularly important in popularising an interpretation of the master/slave relationship which, without drifting towards a literal analysis, is both less psychological and more historically specific than is currently fashionable.[23] Kojève's identification of an existential impasse that develops out of the master's dependency on the slave is also interesting because it would seem to offer an interesting point of departure for the analysis of modern aesthetics. These passages in Hegel and Kojève's influential interpretation of them have been widely taken up in social and psychoanalytic theory, forming, for example, an important part of the background to Richard Wright's Parisian revisions of Marxism and appropriations of phenomenology and existentialism. They have also been of great interest to the feminist writers who have returned to Hegel's allegory (via the Lukacs of *History and Class Consciousness*) as part of their clarifying the possibility of "standpoint epistemologies,"[24] particular sociological or experiential locations from which woman-centred knowledge about the world can proceed. This is a big debate and cannot be reconstructed in its entirety here. It has, however, been brought to bear on modern black history and political culture by a number of feminist authors, in particular Patricia Hill Collins, whose argument for the existence of a black women's standpoint epistemology is conducted in something of the same critical, reconstructive, and revisionist spirit that guides my thinking here.[25]

Hill Collins argues that the western traditions of thinking and thinking about thinking to which the human sciences are bound have systematically tried to separate these privileged activities from mere being. This insight is linked in her argument to criticism of the pernicious effects of the dualistic, binary thinking in which one partner in the cognitive couple is always dominated by its repressed and subjugated other half—male/female, rational/irrational, nature/culture, light/dark.

Though I concur with most of Hill Collins's diagnosis of this state of affairs, I disagree with her responses to it. Her answer to the western separation of thinking (and thinking about thinking) from being is to collapse them back into each other so that they form a functional unity that can be uncritically celebrated. She utilises a feminist version of this reasoning as an analogy for understanding what black women can do to produce a critical theory capable of addressing their experiences of marginalisation from truth-seeking and interpretive activities. This begins in an argument for the social construction of "race" and gender. There is no essential woman or woman in general that can focus the emancipatory project of feminist politics; therefore a feminist epistemology must proceed to construct its own standpoint addressed to that lack. This is done in a spirit disabused of the belief that essentially feminine experience can act as the guarantor of feminist knowledge claims. In the (non-black) feminist discourse, the terms woman and feminist are distinguished and must remain separate for the critique to operate plausibly. There is no open counter-argument from Hill Collins for the superior value of an essentialist understanding of black female subjectivity. However, another version of racial essentialism is smuggled in through the back porch even as Hill Collins loudly banishes it from her front door. In her transposition, the term "black" does a double duty. It covers the positions of knowing and being. Its epistemological and ontological dimensions are entirely congruent. Their simple expressive unity joins an act of political affirmation to this philosophical stance: "being black encompasses both experiencing white domination and individual and group valuation of an independent, long-standing Afrocentric consciousness."[26] Her inconsistent deployment of the term Afrocentric, sometimes appearing as a synonym for black and sometimes as equivalent to the sense of the word "feminist" which was opposed to the word "woman," does little to solve the confusion that results from this: "Even though I will continue to use the term Afrocentric feminist thought interchangeably with the phrase Black feminist thought, I think they are conceptually distinct."[27]

Hill Collins repeatedly emphasises that the standpoint she is exploring is "self-defined." This formulation appears at the point where a classically

"Leninist" version of vanguardism is imported into her writing. The mass of black women have experiences that open the way forward to unique forms of consciousness. However, they are incapable of "articulating" the standpoint and need to be helped to do this by an elite cadre of black female intellectuals who vaccinate ordinary folk with the products of their critical theorising, thereby generating resistance. This group also performs what appears to be a low-intensity disciplinary function in areas of black politics other than feminist struggles: "Black women intellectuals who articulate an autonomous, self-defined standpoint are in a position to examine the usefulness of coalitions with other groups, both scholarly and activist, in order to develop new models for social change."[28] Whatever one thinks of the political strategies implied in all this, it is striking how the image of an integral, humanist, and thoroughly Cartesian racial subject underpins and animates the construct of self that has been situated at the core of this "Black women's standpoint—those experiences and ideas shared by African-American women that provide a unique angle of vision on self, community, and society."[29] The elision of black and African-American in this passage is symptomatic of other problems that will be examined below. But what are we to make of the fact that self always comes first in this litany? What understanding of self is it to supply the subjectivity that can focus the subject of black politics?

Hill Collins's answers to these questions suggest that an embeddedness in Enlightenment assumptions continues despite the ostentatious gestures of disaffiliation. Experience-centred knowledge claims, mediated if at all by input from the intellectual vanguard, simply end up substituting the standpoint of black women for its forerunner rooted in the lives of white men. This may have some value as a short-term corrective, but it is less radical and less stimulating than the possibility that we might move beyond the desire to situate our claims about the world in the lives of these whole and stable, ideal subjects. For all its conspicuous masculinism and Eurocentrism, Hegel's allegory is relational. It can be used to point out the value of incorporating the problem of subject formation into both epistemology and political practice. This would also mean taking a cue from a politicised postmodernism and leaving the categories of enquiry open.[30]

My own interest in the famous section at the start of Hegel's *The Phenomenology of Mind*[31] is twofold: First, it can be used to initiate an analysis of modernity which is abjured by Habermas because it points directly to an approach which sees the intimate association of modernity and slavery as a fundamental conceptual issue. This is significant because it can be used to offer a firm rebuke to the mesmeric idea of history as progress and because it provides an opportunity to re-periodise and reaccentuate accounts of the dialectic of Enlightenment which have not always been concerned to look at modernity through the lenses of colonialism or scientific racism. Second, a return to Hegel's account of the conflict and the forms of dependency produced in the relationship between master and slave foregrounds the issues of brutality and terror which are also too frequently ignored. Taken together, these problems offer an opportunity to transcend the unproductive debate between a Eurocentric rationalism which banishes the slave experience from its accounts of modernity while arguing that the crises of modernity can be resolved from within, and an equally occidental anti-humanism which locates the origins of modernity's current crises in the shortcomings of the Enlightenment project.

Cornel West has pointed out that Hegel was the favourite philosopher of Dr. Martin Luther King, Jr.[32] The point of entry into the discourse of modernity which Hegel affords is doubly significant because, as we shall see, a significant number of intellectuals formed by the black Atlantic have engaged in critical dialogues with his writings. Their difficult and deeply ambivalent relationship to his work and the intellectual tradition in which it stands helps to locate their uncomfortable position relative to western politics and letters and to identify the distinctive perspectives on the modern world that they have expressed. Amiri Baraka's 1963 poem "Hegel" captures this ambivalence and shows that the appropriation of Hegelian themes is by no means always negative:

> I scream for help. And none comes, has ever
> come. No single redeeming hand
> has ever been offered . . .
> no single redeeming word, has come
> wringing out of flesh
> with the imperfect beautiful resolution
> that would release me from this heavy contract
> of emptiness.[33]

In *Being and Nothingness* Sartre makes the point that Hegel's analysis does not deal with lateral relations between masters or within the caste of slaves let alone with the impact of a free non-slave owning population on the institution of slavery.[34] However, despite these contextual failings, its insights and view of slavery as, in a sense, the premise of modernity also give us the chance to reopen discussion of the origins of black politics in the Euro-American age of revolution and the consequent relationship between the contrasting varieties of radicalism which energised the slaves' struggles for emancipation and racial justice, and which endure in the struggles of their dispersed descendants today. Plantation slavery was more than just a system of labour and a distinct mode of racial domination. Whether it encapsulates the inner essence of capitalism or was a vestigial, essentially precapitalist element in a dependant relationship to capitalism proper, it provided the foundations for a distinctive network of economic, social, and political relations. Above all, "its demise threw open the most fundamental questions of economy, society and polity,"[35] and it has retained a central place in the historical memories of the black Atlantic.

The way these populations continue to make creative, communicative use of the memory of slavery points constructively away from the twin positions that have overdetermined the debate on modernity so far—an uncritical and complacent rationalism and a self-conscious and rhetorical antihumanism which simply trivialises the potency of the negative. Moving beyond these options requires consideration of what, following Walter Benjamin, can be called the primal history of modernity.[36] Although Benjamin was not attuned to the possibility that modern history could be seen as fractured along the axis that separates European masters and mistresses from their African slaves, there are elements of his thinking, particularly those which derive from his relationship to Jewish mysticism, which make it a valuable resource for my own critique.[37] The time has come for the primal history of modernity to be reconstructed from the slaves' points of view. These emerge in the especially acute consciousness of both life and freedom which is nurtured by the slave's "mortal terror of his sovereign master" and the continuing "trial by death" which slavery becomes for the male slave.[38] This primal history offers a unique perspective on many of the key intellectual and political issues in the modernity debates. I have already mentioned the idea of history as progress. Apart from that thorny perennial, the slaves' perspectives require a discrete view not just of the dynamics of power and domination in plantation societies dedicated to the pursuit of commercial profit but of such central categories of the Enlightenment project as the idea of universality, the fixity of meaning, the coherence of the subject, and, of course, the foundational ethnocentrism in which these have all tended to be anchored. Each of these issues has an impact on the formation of racial discourse and a relevance in understanding the development of racial politics. These problems aside, the slaves' perspectives necessitate a critical stance on the discourse of bourgeois humanism which several scholars have implicated in the rise and consolidation of scientific racism.[39] Using the memory of slavery as an interpretive device suggests that this humanism cannot simply be repaired by introducing the figures of black folks who had previously been confined to the intermediate category between animal and human that Du Bois identifies as a "tertium quid."[40]

In keeping with the spiritual components which also help to distinguish

them from modern secular rationality, the slaves' perspectives deal only secondarily in the idea of a rationally pursued utopia. Their primary categories
are steeped in the idea of a revolutionary or eschatological apocalypse—
the Jubilee. They provocatively suggest that many of the advances of modernity are in fact insubstantial or pseudo-advances contingent on the
power of the racially dominant grouping and that, as a result, the critique
of modernity cannot be satisfactorily completed from within its own philosophical and political norms, that is, immanently. The representative figures
whose work I shall explore below were all acutely aware of the promise and
potential of the modern world. Nevertheless, their critical perspectives on
it were only partly grounded in its own norms. However uneasily their
work balanced its defences of modernity against its critiques, they drew
deliberately and self-consciously on premodern images and symbols that
gain an extra power in proportion to the brute facts of modern slavery.
These have contributed to the formation of a vernacular variety of unhappy
consciousness which demands that we rethink the meanings of rationality,
autonomy, reflection, subjectivity, and power in the light of an extended
meditation both on the condition of the slaves and on the suggestion that
racial terror is not merely compatible with occidental rationality but cheer-
fully complicit with it. In terms of contemporary politics and social theory,
the value of this project lies in its promise to uncover both an ethics of
freedom to set alongside modernity's ethics of law and the new conceptions of selfhood and individuation that are waiting to be constructed from
the slaves' standpoint—forever disassociated from the psychological and
epistemic correlates of racial subordination. This unstable standpoint is to
be understood in a different way from the clarion calls to epistemological
narcissism and the absolute sovereignty of unmediated experience[41] which
sometimes appear in association with the term. It can be summed up in
Foucault's tentative extension of the idea of a *critical* self-inventory into
the political field. This is made significantly in a commentary upon the
Enlightenment: "The critical ontology of ourselves has to be considered
not, certainly, as a theory, a doctrine, nor even as a permanent body of
knowledge that is accumulating; it has to be conceived as an attitude, an
ethos, a philosophical life in which the critique of what we are is at one
and the same time the historical analysis of the limits that are imposed on
us and an experiment with the possibility of going beyond them."[42]

Having recognised the cultural force of the term "modernity" we must
also be prepared to delve into the special traditions of artistic expression
that emerge from slave culture. As we shall see in the next chapter, art,
particularly in the form of music and dance, was offered to slaves as a substitute for the formal political freedoms they were denied under the planta-

tion regime. The expressive cultures developed in slavery continue to preserve in artistic form needs and desires which go far beyond the mere satisfaction of material wants. In contradistinction to the Enlightenment assumption of a fundamental separation between art and life, these expressive forms reiterate the continuity of art and life. They celebrate the grounding of the aesthetic with other dimensions of social life. The particular aesthetic which the continuity of expressive culture preserves derives not from dispassionate and rational evaluation of the artistic object but from an inescapably subjective contemplation of the mimetic functions of artistic performance in the processes of struggles towards emancipation, citizenship, and eventually autonomy. Subjectivity is here connected with rationality in a contingent manner. It may be grounded in communication, but this form of interaction is not an equivalent and idealised exchange between equal citizens who reciprocate their regard for each other in grammatically unified speech. The extreme patterns of communication defined by the institution of plantation slavery dictate that we recognise the anti-discursive and extra-linguistic ramifications of power at work in shaping communicative acts. There may, after all, be no reciprocity on the plantation outside of the possibilities of rebellion and suicide, flight and silent mourning, and there is certainly no grammatical unity of speech to mediate communicative reason. In many respects, the plantation's inhabitants live non-synchronously. Their mode of communication is divided by the radically opposed political and economic interests that distinguish the master and mistress from their respective human chattels. Under these conditions, artistic practice retains its "cultic functions" while its superior claims to authenticity and historic witness may be actively preserved. It becomes diffuse throughout the subaltern racial collectivity where relations of cultural production and reception operate that are wholly different from those which define the public sphere of the slaveholders. In this severely restricted space, sacred or profane, art became the backbone of the slaves' political cultures and of their cultural history. It remains the means through which cultural activists even now engage in "rescuing critiques" of the present by both mobilising memories of the past and inventing an imaginary past-ness that can fuel their utopian hopes.

We can see now that the arts of darkness appear in the West at the point where modernity is revealed to be actively associated with the forms of terror legitimated by reference to the idea of "race." We must remember that however modern they may appear to be, the artistic practices of the slaves and their descendants are also grounded outside modernity. The invocation of anteriority as anti-modernity is more than a consistent rhetorical flourish linking contemporary Africalogy and its nineteenth-century precursors. These gestures articulate a memory of pre-slave history that can, in turn, operate as a mechanism to distil and focus the counter-power of those held in bondage and their descendants. This artistic practice is therefore inescapably both inside and outside the dubious protection modernity offers. It can be examined in relation to modern forms, themes, and ideas but carries its own distinct critique of modernity, a critique forged out of the particular experiences involved in being a racial slave in a legitimate and avowedly rational system of unfree labour. To put it another way, this artistic and political formation has come to relish its measure of autonomy from the modern—an independent vitality that comes from the syncopated pulse of non-European philosophical and aesthetic outlooks and the fallout from their impact on western norms. This autonomy developed further as slavery, colonialism, and the terror that attended them pitted the vital arts of the slaves against the characteristically modern conditions in which their oppression appeared—as a byproduct of the coerced production of commodities for sale on a world market. This system produced an ungenteel modernity, de-centred from the closed worlds of metropolitan Europe that have claimed the attention of theorists so far.

A preoccupation with the striking doubleness that results from this unique position—in an expanded West but not completely of it—is a definitive characteristic of the intellectual history of the black Atlantic. We will see that it can be traced through the works of a number of modern black thinkers. Frederick Douglass is the first of these representative figures, and his life is an exemplary one as far as this book is concerned. It spanned the Atlantic and involved a record of consistent activism and advocacy on behalf of the slave. There is no space here to discuss the impact of his travels in England and Scotland[43] even though they help to map the spatial dimensions of the black Atlantic world. Unlike the other candidates for the role of progenitor of black nationalism—Martin Delany, Edward Wilmot Blyden, and Alexander Crummell—Douglass had been a slave himself. He is generally remembered for the quality and passion of his political oratory. His writings continue to be a rich resource in the cultural and political analysis of the black Atlantic.[44]

Lord and Bondsman in a Black Idiom

Douglass, who acquired his new post-slave surname from the pages of Sir Walter Scott's *The Lady of the Lake,* published three autobiographies, rewriting his life story and reshaping his public persona at different stages of his life.[45] These texts present a range of important black perspectives on the problem of modernity. Their literary form also raises profound issues about the aesthetic dimensions and periodisation of black modernism. Both lines of inquiry can be extended by some intertextual consideration of the relationship between Douglass's autobiographies and his only venture into fiction, *The Heroic Slave*. His relationship to modernity was a complex and shifting one, particularly in that he retained and developed the religious convictions that lay at the core of his original opposition to the slave system. Yet Douglass would need no lessons from Habermas and his followers as to the incomplete nature of the Enlightenment project or the need for criticism of religion to precede other forms of social criticism. In his writings he repeatedly calls for greater Enlightenment capable of bringing the Illumination of reason to the ethical darkness of slavery. Unlike many of those who were to follow in his footsteps, Douglass conceived of the slave plantation as an archaic institution out of place in the modern world: "[the] plantation is a little nation of its own, having its own language, its own rules, regulations and customs. The laws and institutions of the state, apparently touch it nowhere. The troubles arising here, are not settled by the civil power of the state."[46] The state's lack of access to the plantation illustrated the plantation's general inaccessibility to the varieties of modern, secular political reason necessary to its reform. Douglass compared the slave plantations to the premodern, precapitalist relations of feudal Europe: "In its isolation, seclusion, and self reliant independence [the] plantation resembles what the baronial domains were during the middle ages . . . Grim, cold and unapproachable by all genial influences from communities without, there it stands; full three hundred years behind the age in all that relates to humanity and morals . . . Civilization is shut out."[47] Douglass's own Christianity may have formed the centre of his political outlook, but he was emphatic that the best master he ever had was an atheist: "Were I again to be reduced to the condition of a slave, next to that calamity, I should regard the fact of being the slave of a religious slaveholder, the greatest that could befall me. For all the slaveholders with whom I have ever met, religious slaveholders are the worst."[48]

Douglass advocated the humanity of African slaves and attacked the exclusion of Africa from history in a celebrated ethnological lecture which he delivered in various venues from 1854 on. Later published as "The Claims of the Negro Ethnologically Considered,"[49] this piece offered a coherent challenge to the scientific racism of Douglass's own time. He discussed, among other things, the work of Samuel Morton.[50] It also conveyed the precision of Douglass's attack on the hellenomaniacal excision of Africa from the narrative of civilisation's development. This was an intensely contested issue at a time when scientific understanding was in motion towards a new version of the relationship among Ancient Greece, the Levant, and

Egypt. As Martin Bernal has pointed out,[51] much of this debate turns on the analysis of the Nile Valley civilisations in general and Egypt in particular. Like many African-Americans, Douglass visited Egypt. He travelled there with his second wife, Helen Pitts, during the late 1880s, making it clear that his journey was part of a long-term quest for the facts with which he could support his ethnological opinions.[52] It is obvious that the appeal of Egypt as evidence of the greatness of pre-slave African cultures, like the enduring symbol that Egypt supplies for black creativity and civilisation, has had a special significance within black Atlantic responses to modernity. At the very least, it helped to ground the cultural norms of diaspora politics outside the pathway marked out by the West's own progress from barbarism to civilisation and to show that the path began in Africa rather than Greece. Egypt also provided the symbolic means to locate the diaspora's critique of Enlightenment universals outside the philosophical repertoire of the West.[53] Though Douglass challenged the ethnological implications of Hegel's view of Africa and Africans from the platforms of numerous political meetings, his autobiographies provide a chance to construct critical revisions of Hegel in a rather different form. Douglass was certainly acquainted with the German idealist tradition. We are indebted to Douglass's biographer William McFeely for important details of his intimate relationship with Ottilia Assing, the translator of the German edition of *My Bondage, My Freedom* published in Hamburg in 1860. Assing came from a cultured and intellectual family background. She enjoyed close connections with her uncle's wife, Rahel Levin, an important figure in the Goethe cult. We know that Assing read both Goethe and Feuerbach to Douglass.[54] It would have been surprising if Hegel's name had not been raised in that illustrious company. Assing took her own life in the Bois de Boulogne in 1884 after Douglass's marriage to Helen Pitts.

With this suggestive connection in mind, I want to propose that we read a section of Douglass's narrative as an alternative to Hegel: a supplement if not exactly a trans-coding of his account of the struggle between lord and bondsman. In a rich account of the bitter trial of strength with Edward Covey, the slave breaker to whom he has been sent, Douglass can be read as if he is systematically reworking the encounter between master and slave in a striking manner which inverts Hegel's own allegorical scheme. It is the slave rather than the master who emerges from Douglass's account possessed of "consciousness that exists for itself," while his master becomes the representative of a "consciousness that is repressed within itself." Douglass's transformation of Hegel's metanarrative of power into a metanarrative of emancipation is all the more striking as it is also the occasion for an attempt to specify the difference between a pre-rational, spiritual mode of African thought and his own compound outlook—an uneasy hybrid of the sacred and the secular, the African and the American, formed out of the debilitating experience of slavery and tailored to the requirements of his abolitionism.

In all three versions of the tale, this section of the narrative begins with Douglass being leased into Covey's care by Thomas Auld—his "real" master. Having broken up the Sabbath school that Douglass had organised for his fellow slaves, Auld desired his slave to be "well broken" lest he develop into "another Nat Turner." Unlike Auld, Covey was a poor man steeped in a variety of pseudo-piety that Douglass viewed with special contempt. We are told, significantly, that he was a poor singer and relied mainly on Douglass for raising a hymn in the frequent acts of family worship to which his slaves were party. Douglass continually compares him to a serpent and tells us that his new master was as unreasonable as he was cruel. Without going into the detail of Covey's brutal regime or the nature of the confrontation that he engineered to break Douglass, the conflict between them induced Douglass to flee. He describes the first six months of his stay with Covey in dramatic fashion: "A few months of his discipline tamed me. Mr Covey succeeded in breaking me. I was broken in body, soul and spirit. My natural elasticity was crushed; my intellect languished; the disposition to read departed; the cheerful spark that lingered about my eye died; the dark night of slavery closed in upon me; and behold a man transformed into a brute."[55]

After a particularly severe beating, Douglass returned to Auld to display his wounds and to appeal to him on the grounds that Covey's unjust and brutal regime had endangered a valuable piece of property, namely Douglass himself. Auld found excuses for Covey's behaviour and ordered Douglass to return to his custody. Hidden in the woods, "shut in with nature and nature's God," Douglass prayed, like Madison Washington, the fictional hero of *The Heroic Slave,* for deliverance from slavery in general and Covey in particular. Douglass concedes at this point that he experienced doubt about all religion and believed his prayers to be delusory. As night fell he met another slave who was on his way to spend the Sabbath with his wife, who resided on a neighbouring plantation. Later in Douglass's narratives, readers learn that this man, Sandy, betrayed the slaves when they tried to escape. However, at this point in the tale Douglass looks upon him with respect. He was famous among local slaves for his good nature and his good sense: "He was not only a religious man, but he professed to believe in a system for which I have no name. He was a genuine African, and had inherited some of the so-called magical powers, said to be possessed by African and eastern nations."[56]

Douglass "pour[ed] his grief" into the conjurer's ears and, after a meal, they discussed what strategy was most suitable in circumstances where out-and-out flight was impossible. Sandy's belief in the system of ancient African magic led him to offer Douglass a charmed magic root which, if worn on the right side of his body, would make him invulnerable to Covey's blows. Sandy answered Douglass's Christian scepticism by telling him that his book-learning had not kept Covey off him. He begged the runaway to try the African—I am tempted to say Africentric—alternative, saying that it could certainly do no harm. Douglass took the root from Sandy and returned to the Covey household. He tells the eager reader "a slight gleam or shadow of his superstition had fallen upon me."[57] In view of the fact that Douglass makes such great use of the symbolism of light and darkness, the construction "gleam or shadow" is an interesting evasion. Was it a gleam or a shadow? The two ideas are clear alternatives with strikingly different implications for our reading of the episode. The carefully deployed ambiguity may also be a cryptic acknowledgement of the different ways in which black and white readers were likely to respond to the tale.

On his return, Douglass met Covey and his wife en route to church dressed in their Sunday best. Covey had acquired the countenance of an Angel and smiled so broadly that Douglass began "to think that Sandy's herb had more virtue in it than I, in my pride, had been willing to allow."[58] All went well until Monday morning when Covey, freed from his religious observance, returned to his customary and devious brutality. This was the moment when Douglass resolved, with devastating consequences, to stand up in his own defense. The Hegelian struggle ensued, but this time Douglass discovered an ideal speech situation at the very moment in which he held his tormentor by the throat: "I held him so firmly by the throat that his blood flowed through my nails . . . Are you going to resist you scoundrel" said he. To which, I returned a polite "Yes Sir."[59] The two men were locked together in the Hegelian impasse. Each was able to contain the strength of the other without vanquishing him. Enraged by Douglass's unexpected act of insubordination, Covey then sought to enlist the aid of the other people who were to hand, both slave and free. Covey's cousin Hughes was beaten off by Douglass, then Bill, the hired man, affected ignorance of what Covey wished him to do, and Caroline, the female slave in the Covey household, bravely declined her master's instruction to take hold of Douglass. In the text, each of these supporting characters is addressed by Douglass and Covey in turn. The mutual respect born in their tussle is conveyed by the manner in which they appeal to the others as equals. After two hours, Covey gave up the contest and let Douglass go. The narrator tells us that he was a changed man after that fight, which was "the turning point" in his career as a slave. The physical struggle is also the occasion on which a liberatory definition of masculinity is produced.

> I was nothing before; I was a man now. It [the fight] recalled to life my crushed self-respect and my self confidence, and inspired me with a renewed determination to be a free man. A man without force is without the essential dignity of humanity . . . I was no longer a servile coward, trembling under the frown of a brother worm of the dust, but my long-cowed spirit was roused to an attitude of manly independence. I had reached a point at which I was not afraid to die.[60]

Douglass's tale can be used to reveal a great deal about the difference between the male slave's and the master's views of modern civilisation. In Hegel's allegory, which correctly places slavery at the natal core of modern sociality, we see that one solipsistic combatant in the elemental struggle prefers his conqueror's version of reality to death and submits. He becomes the slave while the other achieves mastery. Douglass's version is quite different. For him, the slave actively prefers the possibility of death to the continuing condition of inhumanity on which plantation slavery depends. He anticipated a point made by Lacan some years later: "death, precisely because it has been drawn into the function of stake in the game . . . shows at the same time how much of the prior rule, as well as of the concluding settlement, has been elided. For in the last analysis it is necessary for the loser not to perish, in order to become a slave. In other words, the pact everywhere precedes violence before perpetuating it."[61]

This turn towards death as a release from terror and bondage and a chance to find substantive freedom accords perfectly with Orlando Patterson's celebrated notion of slavery as a state of "social death."[62] It points to the value of seeing the consciousness of the slave as involving an extended act of mourning. Douglass's preference for death fits readily with archival material on the practice of slave suicide and needs also to be seen alongside other representations of death as agency that can be found in early African-American fiction.[63] Ronald Takaki and others[64] have discussed these passages as part of a wider consideration of Douglass's changing view of the necessity of violence in the cause of black emancipation—a theme that Douglass developed further in *The Heroic Slave*. Douglass's departure from the pacifism that had marked his early work is directly relevant to his critical understanding of modernity. It underscored the complicity of civilisation and brutality while emphasising that the order of authority on which the slave plantation relied cannot be undone without recourse to the counter-violence of the oppressed. Douglass's description of his combat with Covey expresses this once again, offering an interesting though distinctly masculinist resolution of slavery's inner oppositions.

This idea of masculinity is largely defined against the experience of infantilism on which the institutions of plantation slavery rely rather than against women. However, it is interesting that this aspect of Douglass's political stance has been discussed elsewhere among the would-be savants and philosophes of the black Atlantic as a symptom of important differences in the philosophical and strategic orientations of black men and women. In his famous essay "On the Damnation of Women" Du Bois recounts a story told to him by Wendell Phillips which pinpoints the problem with precision:

> Wendell Phillips says that he was once in Faneuil Hall, when Frederick Douglass was one of the chief speakers. Douglass had been describing the wrongs of the Negro race and as he proceeded he grew more and more excited and finally ended by saying that they had no hope of justice from whites, no possible hope except in their own right arms. It must come to blood! They must fight for themselves. Sojourner Truth was sitting, tall and dark, on the very front seat facing the platform, and in the hush of feeling when Douglass sat down she spoke out in her deep, peculiar voice, heard all over the hall: "Frederick, is God dead?"[65]

The question which Sojourner Truth detected in Douglass's fiery oratory and pessimistic political conclusion has an important place in philosophical debates over the value of modernity and the transvaluation of post-sacral, modern values. In Germany at roughly the same time, another Frederick (Nietzsche) was pondering the philosophical and ethical implications of the same question. It remains implicit in the story of Douglass's struggles in and against slavery. It may also be a question that cannot be separated from the distinct mode of masculinity with which it has been articulated. To counter any ambiguity around this point in Douglass's tale, I want to pursue similar philosophical conclusions which appeared elsewhere in the history of the abolitionist movement as an important cipher for its emergent feminist sensibilities shortly after Douglass's own tale was published.

The horrific story of Margaret Garner's attempted escape from slavery in Kentucky can usefully be read in conjunction with Douglass's autobiographical story. A version of this tale is still circulating, both as part of the African-American literary tradition inaugurated by works like Douglass's *The Heroic Slave* and as part of what might be called the black feminist political project. This longevity is testimony not simply to Toni Morrison's conspicuous skill as a writer in reinventing this story in her novel *Beloved*[66] but to the continuing symbolic power of the tale and its importance as an element of the moral critique that anchors black antipathy to the forms of rationality and civilised conduct which made racial slavery and its brutality legitimate.

Contemporary newspaper reports, abolitionist material, and various biographical and autobiographical accounts provide the sources from which this episode can be reconstructed. The simplest details of the case shared by various accounts[67] seem to be as follows. Taking advantage of the winter which froze the Ohio river that usually barred her way to freedom, Margaret Garner, a "mulatto, about five feet high, showing one fourth or one third white blood . . . [with] a high forehead . . . [and] bright and intelligent eyes,"[68] fled slavery on a horse-drawn sleigh in January 1856 with her husband, Simon Garner, Jr., also known as Robert, his parents, Simon and Mary, their four children, and nine other slaves. On reaching Ohio, the family separated from the other slaves, but they were discovered after they had sought assistance at the home of a relative, Elijah Kite. Trapped in his house by the encircling slave catchers, Margaret killed her three-year-old daughter with a butcher's knife and attempted to kill the other children rather than let them be taken back into slavery by their master, Archibald K. Gaines, the owner of Margaret's husband and of the plantation adjacent to her own home. This case initiated a series of legal battles over the scope of the Fugitive Slave Act,[69] Margaret's extradition, her legal subjectivity, and the respective powers of court officers in the different states. Despite pleas that she be placed on trial for the murder of the little girl "whom she probably loved the best,"[70] Margaret's master eventually sent her to the slave market in New Orleans.

The contemporary reports of this episode are contradictory and burdened with the conflicting political interests that framed its central tragedy. One newspaper report suggested that the Garners' original decision to flee from bondage had, for example, been encouraged by a visit to the Gaines household by two English Ladies.[71] The best-known account of the events is set down in the *Reminiscences of Levi Coffin*. Coffin was a local Quaker abolitionist and reputed president of the Underground Railroad who had been peripherally involved in the tragedy. A number of interesting points emerge from that authoritative source as well as from newspaper articles about the case, the American Anti-Slavery Society's annual report, an account given in the biography of Lucy Stone, the distinguished abolitionist and suffragist who visited Margaret Garner in prison and attended the court hearings, and a further version written for the *American Baptist* by one P. S. Bassett, who gave his address as the Fairmount Theological Seminary in Cincinnati.[72]

Hopelessly surrounded by a posse of slave catchers in the house of their kinsman Elijah Kite, Margaret's husband, Simon Garner, Jr., fired several shots from a revolver at the pursuers. In a further struggle that took place after Gaines and his associates had succeeded in entering the house, one marshal had two fingers shot from his hand and lost several teeth from a ricocheting bullet. Coffin writes that "the slave men were armed and fought bravely," while the Anti-Slavery Society makes this resistance a matrimonial rather than gender-based phenomenon: "Robert and Margaret fought bravely and desperately to protect their parents, and their children, in their right to liberty, but were soon overpowered."[73] In this account Margaret's assault on the children takes place between two attacks on the house by Gaines and his henchmen. In Coffin's version of the story it is only *after* Margaret has appreciated the hopelessness of the slaves' besieged position and seen her husband overpowered that she begins her emancipatory assault on her children.

Some newspaper reports said that after almost decapitating the little girl's body in the act of cutting her throat, Margaret called out to her mother-in-law for assistance in slaying the other children, "Mother, help me to kill the children."[74] Bassett, who claimed to have interviewed both the women, quoted Mary Garner as saying that she "neither encouraged nor discouraged her daughter-in-law,—for under similar circumstances she should probably have done the same." What mode of rational, moral calculation may have informed this appeal from one black woman to another? Other papers reported that the older woman could not endure the sight of her grandchildren being murdered and ran to take refuge under a bed. What are we to make of these contrasting forms of violence, one coded as male and outward, directed towards the oppressor, and the other, coded as female, somehow internal, channelled towards a parent's most precious and intimate objects of love, pride, and desire? After her arrest, Margaret Garner is said to have sat in the Hammond Street Police Station House in a shocked and stupefied state. Archibald Gaines took the body of her dead daughter away so that he could bury it in Kentucky on land "consecrated to slavery."[75]

This tale was immediately repeated within the abolitionist movement as important proof of the venal menace posed by the unbridled appetites of the slave masters. From this perspective, much was to be made of the fact that the slain child had been female, killed by her mother lest she fall victim to this licentiousness. Lucy Stone emphasised this point to her biographer: "She was a beautiful woman, chestnut colored, with good features and wonderful eyes. It was no wild desperation that had impelled her, but a calm determination that, if she could not find freedom here, she would get it with the angels . . . Margaret had tried to kill all her children, but she had made sure of the little girl. She had said that her daughter would never suffer as she had."[76]

Stone attended the courtroom deliberations over Margaret's fate and was accused of trying to pass a knife to her while visiting her in prison, so that she could finish the job she had begun. We are told by Coffin that Stone drew tears from many listeners when, in explaining her conduct before the court, she made this argument: "When I saw that poor fugitive, took her toil-hardened hand in mine, and read in her face deep suffering and an ardent longing for freedom, I could not help bid her be of good cheer. I told her that a thousand hearts were aching for her, and that they were glad one child of hers was safe with the angels. Her only reply was a look of deep despair, of anguish such that no words can speak."[77] Stone defended Margaret's conduct as a woman and a Christian, arguing that her infanticide sprung from the deepest and holiest feelings implanted alike in black and white women by their common divine father. Coffin quotes her as likening Margaret's spirit to that of those ancestors to whom the monument at Bunker Hill had been erected. She made the proto-feminist interpretation of Margaret's actions quite explicit: "The faded faces of the Negro Children tell too plainly to what degradation female slaves submit. Rather than give her little daughter to that life, she killed it."[78]

Further indication of the power of this narrative in the development of a distinctly feminine abolitionist discourse comes from the lectures of Sarah Parker Remond, a black abolitionist and physician born free in Salem, Massachusetts, who eventually made her home in Italy.[79] Interestingly, we know that Lucy Stone had visited the Salem Female Anti-Slavery Society, to which Sarah belonged.[80] A version of Remond's account of the Garner story is given in a newspaper report of a packed public meeting that she addressed in the Music Hall, Warrington, England, three years after the incident.[81] Remond had discussed the case with John Jolliffe, Margaret Garner's attorney. Her concern throughout the one-and-a-half-hour lecture was to demonstrate the un-Christian and immoral character of slavery and to reveal its capacity to pervert both civilisation and the natural attributes of human beings. According to the conventions of abolitionist discourse, the image of abusive and coercive white male sexuality was prominently displayed. The perversion of maternity by the institution of slavery was a well-seasoned theme in abolitionist propaganda. Frederick Douglass had made this very point in his *Narrative*, recounting an incident in which a white woman, Mrs. Hicks, murdered her slave—a cousin of Douglass's—for failing to keep the baby she was charged with minding sufficiently quiet during the night.

The offence for which this girl was murdered was this:—She had been set that night to mind Mrs. Hick's baby and during the night she fell asleep and the baby cried. She having lost her rest for several nights previous, did not hear the crying. They were both in the room with Mrs. Hicks. Mrs. Hicks, finding the girl slow to move, jumped from her bed, seized an oak stick of wood by the fireplace, and with it broke the girl's nose and breastbone, and thus ended her life.[82]

These stories raise complex questions about the mediating role of gender categories in racial politics and in particular about the psychological structures of identification facilitated by the idea of maternity. It is impossible to explore these important matters here. The Margaret Garner story corresponds most closely to Douglass's work in her refusal to concede any legitimacy to slavery and thereby initiate the dialectic of intersubjective dependency and recognition that Hegel's allegory presents as modernity's precondition. Like Douglass's, her tale constructs a conception of the slave subject as an agent. What appears in both stories to be a positive preference for death rather than continued servitude can be read as a contribution towards slave discourse on the nature of freedom itself. It supplies a valuable clue towards answering the question of how the realm of freedom is conceptualised by those who have never been free. This inclination towards death and away from bondage is fundamental. It reminds us that in the revolutionary eschatology which helps to define this primal history of modernity, whether apocalyptic or redemptive, it is the moment of jubilee that has the upper hand over the pursuit of utopia by rational means. The discourse of black spirituality which legitimises these moments of violence possesses a utopian truth content that projects beyond the limits of the present. The repeated choice of death rather than bondage articulates a principle of negativity that is opposed to the formal logic and rational calculation characteristic of modern western thinking and expressed in the Hegelian slave's preference for bondage rather than death. As part of his argument against her return to Kentucky, Margaret's lawyer, Mr. Jolliffe, told the court that she and the other fugitives "would all go singing to the gallows" rather than be returned to slavery. The association of this apparent preference for death with song is also highly significant. It joins a moral and political gesture to an act of cultural creation and affirmation. This should be borne in mind when we come to consider how intervention in the memories of slavery is routinely practised as a form of vernacular cultural history.

Douglass's writings and the popularity of the Garner narrative are also notable for marking out the process whereby the division of intellectual labour within the abolitionist movement was transformed. The philosophical material for the abolitionist cause was no longer to be exclusively generated by white commentators who articulated the metaphysical core of simple, factual slave narratives. It is also important to emphasise that these texts offer far more than the reworking and transformation of the familiar Hegelian allegory. They express in the most powerful way a tradition of writing in which autobiography becomes an act or process of simultaneous self-creation and self-emancipation.[83] The presentation of a public persona thus becomes a founding motif within the expressive culture of the African diaspora.[84] The implications that this has for the inner aesthetic character of black Atlantic modernity will be explored in greater detail below. It is important to note here that a new discursive economy emerges with the refusal to subordinate the particularity of the slave experience to the totalising power of universal reason held exclusively by white hands, pens, or publishing houses. Authority and autonomy emerge directly from the deliberately personal tone of this history. Eagerly received by the movement to which they were addressed, these tales helped to mark out a dissident space within the bourgeois public sphere which they aimed to suffuse with their utopian content. The autobiographical character of many statements like this is thus absolutely crucial. It appeals in special ways to the public opinion of the abolitionist movement against the arbitrary power intrinsic to a slave system which is both unreasonable and un-Christian. What Richard Wright would later identify as the aesthetics of personalism flows from these narratives and shows that in the hands of slaves the particular can wear the mantle of truth and reason as readily as the universal.

It is worth pausing for a moment to examine an especially significant passage at the end of the fifth chapter of Douglass's narrative which has been pointed out by William Andrews in his absorbing book *To Tell a Free Story*.[85] In this passage, Douglass is reflecting on a turning point in his life when, at the age of seven or eight, he was sent by his master to Baltimore to live with the Aulds. Looking back on this event, Douglass describes it as the first plain manifestation of a special providence which has attended him ever since. He acknowledges that the white reader is likely to respond sceptically to his claim to have been singled out for this special destiny: "I may be deemed superstitious, and even egotistical, in regarding this event as a special interposition of divine providence in my favour. But I should be false to the earliest sentiments of my soul if I suppressed the opinion. I prefer to be true to myself even at the hazard of incurring the ridicule of others, rather than to be false and incur my own abhorrence."[86] Andrews points out that Douglass does not appeal to *divine* authority to legitimate this declaration of independence in the interpretation of his own life. The passage underscores the link between autobiographical writing and the project of self-liberation. Its fundamental importance lies in the clarity of its announcement that truth to the self takes priority over what the readers may think is acceptable or appropriate to introduce into an abolitionist discourse. However, I believe that there is a deeper argument here concerning the status of truth and reason as universal concepts and the need to depart from absolute standards if the appropriate qualities of racial authenticity and personal witness are to be maintained. The distinctive pattern of self-creation evident in this text and many similar texts of the period is not, as some of the aspiring post-structuralist literary critics would have it, simply the inauguration of a new and vital literary genre. Douglass's conclusions direct the reader's attention to a distinct and compelling variety of metaphysical, philosophical commentary. They point to the initiation and reproduction of a distinctive political perspective in which autopoiesis articulates with poetics to form a stance, a style, and a philosophical mood that have been repeated and reworked in the political culture of the black Atlantic ever since. The vernacular components of black expressive culture are thus tied to the more explicitly philosophical writings of black modernist writers like Wright and Du Bois. They develop this line of enquiry by seeking to answer the metaphysical questions "Who am I?" and "When am I most myself?"

Some years later, Du Bois echoed Douglass with a disarming precision. He developed the argument implied in the earlier text, elevating it to a new level of abstraction:

> This the American black man knows: his fight here is a fight to the finish. Either he dies or wins. If he wins it will be by no subterfuge or evasion of amalgamation. He will enter modern civilisation here in America as a black man on terms of perfect and unlimited equality with any white man, or he will not enter at all. Either extermination root and branch, or absolute equality. There can be no compromise. This is the last great battle of the West.[87]

Like Douglass, Du Bois wanted to establish that the history of blacks in the new world, particularly the experiences of the slave trade and the plantation, were a legitimate part of the moral history of the West as a whole. They were not unique events—discrete episodes in the history of a minority—that could be grasped through their exclusive impact on blacks themselves, nor were they aberrations from the spirit of modern culture that were likely to be overcome by inexorable progress towards a secular, rational utopia. The continuing existence of racism belied both these verdicts, and it requires us to look more deeply into the relationship of racial terror and subordination to the inner character of modernity. This is the path indicated by Wright, James, Du Bois, and a host of others who have contributed in a variety of ways to the hermeneutics which distinguishes the grounded aesthetics of the black Atlantic. This hermeneutics has two interrelated dimensions—it is both a hermeneutics of suspicion and a hermeneutics of memory. Together they have nurtured a redemptive critique.

In the period after slavery, the memory of the slave experience is itself recalled and used as an additional, supplementary instrument with which to construct a distinct interpretation of modernity. Whether or not these memories invoke the remembrance of a terror which has moved beyond the grasp of ideal, grammatical speech, they point out of the present towards a utopian transformation of racial subordination. We must enquire then whether a definition of modern rationality such as that employed by Habermas leaves room for a liberatory, aesthetic moment which is emphatically anti- or even pre-discursive? In other words, in what follows, the critique of bourgeois ideology and the fulfilment of the Enlightenment project under the banner of working-class emancipation which goes hand in hand with it is being complemented by another struggle — the battle to represent a redemptive critique of the present in the light of the vital memories of the slave past. This critique is constructed only partly from within the normative structures provided by modernity itself. We can see this from the way it mobilises an idea of the ancient pre-slave past, often in the form of a concern with Egyptian history and culture, and uses this to anchor its dissident assessments of modernity's achievements.

3

"Jewels Brought from Bondage": Black Music and the Politics of Authenticity

My nationality is reality.
Kool G Rap

Since the mid-nineteenth century a country's music has become a political ideology by stressing national characteristics, appearing as a representative of the nation, and everywhere confirming the national principle . . . Yet music, more than any other artistic medium, expresses the national principle's antinomies as well.
T. W. Adorno

O black and unknown bards of long ago,
How came your lips to touch the sacred fire?
How in your darkness, did you come to know
The power and beauty of the minstrel's lyre?
Who first from midst his bonds lifted his eyes?
Who first from out the still watch, lone and long,
Feeling the ancient faith of prophets rise
Within his dark-kept soul burst into song?

Heart of what slave poured out such melody
As "Steal away to Jesus"? On its strains
His spirit must have nightly floated free,
Though still about his hands he felt his chains.
Who heard great "Jordan Roll"? Whose starward eye
Saw chariot "swing low"? And who was he
That breathed that comforting melodic sigh,
"Nobody knows de trouble I see"?
James Weldon Johnson

THE CONTEMPORARY debates over modernity and its possible eclipse cited in the last chapter have largely ignored music. This is odd given that the modern differentiation of the true, the good, and the beautiful was conveyed directly in the transformation of public use of culture in general and the increased public importance of all kinds of music.[1] I have suggested that the critiques of modernity articulated by successive generations of black intellectuals had their rhizomorphic systems of propagation anchored in a continued proximity to the unspeakable terrors of the slave experience. I argued that this critique was nurtured by a deep sense of the complicity of racial terror with reason. The resulting ambivalence towards modernity has constituted some of the most distinctive forces shaping black Atlantic political culture. What follows will develop this argument in a slightly different direction by exploring some of the ways in which closeness to the ineffable terrors of slavery was kept alive—carefully cultivated—in ritualised, social forms. This chapter begins a shift that will be developed further in Chapter 4, where my concern with black responses to modernity begins to be complemented by an interest in the development of black modernisms.

The question of racial terror always remains in view when these modernisms are discussed because imaginative proximity to terror is their inaugural experience. This focus is refined somewhat in the progression from slave society into the era of imperialism. Though they were unspeakable, these terrors were not inexpressible, and my main aim here is to explore how residual traces of their necessarily painful expression still contribute to historical memories inscribed and incorporated into the volatile core of Afro-Atlantic cultural creation. Thinking about the primary object of this chapter—black musics—requires this reorientation towards the phatic and the ineffable.

Through a discussion of music and its attendant social relations, I want to clarify some of the distinctive attributes of black cultural forms which are both modern and modernist. They are modern because they have been marked by their hybrid, creole origins in the West, because they have struggled to escape their status as commodities and the position within the cultural industries it specifies, and because they are produced by artists whose understanding of their own position relative to the racial group and of the role of art in mediating individual creativity with social dynamics is shaped by a sense of artistic practice as an autonomous domain either reluctantly or happily divorced from the everyday lifeworld.

These expressive cultural forms are thus western and modern, but this is not all they are. I want to suggest that, rather like the philosophical critique examined in Chapter 2, their special power derives from a doubleness, their unsteady location simultaneously inside and outside the conventions, assumptions, and aesthetic rules which distinguish and periodise modernity. These musical forms and the intercultural conversations to which they contribute are a dynamic refutation of the Hegelian suggestions that thought and reflection have outstripped art and that art is opposed to philosophy as the lowest, merely sensuous form of reconciliation between nature and finite reality.[2] The stubborn modernity of these black musical forms would require a reordering of Hegel's modern hierarchy of cultural achievements. This might claim, for example, that music should enjoy higher status because of its capacity to express a direct image of the slaves' will.

The anti-modernity of these forms, like their anteriority, appears in the (dis)guise of a premodernity that is both actively reimagined in the present and transmitted intermittently in eloquent pulses from the past. It seeks not simply to change the relationship of these cultural forms to newly autonomous philosophy and science but to refuse the categories on which the relative evaluation of these separate domains is based and thereby to transform the relationship between the production and use of art, the everyday world, and the project of racial emancipation.

The topos of unsayability produced from the slaves' experiences of racial terror and figured repeatedly in nineteenth-century evaluations of slave music has other important implications. It can be used to challenge the privileged conceptions of both language and writing as preeminent expressions of human consciousness. The power and significance of music within the black Atlantic have grown in inverse proportion to the limited expressive power of language. It is important to remember that the slaves' access to literacy was often denied on pain of death and only a few cultural opportunities were offered as a surrogate for the other forms of individual autonomy denied by life on the plantations and in the barracoons. Music becomes vital at the point at which linguistic and semantic indeterminacy/polyphony arise amidst the protracted battle between masters, mistresses, and slaves. This decidedly modern conflict was the product of circumstances where language lost something of its referentiality and its privileged relationship to concepts.[3] In his narrative, Frederick Douglass raised this point when discussing Gore, the overseer who illustrates the relationship between the rationalism of the slave system and its terror and barbarity:

> Mr Gore was a grave man, and, though a young man, he indulged in no jokes, said no funny words, seldom smiled. His words were in perfect keeping with his looks, and his looks were in perfect keeping with his words. Overseers will sometimes indulge in a witty word, even with the slaves; not so with Mr Gore. He spoke but to command, and commanded but to be obeyed; he dealt sparingly with words, and bountifully with his whip, never using the former where the latter would answer as well . . . His savage barbarity was equalled only by the consummate coolness with which he committed the grossest and most savage deeds upon the slaves under his charge.[4]

Examining the place of music in the black Atlantic world means surveying the self-understanding articulated by the musicians who have made it, the symbolic use to which their music is put by other black artists and writers, and the social relations which have produced and reproduced the unique expressive culture in which music comprises a central and even foundational element. I want to propose that the possible commonality of post-slave, black cultural forms be approached via several related problems which converge in the analysis of black musics and their supporting social relations. One particularly valuable pathway into this is provided by the distinctive patterns of language use that characterise the contrasting populations of the modern, western, African diaspora.[5] The oral character of the cultural settings in which diaspora musics have developed presupposes a distinctive relationship to the body—an idea expressed with exactly the right amount of impatience by Glissant: "It is nothing new to declare that for us music, gesture, dance are forms of communication, just as important as the gift of speech. This is how we first managed to emerge from the plantation: aesthetic form in our cultures must be shaped from these oral structures."[6]

The distinctive kinesics of the post-slave populations was the product of these brutal historical conditions. Though more usually raised by analysis of sports, athletics, and dance it ought to contribute directly to the under standing of the traditions of performance which continue to characterise the production and reception of diaspora musics. This orientation to the specific dynamics of performance has a wider significance in the analysis of black cultural forms than has so far been supposed. Its strengths are evident when it is contrasted with approaches to black culture that have been premised exclusively on textuality and narrative rather than dramaturgy, enunciation, and gesture—the pre- and anti-discursive constituents of black metacommunication.

Each of these areas merits detailed treatment in its own right.[7] All of them are configured by their compound and multiple origins in the mix of African and other cultural forms sometimes referred to as creolisation. However, my main concern in this chapter is less with the formal attributes of these syncretic expressive cultures than with the problem of how critical, evaluative, axiological, (anti)aesthetic judgements on them can be made and with the place of ethnicity and authenticity within these judgements. What special analytical problems arise if a style, genre, or particular performance of music is identified as being expressive of the absolute essence of the group that produced it? What contradictions appear in the transmission and adaptation of this cultural expression by other diaspora populations, and how will they be resolved? How does the hemispheric displacement and global dissemination of black music get reflected in localised traditions of critical writing, and, once the music is perceived as a world phenomenon, what value is placed upon its origins, particularly if they come into opposition against further mutations produced during its contingent loops and fractal trajectories? Where music is thought to be emblematic and constitutive of racial difference rather than just associated with it, how is music used to specify general issues pertaining to the problem of racial authenticity and the consequent self-identity of the ethnic group? Thinking about music—a non-representational, non-conceptual form—raises aspects of embodied subjectivity that are not reducible to the cognitive and the ethical. These questions are also useful in trying to pinpoint the distinctive aesthetic components in black communication.

The invented traditions of musical expression which are my object here are equally important in the study of diaspora blacks and modernity because they have supported the formation of a distinct, often priestly caste of organic intellectuals[8] whose experiences enable us to focus upon the crisis of modernity and modern values with special clarity. These people have often been intellectuals in the Gramscian sense, operating without the benefits that flow either from a relationship to the modern state or from secure institutional locations within the cultural industries. They have often pursued roles that escape categorisation as the practice of either legislators or interpreters and have advanced instead as temporary custodians of a distinct and embattled cultural sensibility which has also operated as a political and philosophical resource. The irrepressible rhythms of the once forbidden drum are often still audible in their work. Its characteristic syncopations still animate the basic desires—to be free and to be oneself—that are revealed in this counterculture's unique conjunction of body and music. Music, the grudging gift that supposedly compensated slaves not only for their exile from the ambiguous legacies of practical reason but for their complete exclusion from modern political society, has been refined and developed so that it provides an enhanced mode of communication beyond the petty power of words—spoken or written.

Paradoxically, in the light of their origins in the most modern of social relations at the end of the eighteenth century, modernity's ethnocentric aesthetic assumptions have consigned these musical creations to a notion of the primitive that was intrinsic to the consolidation of scientific racism. The creators of this musically infused subculture and counter-power are perhaps more accurately described as midwives, an appropriate designation following Julia Kristeva's provocative pointers towards the "feminisation" of the ethical bases from which dissident political action is possible.[9] They stand their ground at the social pivot of atavistic nature and rational culture. I want to endorse the suggestion that these subversive music makers and users represent a different kind of intellectual not least because their self-identity and their practice of cultural politics remain outside the dialectic of pity and guilt which, especially among oppressed people, has so often governed the relationship between the writing elite and the masses of people who exist outside literacy. I also want to ask whether for black cultural theory to embrace or even accept this mediated, tactical relationship to the unrepresentable, the pre-rational, and the sublime would be to sip from a poisoned chalice. These questions have become politically decisive since these cultural forms have colonised the interstices of the cultural industry on behalf not just of black Atlantic peoples but of the poor, exploited, and downpressed everywhere.

The current debate over modernity centres either on the problematic relationships between politics and aesthetics or on the question of science and its association with the practice of domination.[10] Few of these debates operate at the interface of science and aesthetics which is the required starting point of contemporary black cultural expression and the digital technology of its social dissemination and reproduction. These debates over modernity conventionally define the political instance of the modern social totality through a loose invocation of the achievements of bourgeois democracy. The discrete notion of the aesthetic, in relation to which this self-sustaining political domain is then evaluated, is constructed by the idea and the ideology of the text and of textuality as a mode of communicative practice which provides a model for all other forms of cognitive exchange and social interaction. Urged on by the post-structuralist critiques of the metaphysics of presence, contemporary debates have moved beyond citing language as the fundamental analogy for comprehending all signifying practices to a position where textuality (especially when wrenched open through the concept of difference) expands and merges with totality. Paying careful attention to the structures of feeling which underpin black expressive cultures can show how this critique is incomplete. It gets blocked by this invocation of all-encompassing textuality. Textuality becomes a means to evacuate the problem of human agency, a means to specify the death (by fragmentation) of the subject and, in the same manoeuvre, to enthrone the literary critic as mistress or master of the domain of creative human communication.

At the risk of appearing rather esoteric, I want to suggest that the history and practice of black music point to other possibilities and generate other plausible models. This neglected history is worth reconstructing, whether or not it supplies pointers to other more general cultural processes. However, I want to suggest that bourgeois democracy in the genteel metropolitan guise in which it appeared at the dawn of the public sphere should not serve as an ideal type for all modern political processes. Secondly, I want to shift concern with the problems of beauty, taste, and artistic judgement so that discussion is not circumscribed by the idea of rampant, invasive textuality. Foregrounding the history of black music making encourages both of these propositions. It also requires a different register of analytic concepts. This demand is amplified by the need to make sense of musical performances in which identity is fleetingly experienced in the most intensive ways and sometimes socially reproduced by means of neglected modes of signifying practice like mimesis, gesture, kinesis, and costume. Antiphony (call and response) is the principal formal feature of these musical traditions. It has come to be seen as a bridge from music into other modes of cultural expression, supplying, along with improvisation, montage, and dramaturgy, the hermeneutic keys to the full medley of black artistic practices. Toni Morrison eloquently states her view of this important relationship.

> Black Americans were sustained and healed and nurtured by the translation of their experience into art above all in the music. That was functional . . . My parallel is always the music because all of the strategies of the art are there. All of the intricacy, all of the discipline. All the work that must go into improvisation so that it appears that you've never touched it. Music makes you hungry for more of it. It never really gives you the whole number. It slaps and it embraces, it slaps and it embraces. The literature ought to do the same thing. I've been very deliberate about that. The power of the word is not music, but in terms of aesthetics, the music is the mirror that gives me the necessary clarity . . . The major things black art has to have are these: it must have the ability to use found objects, the appearance of using found things, and it must look effortless. It must look cool and easy. If it makes you sweat, you haven't done the work. You shouldn't be able to see the seams and stitches. I have wanted always to develop a way of writing that was irrevocably black. I don't have the resources of a musician but I thought that if it was truly black literature it would not be black because I was, it would not even be black because of its subject matter. It would be something intrinsic, indigenous, something in the way it was put together—the sentences, the structure, texture and tone—so that anyone who read it would realise. I use the analogy of the music because you can range all over the world and it's still black . . . I don't imitate it, but I am informed by it. Sometimes I hear blues, sometimes spirituals or jazz and I've appropriated it. I've tried to reconstruct the texture of it in my writing—certain kinds of repetition—its profound simplicity . . . What has already happened with the music in the States, the literature will do one day and when that happens it's all over.[11]

The intense and often bitter dialogues which make the black arts movement move offer a small reminder that there is a democratic, communitar-
ian moment enshrined in the practice of antiphony which symbolises and
anticipates (but does not guarantee) new, non-dominating social relationships. Lines between self and other are blurred and special forms of pleasure are created as a result of the meetings and conversations that are established between one fractured, incomplete, and unfinished racial self and
others. Antiphony is the structure that hosts these essential encounters.
Ralph Ellison's famous observation on the inner dynamics of jazz production uses visual art as its central analogy but it can be readily extended
beyond the specific context it was written to illuminate:

> There is in this a cruel contradiction implicit in the art form itself. For
> true jazz is an art of individual assertion within and against the group.
> Each true jazz moment . . . springs from a contest in which the artist
> challenges all the rest; each solo flight, or improvisation, represents
> (like the canvasses of a painter) a definition of his [*sic*] identity: as
> individual, as member of the collectivity and as a link in the chain of
> tradition. Thus because jazz finds its very life in improvisation upon
> traditional materials, the jazz man must lose his identity even as he
> finds it . . .[12]

This quote offers a reminder that apart from the music and the musicians
themselves, we must also take account of the work of those within the
expressive culture of the black Atlantic who have tried to use its music as
an aesthetic, political, or philosophical marker in the production of what
might loosely be called their critical social theories. Here it is necessary to
consider the work of a whole host of exemplary figures: ex-slaves, preach-
ers, self-educated scholars and writers, as well as a small number of profes-
sionals and the tiny minority who managed to acquire some sort of academic position in essentially segregated educational systems or took
advantage of opportunities in Liberia, Haiti, and other independent states.
This company spreads out in discontinuous, transverse lines of descent that
stretch outwards across the Atlantic from Phyllis Wheatley onwards. Its
best feature is an anti-hierarchical tradition of thought that probably culminates in C. L. R. James's idea that ordinary people do not need an intellectual vanguard to help them to speak or to tell them what to say.[13] Repeatedly, within this expressive culture it is musicians who are presented as
living symbols of the value of self-activity.[14] This is often nothing more or
less than a question of style.

The basic labours of archaeological reconstruction and periodisation
aside, working on the contemporary forms of black expressive culture involves struggling with one problem in particular. It is the puzzle of what

analytic status should be given to the variation within black communities and between black cultures which their musical habits reveal. The tensions produced by attempts to compare or evaluate differing black cultural formations can be summed up in the following question: How are we to think critically about artistic products and aesthetic codes which, though they may be traceable back to one distinct location, have been changed either by the passage of time or by their displacement, relocation, or dissemination through networks of communication and cultural exchange? This question serves as a receptacle for several even more awkward issues. They include the unity and differentiation of the creative black self, the vexed matter of black particularity, and the role of cultural expression in its formation and reproduction. These problems are especially acute because black thinkers have been unable to appeal to the authoritative narratives of psychoanalysis as a means to ground the cross-cultural aspirations of their theories. With a few noble exceptions, critical accounts of the dynamics of black subordination and resistance have been doggedly monocultural, national, and ethnocentric. This impoverishes modern black cultural history because the transnational structures which brought the black Atlantic world into being have themselves developed and now articulate its myriad forms into a system of global communications constituted by flows. This fundamental dislocation of black culture is especially important in the recent history of black musics which, produced out of the racial slavery which made modern western civilisation possible, now dominate its popular cultures.

In the face of the conspicuous differentiation and proliferation of black cultural styles and genres, a new analytic orthodoxy has begun to grow. In the name of anti-essentialism and theoretical rigour it suggests that since black particularity is socially and historically constructed, and plurality has become inescapable, the pursuit of any unifying dynamic or underlying structure of feeling in contemporary black cultures is utterly misplaced. The attempt to locate the cultural practices, motifs, or political agendas that might connect the dispersed and divided blacks of the new world and of Europe with each other and even with Africa is dismissed as essentialism or idealism or both.[15]

The alternative position sketched out in this the rest of this chapter offers a tentative rebuke to that orthodoxy which I regard as premature in its dismissal of the problem of theorising black identity. I suggest that weighing the similarities and differences between black cultures remains an urgent concern. This response relies crucially on the concept of diaspora,[16] which will be discussed in more detail in Chapter 6. For present purposes I want to state that diaspora is still indispensable in focusing on the political and ethical dynamics of the unfinished history of blacks in the modern world. The dangers of idealism and pastoralisation associated with this concept ought, by now, to be obvious, but the very least that it offers is an heuristic means to focus on the relationship of identity and non-identity in black political culture. It can also be employed to project the plural richness of black cultures in different parts of the world in counterpoint to their common sensibilities—both those residually inherited from Africa and those generated from the special bitterness of new world racial slavery. This is not an easy matter. The proposition that the post-slave cultures of the Atlantic world are in some significant way related to one another and to the African cultures from which they partly derive has long been a matter of great controversy capable of arousing intense feeling which goes far beyond dispassionate scholastic contemplation. The situation is rendered even more complex by the fact that the fragile psychological, emotional, and cultural correspondences which connect diaspora populations in spite of their manifest differences are often apprehended only fleetingly and in ways that persistently confound the protocols of academic orthodoxy. There is, however, a great body of work which justifies the proposition that some cultural, religious, and linguistic affiliations can be identified even if their contemporary political significance remains disputed. There are also valuable though underutilised leads to be found in the work of the feminist political thinkers, cultural critics, and philosophers who have formulated stimulating conceptions of the relationship between identity and difference in the context of advancing the political projects of female emancipation.[17]

UK Blak

The issue of the identity and non-identity of black cultures has acquired a special historical and political significance in Britain. Black settlement in that country goes back many centuries, and affirming its continuity has become an important part of the politics that strive to answer contemporary British racism. However, the bulk of today's black communities are of relatively recent origin, dating only from the post–World War II period. If these populations are unified at all, it is more by the experience of migration than by the memory of slavery and the residues of plantation society. Until recently, this very newness and conspicuous lack of rootedness in the "indigenous" cultures of Britain's inner cities conditioned the formation of racial subcultures which drew heavily from a range of "raw materials" supplied by the Caribbean and black America. This was true even where these subcultures also contributed to the unsteady equilibrium of antagonistic class relationships into which Britain's black settlers found themselves inserted as racially subordinated migrant labourers but also as working-class black settlers.

The musics of the black Atlantic world were the primary expressions of cultural distinctiveness which this population seized upon and adapted to its new circumstances. It used the separate but converging musical traditions of the black Atlantic world, if not to create itself anew as a conglomeration of black communities, then as a means to gauge the social progress of spontaneous self-creation which was sedimented together by the endless pressures of economic exploitation, political racism, displacement, and exile. This musical heritage gradually became an important factor in facilitating the transition of diverse settlers to a distinct mode of lived blackness. It was instrumental in producing a constellation of subject positions that was openly indebted for its conditions of possibility to the Caribbean, the United States, and even Africa. It was also indelibly marked by the British conditions in which it grew and matured.

It is essential to appreciate that this type of process has not been confined to settlers of Afro-Caribbean descent. In reinventing their own ethnicity, some of Britain's Asian settlers have also borrowed the sound system culture of the Caribbean and the soul and hip hop styles of black America, as well as techniques like mixing, scratching, and sampling as part of their invention of a new mode of cultural production with an identity to match.[18] The popularity of Apache Indian[19] and Bally Sagoo's[20] attempts to fuse Punjabi music and language with reggae music and raggamuffin style raised debates about the authenticity of these hybrid cultural forms to an unprecedented pitch. The experience of Caribbean migrants to Britain provides further examples of complex cultural exchange and of the ways in which a self-consciously synthetic culture can support some equally novel political identities. The cultural and political histories of Guyana, Jamaica, Barbados, Grenada, Trinidad, and St. Lucia, like the economic forces at work in generating their respective migrations to Europe, are widely dissimilar. Even if it were possible, let alone desirable, their synthesis into a single black British culture could never have been guaranteed by the effects of racism alone. Thus the role of external meanings around blackness, drawn in particular from black America, became important in the elaboration of a connective culture which drew these different "national" groups together into a new pattern that was not ethnically marked in the way that their Caribbean cultural inheritances had been. Reggae, a supposedly stable and authentic category, provides a useful example here. Once its own hybrid origins in rhythm and blues were effectively concealed,[21] it ceased, in Britain, to signify an exclusively ethnic, Jamaican style and derived a different kind of cultural legitimacy both from a new global status and from its expression of what might be termed a pan-Caribbean culture.

The style, rhetoric, and moral authority of the civil rights movement and of Black Power suffered similar fates. They too were detached from their original ethnic markers and historical origins, exported and adapted, with evident respect but little sentimentality, to local needs and political climates. Appearing in Britain through a circulatory system that gave a central place to the musics which had both informed and recorded black struggles in other places, they were rearticulated in distinctively European conditions. How the appropriation of these forms, styles, and histories of struggle was possible at such great physical and social distance is in itself an interesting question for cultural historians. It was facilitated by a common fund of urban experiences, by the effect of similar but by no means identical forms of racial segregation, as well as by the memory of slavery, a legacy of Africanisms, and a stock of religious experiences defined by them both. Dislocated from their original conditions of existence, the sound tracks of this African-American cultural broadcast fed a new metaphysics of blackness elaborated and enacted in Europe and elsewhere within the underground, alternative, public spaces constituted around an expressive culture that was dominated by music.

The inescapably political language of citizenship, racial justice, and equality was one of several discourses which contributed to this transfer of cultural and political forms and structures of feeling. A commentary on the relationship of work to leisure and the respective forms of freedom with which these opposing worlds become identified provided a second linking principle. A folk historicism animating a special fascination with history and the significance of its recovery by those who have been expelled from the official dramas of civilisation was a third component here. The representation of sexuality and gender identity, in particular the ritual public projection of the antagonistic relationship between black women and men in ways that invited forms of identification strong enough to operate across the line of colour, was the fourth element within this vernacular cultural and philosophical formation dispersed through the musics of the black Atlantic world.

The conflictual representation of sexuality has vied with the discourse of racial emancipation to constitute the inner core of black expressive cultures. Common rhetorical strategies developed through the same repertory of enunciative procedures have helped these discourses to become interlinked. Their association was pivotal, for example, in the massive secularisation that produced soul out of rhythm and blues, and it persists today. It can be easily observed in the bitter conflict over the misogynist tone and masculinist direction of hip hop. Hip hop culture has recently provided the raw material for a bitter contest between black vernacular expression and repressive censorship of artistic work. This has thrown some black commentators into a quandary which they have resolved by invoking the rheto-

ric of cultural insiderism and drawing the comforting cloak of absolute
ethnicity even more tightly around their anxious shoulders. The most significant recent illustration of this is provided by the complex issues stemming from the obscenity trial of 2 Live Crew, a Florida-based rap act led
by Luther Cambell, a commercially minded black American of Jamaican
descent. This episode is not notable because the forms of misogyny that
attracted the attention of the police and the district attorneys were new.[22]
Its importance lay in the fact that it was the occasion for an important
public intervention by black America's best known academic and cultural
critic, Henry Louis Gates, Jr.[23] Gates went beyond simply affirming the
artistic status of this particular hip hop product, arguing in full effect that
the Crew's material was a manifestation of distinctively black cultural traditions which operated by particular satirical codes where one man's misogyny turns out to be another man's parodic play. Rakim, the most gifted rap
poet of the eighties, had a very different perspective on the authenticity of
2 Live Crew's output.

> That [the 2 Live Crew situation] ain't my problem. Some people
> might think it's our problem because rap is one big happy family.
> When I make my bed, I lay on it. I don't say nothin' I can't stand up
> for. 'cause I seen one interview, where they asked him [Luther Cam-
> bell] a question and he started talkin' all this about black culture. That
> made everybody on the rap tip look kinda dense. He was sayin' "Yo
> this is my culture." That's not culture at all.[24]

It is striking that apologists for the woman-hating antics of 2 Live Crew
and other similar performers have been so far unconcerned that the vernacular tradition they rightly desire to legitimise and protect has its own record
of reflection on the specific ethical obligations and political responsibilities
which constitute the unique burden of the black artist. Leaving the question of misogyny aside for a moment, to collude in the belief that black
vernacular is *nothing* other than a playful, parodic cavalcade of Rabelaisian
subversion decisively weakens the positions of the artist, the critical commentator, and the community as a whole. What is more significant is surely
the failure of either academic or journalistic commentary on black popular
music in America to develop a reflexive political aesthetics capable of distin-
guishing 2 Live Crew and their ilk from their equally authentic but possibly
more compelling and certainly more constructive peers.

I am not suggesting that the self-conscious racial pedagogy of recognisably political artists like KRS1, the Poor Righteous Teachers, Lakim Sha-
bazz, or the X Clan should be straightforwardly counterposed against the
carefully calculated affirmative nihilism of Ice Cube, Tim Dog, the Ghetto

Boys, Above the Law, and Compton's Most Wanted. The different styles and political perspectives expressed within the music are linked both by the bonds of a stylised but aggressively masculinist discourse and by formal borrowings from the linguistic innovations of Jamaica's distinct modes of "kinetic orality."[25] This debt to Caribbean forms, which can only undermine the definition of hip hop as an exclusively American product, is more openly acknowledged in the ludic Africentrisms of the Jungle Brothers, De La Soul, and A Tribe Called Quest, which may represent a third alternative—both in its respectful and egalitarian representation of women and in its more ambivalent relationship to America and Americanism. The stimulating and innovative work of this last group of artists operates a rather different, eccentric conception of black authenticity that effectively contrasts the local (black nationalism) with the global (black internationalism) and measures Americanism against the appeal of Ethiopianism and pan-Africanism. It is important to emphasise that all three strands within hip hop—pedagogy, affirmation, and play—contribute to a folk-cultural constellation where neither the political compass of weary leftism nor the shiny navigational instruments of premature black postmodernism[26] in aesthetics have so far offered very much that is useful.

In dealing with the relationship of race to class it has been commonplace to recall Stuart Hall's suggestive remark that the former is the modality in which the latter is lived. The tale of 2 Live Crew and the central place of sexuality in the contemporary discourses of racial particularity point to an analogous formulation that may prove equally wieldy: gender is the modality in which race is lived. An amplified and exaggerated masculinity has become the boastful centrepiece of a culture of compensation that self-consciously salves the misery of the disempowered and subordinated. This masculinity and its relational feminine counterpart become special symbols of the difference that race makes. They are lived and naturalised in the distinct patterns of family life on which the reproduction of the racial identities supposedly relies. These gender identities come to exemplify the immutable cultural differences that apparently arise from absolute ethnic difference. To question them and their constitution of racial subjectivity is at once to be ungendered and to place oneself outside of the racial kin group. This makes these positions hard to answer, let alone criticise. Experiencing racial sameness through particular definitions of gender and sexuality has also proved to be eminently exportable. The forms of connectedness and identification it makes possible across space and time cannot be confined within the borders of the nation state and correspond closely to lived experience. They may even create new conceptions of nationality in the conflictual interaction between the women who quietly and privately reproduce the black national community and the men who aspire to be its public soldier citizens.

These links show no sign of fading, but the dependence of blacks in Britain on black cultures produced in the new world has recently begun to change. The current popularity of Jazzie B and Soul II Soul, Maxi Priest, Caron Wheeler, Monie Love, the Young Disciples, and others in the United States confirms that during the eighties black British cultures ceased to simply mimic or reproduce wholesale forms, styles, and genres which had been lovingly borrowed, respectfully stolen, or brazenly high-jacked from blacks elsewhere. Critical space/time cartography of the diaspora needs therefore to be readjusted so that the dynamics of dispersal and local autonomy can be shown alongside the unforeseen detours and circuits which mark the new journeys and new arrivals that, in turn, release new political and cultural possibilities.[27]

At certain points during the recent past, British racism has generated turbulent economic, ideological, and political forces that have seemed to act upon the people they oppressed by concentrating their cultural identities into a single powerful configuration. Whether these people were of African, Caribbean, or Asian descent, their commonality was often defined by its reference to the central, irreducible sign of their common racial subordination—the colour black. More recently, though, this fragile unity in action has fragmented and their self-conception has separated into its various constituent elements. The unifying notion of an open blackness has been largely rejected and replaced by more particularistic conceptions of cultural difference. This retreat from a politically constructed notion of racial solidarity has initiated a compensatory recovery of narrowly ethnic culture and identity. Indeed, the aura of authentic ethnicity supplies a special form of comfort in a situation where the very historicity of black experience is constantly undermined.

These political and historical shifts are registered in the cultural realm. The growth of religious fundamentalism among some Asian-descended populations is an obvious sign of their significance, and there may be similar processes at work in the experience of the peoples of Caribbean descent for whom an equivalent retreat into pure ethnicity has acquired pronounced generational features. Their desire to anchor themselves in racial particularity is not dominated by the longing to return to the Victorian certainties and virtues of Caribbean cultural life. However, in conjunction with the pressures of economic recession and populist racism, this yearning has driven many older settlers to return to the lands in which they were born. Among their descendants, the same desire to withdraw has achieved a very different form of expression. It has moved towards an overarching

Africentrism which can be read as inventing its own totalising conception of black culture. This new ethnicity is all the more powerful because it corresponds to no actually existing black communities. Its radical utopianism, often anchored in the ethical bedrock provided by the history of the Nile Valley civilisations, transcends the parochialism of Caribbean memories in favour of a heavily mythologised Africanity that is itself stamped by its origins not in Africa but in a variety of pan-African ideology produced most recently by black America. The problems of contemporary Africa are almost completely absent from its concerns. This complex and sometimes radical sensibility has been recently fostered by the more pedagogic and self-consciously politicised elements within hip hop. The "college-boy rap" of the more edutainment minded groups represents one pole in the field that reproduced it, while the assertive stance of hip hop's narrow nationalists represents the other. This political change can be registered in the deepening splits within hip hop over the language and symbols appropriate for black self-designation and over the relative importance of opposing racism on the one hand, and of elaborating the symbolic forms of black identity on the other. These necessary tasks are not synonymous or even co-extensive though they can be rendered compatible. What is more significant for present purposes is that in the Africentric discourse on which both sides of opinion draw, the idea of a diaspora composed of communities that are both similar *and* different tends to disappear somewhere between the invocations of an African motherland and the powerful critical commentaries on the immediate, local conditions in which a particular performance of a piece of music originates. These complexities aside, hip hop culture is best understood as the latest export from black America to have found favour in black Britain. It is especially interesting then that its success has been built on transnational structures of circulation and intercultural exchange established long ago.

The Jubilee Singers and the Transatlantic Route

I want to illustrate these arguments further by briefly bringing forward some concrete historical instances in which the musical traditions of the black Atlantic world can be seen to have acquired a special political valency and in which the idea of authentic racial culture has been either contested or symptomatically overlooked. These examples are simultaneously both national, in that they had a direct impact on life in Britain, and diasporic, in that they tell us something fundamental about the limits of that national perspective. They are not, of course, the only examples I could have chosen. They have been selected somewhat at random, though I hope that the fact that they span a century will be taken as further evidence for the existence of fractal[28] patterns of cultural and political affiliation to which I pointed in Chapter 1. In rather different ways, these examples reflect the special position of Britain within the black Atlantic world, standing at the apex of the semi-triangular structure which saw commodities and people shipped to and fro across the ocean.

The first relates to the visits by the Fisk University Jubilee Singers[29] to England, Ireland, Wales, and Scotland in the early 1870s under the philanthropic patronage of the Earl of Shaftesbury. The Fisk Singers have a profound historical importance because they were the first group to perform spirituals on a public platform, offering this form of black music as popular culture.[30] In the story of this choir we can discover that the distinctive patterns of cross-cultural circulation, on which the rise of more recent phenomena like Africentric rap has relied, precede the consolidation of coherent youth cultures and subcultures after the 1939–1945 war.

I believe that these circulatory systems can be traced right back to the beginnings of black music's entry into the public domain of late-nineteenth-century mass entertainment. The world-wide travels of the Fisk Jubilee Singers provide a little-known but nonetheless important example of the difficulties that, from the earliest point, attended the passage of African-American folk forms into the emergent popular-cultural industries of the overdeveloped countries. At that time, the status of the Jubilee Singers' art was further complicated by the prominence and popularity of minstrelsy.[31] One review of the earliest performances by the group was headlined "Negro Minstrelsy in Church—Novel Religious Exercise," while another made much of the fact that this band of Negro minstrels were, in fact, "genuine negroes."[32] Doug Seroff quotes another contemporary American review of a concert by the group: "Those who have only heard the burnt cork caricatures of negro minstrelsy have not the slightest conception of what it really is."[33] Similar problems arose in the response of European audiences and critics: "From the first the Jubilee music was more or less of a puzzle to the critics; and even among those who sympathised with their mission there was no little difference of opinion as to the artistic merit of their entertainments. Some could not understand the reason for enjoying so thoroughly as almost everyone did these simple *unpretending* songs" (emphasis added).[34]

The role of music and song within the abolitionist movement is an additional and equally little known factor which must have prefigured some of the Jubilees' eventual triumphs.[35] The choir, sent forth into the world with economic objectives which must have partially eclipsed their pursuit of aesthetic excellence in their musical performances, initially struggled to win an audience for black music produced by blacks from a constituency which had been created by fifty years of "blackface" entertainment. Needless to say, the aesthetic and political tensions involved in establishing the credibility and appeal of their own novel brand of black cultural expression were not confined to the concert halls. Practical problems arose in the mechanics of touring when innkeepers refused the group lodgings having taken their bookings on the assumption that they were a company of "nigger minstrels" (that is, white). One landlord did not discover that "their faces were coloured by their creator and not by burnt cork"[36] until the singers were firmly established in their bedrooms. He still turned them into the street.

The choir's progress was predictably dogged by controversies over the relative value of their work when compared to the output of the white "minstrel" performers. The Fisk troupe also encountered the ambivalence and embarrassment of black audiences unsure or uneasy about serious, sacred music being displayed to audiences conditioned by the hateful antics of Zip Coon, Jim Crow, and their odious supporting cast. Understandably, blacks were protective of their unique musical culture and fearful of how it might be changed by being forced to compete on the new terrain of popular culture against the absurd representations of blackness offered by minstrelsy's pantomime dramatisation of white supremacy.

The Fisk Singers' own success spawned a host of other companies who took to the road in Europe, South Africa, and elsewhere offering a similar musical fare in the years after 1871.[37] Their success is especially significant amidst the changed cultural and ideological circumstances that attended the remaking of the English working class in the era of imperialism.[38] In explicit opposition to minstrelsy, which was becoming an established element in popular culture by this time,[39] the Fisk Singers constructed an aura of seriousness around their activities and projected the memory of slavery outwards as the means to make their musical performances intelligible and pleasurable. The choir had taken to the road seven years after the founding of their alma mater to raise funds. They produced books to supplement the income from their concert performances, and these volumes ran to more than 60,000 copies sold between 1873 and the end of the century. Interestingly, these publications included a general historical account of Fisk and its struggles, some unusual autobiographical statements from the members of the choir, and the music and lyrics of between 104 and 139 songs from their extensive repertoire. In my opinion, this unusual combination of communicative modes and genres is especially important for anyone seeking to locate the origins of the polyphonic montage technique developed by Du Bois in *The Souls of Black Folk*.

The Singers' texts describe an austere Queen Victoria listening to "John Brown's Body" "with manifest pleasure," the Prince of Wales requesting "No More Auction Block for Me," and the choir being waited upon by Mr. and Mrs. Gladstone after their servants had been dismissed.[40] These images are important, though the history of the choir's performances to enormous working-class audiences in British cities may be more valuable to beleaguered contemporary anti-racism which is struggling to find precedents and to escape the strictures of its own apparent novelty. It is clear that for their liberal patrons the music and song of the Fisk Jubilee Singers offered an opportunity to feel closer to God and to redemption while the memory of slavery recovered by their performances entrenched the feelings of moral rectitude that flowed from the commitment to political reform for which the imagery of elevation from slavery was emblematic long after emancipation. The Jubilee Singers' music can be shown to have communicated what Du Bois called "the articulate message of the slave to the world"[41] into British culture and society at several distinct and class-specific points. The spirituals enforced the patrician moral concerns of Shaftesbury and Gladstone but also introduced a specific moral sensibility into the lives of the lower orders who, it would appear, began to create jubilee choirs of their own.[42]

The meaning of this movement of black singers for our understanding of the Reconstruction period in the United States also remains to be explored. It will complement and extend work already done on representations of blackness during this era[43] and promises to go far beyond the basic argument I want to emphasise here. Black people singing slave songs as mass entertainment set new public standards of authenticity for black cultural expression. The legitimacy of these new cultural forms was established precisely through their distance from the racial codes of minstrelsy. The Jubilee Singers' journey out of America was a critical stage in making this possible.

The extraordinary story of the Jubilee Singers and their travels is also worth considering because it made a great impression on successive generations of black cultural analysts and commentators. Du Bois, who was a student at Fisk, devoted a chapter to their activities in *The Souls of Black Folk*. He discovered a symbol with which to reconcile the obligations of the talented tenth with those of the black poor and peasantry in the way that the Jubilees were able to turn the black university into a place of music and song. We shall see in the next chapter that *The Souls* is a key text. It underpins all that follows it, and its importance is marked by the way Du Bois places black music as the central sign of black cultural value, integrity, and autonomy. Each chapter was introduced with a fragment of slave song which both accompanied and signified on the Euro-American romantic poetry that comprised the other part of these double epigraphs. *The Souls* is the place where slave music is signalled in its special position of privileged signifier of black authenticity. The double consciousness which *The Souls* argues is the founding experience of blacks in the West is itself expressed in the double value of these songs which are always both American and black. In his essay on the songs in *The New Negro* anthology which supplied the manifesto for the Harlem Renaissance, the philosopher Alain Locke makes this point clear:

> The spirituals are really the most characteristic product of the race genius as yet in America. But the very elements which make them uniquely expressive of the Negro make them at the same time deeply representative of the soil that produced them. Thus, as unique spiritual products of American life, they become nationally as well as racially characteristic. It may not be readily conceded now that the song of the negro is America's folk song; but if the spirituals are what we think them to be, a classic folk expression, then this is their ultimate destiny. Already they give evidence of this classic quality . . . The universality of the spirituals looms more and more as they stand the test of time.[44]

This doubleness has proved awkward and embarrassing for some commentators since it forces the issues of cultural development, mutation, and change into view and requires a degree of conceptual adjustment in order to account for the tension that is introduced between the same and the other or the traditional and the modern. This has caused problems, particularly for those thinkers whose strategy for legitimating their own position as critics and artists turns on an image of the authentic folk as custodians of an essentially invariant, anti-historical notion of black particularity to which they alone somehow maintain privileged access. As Hazel Carby[45] has pointed out, Zora Neale Hurston was one black intellectual who favoured these tactics. She too recognised the story of the Fisk Jubilee Singers as an important turning point in the development of black political culture, but the lesson she drew from the allegory that their travels could be made to generate was very different from what the same story offered Du Bois and Locke. For Hurston, the success of the Fisk choir represented the triumph of musicians' tricks over the vital, untrained, angular spirit of the rural folk who "care nothing about pitch" and "are bound by no rules."[46] She dismissed Du Bois's suggestion that the body of spirituals could be described as "sorrow songs" as "ridiculous" and hinted that he had his own doubtful reasons for needing to represent them in this unremittingly mournful guise. She attacked the choir's performances as inauthentic in one of her rich and thoughtful contributions to Nancy Cunard's anthology *Negro:*

> In spite of the goings up and down on the earth, from the original Fisk Jubilee singers down to the present, there has been no genuine presentation of Negro songs to white audiences. The spirituals that have been sung around the world are Negroid to be sure, but so full of musicians tricks that Negro congregations are highly entertained when they hear their old songs so changed. They never use the new style songs, and these are never heard unless perchance some daughter or son has been off to college and returns with one of the old songs with its face lifted, so to speak.
>
>   I am of the opinion that this trick style of delivery was originated by the Fisk Singers . . . This Glee Club style has gone on for so long and become so fixed among concert singers that it is considered quite authentic. But I say again, that not one concert singer in the world is singing the songs as the Negro song makers sing them.[47]

I should emphasise that as far as this chapter is concerned, whether Hurston was right or wrong about the Fisk Singers is not the primary question. The issue which interests me more than her correctness is her strongly felt need to draw a line around what is and isn't authentically, genuinely, and really black and to use music as the medium which makes these distinctions credible. Hurston's sometime adversary and competitor Richard Wright was yet another who became absorbed by the story of the Jubilee Singers. In the early forties, when both writers were trying to make the leap from literature to Hollywood, he produced a film script, "Melody Limited," which was based on the singers' travels in Europe. He explained that the aim of the film "would be to depict the romantic and adventurous manner in which the first Negro Educational Institutions were built and the part and role Negro Folk songs, religious and secular, played in their building."[48] Wright, who felt that the impression left by the singers was "still extant in Europe and America," presented their music as mediating the relationship between an outmoded abolitionist politics and the nascent struggles of ex-slaves towards citizenship and progress through education. He felt that the film would "give vent and scope to Negro singing talent," "refresh the memory of the nation with a conceptual sense of the Negro in our society," and "recapture some of the old dignity and barbaric grandeur of the songs." His travelling singers are refused passage to Europe on a segregated steamer but make their way eventually to England. Their popular triumphs there lead to prestigious performances in front of the royal family and the prime minister, who are held spellbound by their sublime art. In the script's central scene, the black choir competes against a similar Irish ensemble who on purely racist grounds are awarded the victor's trophy for an impressive but inferior performance. This illegitimate result precipitates the sudden death of one elderly member of the black group, and in their mourning for her the Jubilee choir improvise a "half African, half slave" song which even the watching Mr. Gladstone recognises as capable of conquering death itself: "The ring shout mounts, and as it does so, it transforms itself into a song of wild, barbaric beauty to death."

Almost one hundred years after the Jubilees set sail from Boston for England on the Cunard ship Batavia, another black American musician made the transatlantic journey to London. Jimi Hendrix's importance in the history of African-American popular music has increased since his untimely death in 1970. The European triumph which paved the way for Hendrix's American successes presents another interesting but rather different case of the political aesthetics implicated in representations of racial authenticity. A seasoned, if ill-disciplined, rhythm and blues sideman, Hendrix was reinvented as the essential image of what English audiences felt a black American performer should be: wild, sexual, hedonistic, and dangerous. His biographers agree that the updated minstrel antics of his stage shows became a fetter on his creativity and that the irrepressible issue of racial politics intervened bitterly in his fluctuating relationships with the English musicians who provided the bizarre backdrop to his blues-rooted creativity.[49] Jimi's shifting relationship to black cultural forms and political movements caused substantial problems when he returned to play in the United States and was denounced as a "white nigger" by some of the Black Power activists who could not fathom his choices in opting to cultivate an almost exclusively white, pop audience that found the minstrel stance a positive inducement to engage with his transgressive persona if not his music. Charles Shaar Murray quotes the following diagnosis of Hendrix's success by the rival English blues guitarist Eric Clapton: "You know English people have a very big thing towards a spade. They really love that magic thing. They all fall for that kind of thing. Everybody and his brother in England still think that spades have big dicks. And Jimi came over and exploited that to the limit . . . and everybody fell for it."[50] Sexuality and authenticity have been intertwined in the history of western culture for several hundred years.[51] The overt sexuality of Hendrix's neo-minstrel buffoonery seems to have been received as a sign of his authentic blackness by the white rock audiences on which his burgeoning pop career was so solidly based. Whether or not Hendrix's early performances were parodic of the minstrel role or undeniable confirmation of its enduring potency, his negotiation of its vestigial codes points to the antagonism between different local definitions of what blackness entailed and to the combined and uneven character of black cultural development. The complexity of his relationship to the blues and his fluctuating commitment to the politics of racial protest which had set American cities on fire during this period extend and underscore this point. The creative opposition in his work between obvious reverence for blues-based traditions and an assertively high-tech, futuristic spirituality distils a wider conflict not simply between pre-modern or anti-modern and the modern but between the contending definitions of authenticity which are appropriate to black cultural creation on its passage into international pop commodification. Nelson George, the respected historian and critic of African-American music, resolves this problem in his assessment of Hendrix by expelling the innovative guitarist from his canonical reconstruction of the black musical idiom and making Hendrix's racial alienation literal: "Jimi's music was, if not from another planet, definitely from another country."[52] In a thoughtful and solidly intelligent biography, the only book to treat Hendrix's political sensibilities seriously, another black American writer, the poet David Henderson, is more insightful and more tuned in to the possibilities for innovation opened up for Hendrix simply by his being in London rather than New York. The multiple ironies in this location come across not only in Henderson's account of Hendrix's relationship with Rahsaan Roland Kirk but in his outsider's attempts to place the guitarist's image in a wider structure of cultural relationships perceived to be shaped by class rather than race and ethnicity: "The Hendrix Hairdo, frizzy and bountiful, was viewed by many cultural onlookers as one of the most truly remarkable visual revolts of London. For the British trendy public, who hardly ever outwardly acculturated another race's appearance, another culture, to have their youths sporting bouffant Afros and digging blues was a bit much."[53] Hendrix would later rationalise his ambivalence towards both blackness and America through the nomadic ideology of the gypsy that appeared in his work as an interestingly perverse accompaniment to the decision to play funkier and more politically engaged music with an all-black band.

Authenticity is not so hotly contested in my third example of transnational, diasporic cultural innovation centred on London. It is provided by a song that circulated across the black Atlantic network rather than an individual artist or group. It is included here precisely because the right to borrow, reconstruct, and redeploy cultural fragments drawn from other black settings was not thought to be a problem by those who produced and used the music. This is also a more contemporary example, though it relates to the piece "I'm So Proud," originally written and performed by the Chicagoan vocal trio the Impressions, at the peak of their artistic and commercial success in the mid-1960s. The group's sixties hits like "Gypsy Woman," "Grow Closer Together," "Minstrel and Queen," and "People Get Ready" were extremely popular among blacks in Britain and in the Caribbean. In Jamaica, the male vocal trio format popularised by the band inaugurated a distinct genre within the vernacular musical form which would eventually be marketed internationally as reggae.[54] The Wailers were only the best known of many groups that patterned themselves on the Impressions and strove to match the singing of the Americans in its rich harmonic textures, emotional dynamics, and black metaphysical grace.

A new version of the Impressions' hit "I'm So Proud" topped the reggae charts in Britain during 1990. Retitled "Proud of Mandela," it was performed in interperformative tandem by the Brummie toaster Macka B and the Lovers' Rock singer Kofi, who had produced her own version of the tune closely patterned on another, soft soul version that had been issued by the American singer Deniece Williams in 1983. I want to make no special claims for the formal, musical merits of this particular record, but I think it is a useful example in that it brings Africa, America, Europe, and the Caribbean seamlessly together. It was produced in Britain by the children of Caribbean and African settlers from raw materials supplied by black Chicago but filtered through Kingstonian sensibility in order to pay tribute to a black hero whose global significance lies beyond the limits of his partial South African citizenship and the impossible national identity which goes with it. The very least which this music and its history can offer us today is an analogy for comprehending the lines of affiliation and association which take the idea of the diaspora beyond its symbolic status as the fragmentary opposite of some imputed racial essence. Thus foregrounding the role of music allows us to see England, or more accurately London, as an important junction point or crossroads on the webbed pathways of black Atlantic political culture. It is revealed to be a place where, by virtue of local factors like the informality of racial segregation, the configuration of class relations, and the contingency of linguistic convergences, global phenomena such as anti-colonial and emancipationist political formations are still being sustained, reproduced, and amplified. This process of fusion and intermixture is recognised as an enhancement to black cultural production by the black public who make use of it. Its authenticity or artificiality was not thought to be a problem partly because it was content to remain inside the hidden spaces of the black cultural underground and also because of the difference made by the invocation of Nelson Mandela. The name of Mandela became a paternal talisman that could suspend and refocus intra-racial differences that might prove difficult and even embarrassing in other

circumstances. His release from prison projected an unchallenged, patriarchal voice, a voice rooted in the most intense political conflict between
blacks and whites on this planet, the final frontier of white supremacy on
the African continent, out across the relay systems of the black Atlantic.
The heroic, redemptive authenticity that enveloped the image of Mandela
in these locations was nicely deconstructed in a speech that he himself
made in Detroit on his first visit to the United States. Mandela answered
the Africentric expectations of his audience by confiding that he had found
solace in listening to Motown music while in jail on Robben Island. Quot-
ing from Marvin Gaye's "What's Going On?" he explained, "When we
were in prison, we appreciated and obviously listened to the sound of Detroit."[55] The purist idea of one-way flow of African culture from east to
west was instantly revealed to be absurd. The global dimensions of diaspora
dialogue were momentarily visible and, as his casual words lit up the black
Atlantic landscape like a flash of lightning on a summer night, the value
of music as the principal symbol of racial authenticity was simultaneously
confirmed and placed in question.

Music Criticism and the Politics of Racial Authenticity

The problem of cultural origins and authenticity to which these examples
point has persisted and assumed an enhanced significance as mass culture
has acquired new technological bases and black music has become a truly
global phenomenon. It has taken on greater proportions as original, folk,
or local expressions of black culture have been identified as authentic and
positively evaluated for that reason, while subsequent hemispheric or
global manifestations of the same cultural forms have been dismissed as
inauthentic and therefore lacking in cultural or aesthetic value precisely
because of their distance (supposed or actual) from a readily identifiable
point of origin. In his book-jacket comments on Nelson George's *The
Death of Rhythm and Blues,* Spike Lee, a well-known exponent of cultural
protectionism, makes the obvious contemporary version of these arguments. "Once again Nelson George has shown the the direct correlation
between the music of black people and their condition. It's a shame that
the more we progress as a people, the more diluted the music gets. What
is the answer?"[56]

The fragmentation and subdivision of black music into an ever-
increasing proliferation of styles and genres which makes a nonsense of this
polar opposition between progress and dilution has also contributed to a
situation in which authenticity emerges among the music makers as a
highly charged and bitterly contested issue. The conflict between the trum-

peters Wynton Marsalis and Miles Davis is worth citing here as yet another example of how these conflicts can be endowed with a political significance. Marsalis argued that jazz provides an essential repository for wider black cultural values while Davis insisted upon prioritising the restless creative energies that could keep the corrosive processes of reification and commodification at bay. Marsalis's assertive, suit-wearing custodianship of "jazz tradition" was dismissed by Davis as a safe, technically sophisticated pastiche of earlier styles. This was done not on the grounds that it was inauthentic, which had been Marsalis's critical charge against Davis's "fusion" output, but because it was felt to be anachronistic:

> What's he doin' messing with the past? A player of his calibre should just wise up and realize its over. The past is dead. Jazz is dead . . . Why get caught up in that old shit? . . . Don't nobody tell me the way it was. Hell, I was there . . . no one wanted to hear us when we were playing jazz . . . Jazz is dead, God damn it. That's it finito! its over and there's no point apeing the shit.[57]

There are many good reasons why black cultures have had great difficulty in seeing that the displacements and transformations celebrated in Davis's work after "In a Silent Way" are unavoidable and that the developmental processes regarded by conservatives as cultural contamination may actually be enriching or strengthening. The effects of racism's denials not only of black cultural integrity but of the capacity of blacks to bear and reproduce any culture worthy of the name are clearly salient here. The place prepared for black cultural expression in the hierarchy of creativity generated by the pernicious metaphysical dualism that identifies blacks with the body and whites with the mind is a second significant factor. However, beyond these general questions lies the need to project a coherent and stable racial culture as a means to establish the political legitimacy of black nationalism and the notions of ethnic particularity on which it has come to rely. This defensive reaction to racism can be said to have taken over its evident appetite for sameness and symmetry from the discourses of the oppressor. European romanticism and cultural nationalism contributed directly to the development of modern black nationalism. It can be traced back to the impact of European theories of nationhood, culture, and civilisation on elite African-American intellectuals in the early and mid-nineteenth century.[58] Here, the image of the nation as an accumulation of symmetrical family units makes a grim appearance amidst the drama of ethnic identity-construction. Alexander Crummell's endorsement of Lord Beaconsfield's views on the fundamental importance of race as "the key to history" should sound a cautionary note to contemporary cultural critics who would give artists the job of refining the ethnic distinctiveness of the group and who are tempted to use the analogy of family not only to comprehend the meaning of race but to make these rather authoritarian gestures: "Races, like families are the organisms and the ordinance of God; and race feeling, like family feeling, is of divine origin. The extinction of race feeling is just as possible as the extinction of family feeling. Indeed race is family. The principle of continuity is as masterful in races as it is in families—as it is in nations."[59]

Du Bois pointed out long ago that "the negro church antedates the negro home,"[60] and all black Atlantic appeals to the integrity of the family should be approached with his wise observation in mind. The family is something more than merely a means to naturalise and expel from historical time relationships that should be seen as historical and contingent. This link between family, cultural reproduction, and ethno-hermeneutics has been expressed eloquently by Houston A. Baker, Jr., the leading African-American literary critic who has advanced the trope of the family as a means to situate and periodise the whole history of black cultural production and more importantly as a kind of interpretive filter for those who would approach black cultures.

> My tale, then, to say again what I have said, is of a complex field of sounding strategies in Afro-America that are part of a family. The family's history always no matter how it is revised, purified, distorted, emended—begins in an economics of slavery. The modernity of our family's sounding strategies resides in their deployment for economic (whether to ameliorate desire or to secure material advantage) advancement. The metaphor that I used earlier seems more than apt for such salvific soundings—they are, indeed blues geographies that can *never be understood* outside a family commitment.[61] (emphasis added)

Baker's position is in many ways a sophisticated restatement of the absolutist approach to "race" and ethnicity which animated black nationalism during the sixties but which has run into trouble more recently. This position has not always found it easy to accommodate the demands and priorities of feminisms, many of which see the family relations that sustain the race as playing a less innocent role in the subordination of its female members. This position has also failed when faced with the need to make sense of the increasingly distinct forms of black culture produced from different diaspora populations. It bears repetition that even where African-American forms are borrowed and set to work in new locations they have often been deliberately reconstructed in novel patterns that do not respect their originators' proprietary claims or the boundaries of discrete nation states and the supposedly natural political communities they express or simply contain. My point here is that the unashamedly hybrid character of these black Atlantic cultures continually confounds any simplistic (essentialist or anti-essentialist) understanding of the relationship between racial identity and racial non-identity, between folk cultural authenticity and pop cultural betrayal. Here the idea of the racial community as a family has been invoked and appealed to as a means to signify connectedness and experiential continuity that is everywhere denied by the profane realities of black life amidst the debris of de-industrialisation. I want to ask whether the growing centrality of the family trope within black political and academic discourse points to the emergence of a distinctive and emphatically post-national variety of racial essentialism. The appeal to family should be understood as both the symptom and the signature of a neo-nationalist outlook that is best understood as a flexible essentialism. The relationship between this ideal, imaginary, and pastoral black family and utopian as well as authoritarian representations of blackness will be considered again in the concluding chapter.

Pop culture has been prepared to provide selective endorsements for the premium that some black thinkers wish to place on authenticity and has even set this special logic to work in the marketing of so-called World Music. Authenticity enhances the appeal of selected cultural commodities and has become an important element in the mechanism of the mode of racialisation necessary to making non-European and non-American musics acceptable items in an expanded pop market. The discourse of authenticity has been a notable presence in the mass marketing of successive black folk-cultural forms to white audiences. The distinction between rural and urban blues provides one good example of this, though similar arguments are still made about the relationship between authentic jazz and "fusion" styles supposedly corroded by the illegitimate amalgamation of rock influences or the struggle between real instruments and digital emulators. In all these cases it is not enough for critics to point out that representing authenticity always involves artifice. This may be true, but it is not helpful when trying to evaluate or compare cultural forms let alone in trying to make sense of their mutation. More important, this response also misses the opportunity to use music as a model that can break the deadlock between the two unsatisfactory positions that have dominated recent discussion of black cultural politics.

Soul Music and the Making of Anti-Anti-Essentialism

As I argued in the opening chapter, critical dialogue and debate on these questions of identity and culture currently stage a confrontation between two loosely organised perspectives which, in opposing each other, have become locked in an entirely fruitless relationship of mutual interdependency. Both positions are represented in contemporary discussions of black music, and both contribute to staging a conversation between those who see the music as the primary means to explore critically and reproduce politically the necessary ethnic essence of blackness and those who would dispute the existence of any such unifying, organic phenomenon. Wherever the confrontation between these views is staged, it takes the basic form of conflict between a tendency focused by some variety of exceptionalist claim (usually though not always of a nationalist nature) and another more avowedly pluralistic stance which is decidedly sceptical of the desire to totalise black culture, let alone to make the social dynamics of cultural integration synonymous with the practice of nation building and the project of racial emancipation in Africa and elsewhere.

The first option typically identifies music with tradition and cultural continuity. Its conservatism is sometimes disguised by the radical nature of its affirmative political rhetoric and by its laudable concern with the relationship between music and the memory of the past. It currently announces its interpretive intentions with the popular slogan "It's a Black thing you wouldn't understand." But it appears to have no great enthusiasm for the forbidding, racially prescriptive musical genres and styles that could make this bold assertion plausible. There has been no contemporary equivalent to the provocative, hermetic power of dub which supported the radical Ethiopianism of the seventies or of the anti-assimilationist unintelligibility of bebop in the forties. The usually mystical "Africentrism" which animates this position perceives no problem in the internal differentiation of black cultures. Any fragmentation in the cultural output of Africans at home and abroad is *only* apparent rather than real and cannot therefore forestall the power of the underlying racial aesthetic and its political correlates.

This exceptionalist position shares elitism and contempt for black popular culture with the would-be postmodern pragmatism which routinely and inadequately opposes it. Something of the spirit of the second "anti-essentialist" perspective is captured in the earlier but equally historic black vernacular phrase "Different strokes for different folks." This notional pluralism is misleading. Its distaste for uncomfortable questions of class and power makes political calculation hazardous if not impossible. This second position refers pejoratively to the first as racial essentialism. It moves towards a casual and arrogant deconstruction of blackness while ignoring the appeal of the first position's powerful, populist affirmation of black culture. The brand of elitism which would, for example, advance the white noise of Washington, D.C.'s Rasta thrash punk band the Bad Brains as the last word in black cultural expression is clearly itching to abandon the ground of the black vernacular entirely. This abdication can only leave that space open to racial conservationists who veer between a volkish, proto-fascist sensibility and the misty-eyed sentimentality of those who would shroud themselves in the supposed moral superiority that goes with victim status. It is tantamount to ignoring the undiminished power of racism itself and forsaking the mass of black people who continue to comprehend their lived particularity through what it does to them. Needless to say, the lingering effects of racism institutionalised in the political field are overlooked just as its inscription in the cultural industries which provide the major vehicle for this exclusively aesthetic radicalism passes unremarked upon.

It is ironic, given the importance accorded to music in the habitus of diaspora blacks, that neither pole in this tense conversation takes the music very seriously. The narcissism which unites both standpoints is revealed by the way that they both forsake discussion of music and its attendant drama-turgy, performance, ritual, and gesture in favour of an obsessive fascination with the bodies of the performers themselves. For the unashamed essen-tialists, Nelson George denounces black musicians who have had facial sur-gery and wear blue or green contact lenses, while in the opposite camp, Kobena Mercer steadily reduces Michael Jackson's voice first to his body, then to his hair, and eventually to his emphatically disembodied image.[62] I want to emphasise that even though it may have once been an important factor in shaping the intellectual terrain on which politically engaged anal-ysis of black culture takes place, the opposition between these rigid per-spectives has become an obstacle to critical theorising.

The syncretic complexity of black expressive cultures alone supplies pow-erful reasons for resisting the idea that an untouched, pristine Africanity resides inside these forms, working a powerful magic of alterity in order to trigger repeatedly the perception of absolute identity. Following the lead established long ago by Leroi Jones, I believe it is possible to approach the music as a *changing* rather than an unchanging same. Today, this involves the difficult task of striving to comprehend the reproduction of cultural traditions not in the unproblematic transmission of a fixed essence through time but in the breaks and interruptions which suggest that the invocation of tradition may itself be a distinct, though covert, response to the desta-bilising flux of the post-contemporary world. New traditions have been invented in the jaws of modern experience and new conceptions of moder-nity produced in the long shadow of our enduring traditions—the African ones and the ones forged from the slave experience which the black vernac-ular so powerfully and actively remembers. This labour also necessitates far closer attention to the rituals of performance that provide prima facie evidence of linkage between black cultures.

Because the self-identity, political culture, and grounded aesthetics that distinguish black communities have often been constructed through their music and the broader cultural and philosophical meanings that flow from its production, circulation, and consumption, music is especially important in breaking the inertia which arises in the unhappy polar opposition between a squeamish, nationalist essentialism and a sceptical, saturnalian pluralism which makes the impure world of politics literally unthinkable. The preeminence of music within the diverse black communities of the Atlantic diaspora is itself an important element in their essential connectedness. But the histories of borrowing, displacement, transformation, and continual reinscription that the musical culture encloses are a living legacy that should not be reified in the primary symbol of the diaspora and then employed as an alternative to the recurrent appeal of fixity and rootedness.

Music and its rituals can be used to create a model whereby identity can be understood neither as a fixed essence nor as a vague and utterly contingent construction to be reinvented by the will and whim of aesthetes, symbolists, and language gamers. Black identity is not simply a social and political category to be used or abandoned according to the extent to which the rhetoric that supports and legitimises it is persuasive or institutionally powerful. Whatever the radical constructionists may say, it is lived as a coherent (if not always stable) experiential sense of self. Though it is often felt to be natural and spontaneous, it remains the outcome of practical activity: language, gesture, bodily significations, desires. We can use Foucault's insightful comments to illuminate this necessarily political relationship. They point towards an anti-anti-essentialism that sees racialised subjectivity as the product of the social practices that supposedly derive from it:[63] "Rather than seeing [the modern soul] as the reactivated remnants of an ideology, one would see it as the present correlative of a certain technology of power over the body. It would be wrong to say that the soul is an illusion, or an ideological effect. On the contrary it exists, it has a reality, it is produced permanently around, on, within the body by the functioning of power that is exercised."[64]

These significations can be condensed in the process of musical performance though it does not, of course, monopolise them. In the black Atlantic context, they produce the imaginary effect of an internal racial core or essence by acting on the body through the specific mechanisms of identification and recognition that are produced in the intimate interaction of performer and crowd. This reciprocal relationship can serve as an ideal communicative situation even when the original makers of the music and its eventual consumers are separated in space and time or divided by the technologies of sound reproduction and the commodity form which their art has sought to resist. I have explored elsewhere how the struggle against the commodity form has been taken over into the very configurations that black mass cultural creation assumes. Negotiations with that status are revealed openly and have become a cornerstone in the anti-aesthetic which governs those forms. The aridity of those three crucial terms—production, circulation, and consumption—does scant justice to the convoluted outernational processes to which they now refer. Each of them, in contrasting ways, hosts a politics of race and power which is hard to grasp, let alone fully appreciate, through the sometimes crude categories that political economy and European cultural criticism deploy in their tentative analyses of ethnicity and culture. The term "consumption" has associations that are particularly problematic, and needs to be carefully unpacked. It accentuates the passivity of its agents and plays down the value of their creativity as well as the micro political significance of their actions in understanding the forms of anti-discipline and resistance conducted in everyday life. Michel de Certeau has made this point at a general level:

> Like law [one of its models], culture articulates conflicts and alternately legitimises, displaces or controls the superior force. It develops in an atmosphere of tensions, and often of violence, for which it provides symbolic balances, contracts of compatibility and compromises, all more or less temporary. The tactics of consumption, the ingenious ways in which the weak make use of the strong, thus lend a political dimension to everyday practices."[65]

Some Black Works of Art in the Age of Digital Simulation

I suggested in Chapter 1 that hip hop culture grew out of the cross-fertilisation of African-American vernacular cultures with their Caribbean equivalents rather than springing fully formed from the entrails of the blues. The immediate catalyst for its development was the relocation of Clive "Kool DJ Herc" Campbell from Kingston to 168th Street in the Bronx. The syncretic dynamics of the form were complicated further by a distinctly Hispanic input into and appropriation of the break dance moves which helped to define the style in its early stages. But hip hop was not just the product of these different, though converging, black cultural traditions. The centrality of "the break" within it, and the subsequent refinement of cutting and mixing techniques through digital sampling which took the form far beyond the competence of hands on turntables, mean that the aesthetic rules which govern it are premised on a dialectic of rescuing appropriation and recombination which creates special pleasures and is not limited to the technological complex in which it originated. The deliberately fractured form of these musical pieces is worth considering for a moment. It recalls the characteristic flavour of Adorno's remarks in another, far distant setting:

> They call [it] uncreative because [it] suspends their concept of creation itself. Everything with which [it] occupies itself is already there . . . in vulgarised form; its themes are expropriated ones. Nevertheless nothing sounds as it was wont to do; all things are diverted as if by a magnet. What is worn out yields pliantly to the improvising hand; the used parts win second life as variants. Just as the chauffeur's knowledge of his old second hand car can enable him to drive it punctually and unrecognised to its intended destination, so can the expression of an up beat melody . . . arrive at places which the approved musical language could never safely reach.[66]

Acoustic and electric instruments are disorganically combined with digital sound synthesis, a variety of found sounds: typically screams, pointed fragments of speech or singing, and samples from earlier recordings—both vocal and instrumental—whose open textuality is raided in playful affirmations of the insubordinate spirit which ties this radical form to one important definition of blackness. The non-linear approach which European cultural criticism refers to as montage is a useful principle of composition in trying to analyse all this. Indeed it is tempting to endorse the Brechtian suggestion that some version of "montage" corresponds to an unprecedented type of realism, appropriate to the extreme historical conditions which form it. But these dense, implosive combinations of diverse and dissimiliar sounds amount to more than the technique they employ in their joyously artificial reconstruction of the instability of lived, profane racial identity. An aesthetic stress is laid upon the sheer social and cultural distance which formerly separated the diverse elements now dislocated into novel meanings by their provocative aural juxtaposition.

Ronnie Laws's recent instrumental single release "Identity"[67] is worth citing here. Produced in a low-tech setting for an independent record company, the record is notable not just for its title but as an up-to-date case of the more radical possibilities opened up by this new form of the old genre which demands that the past be made audible in the present. The architect of the tune, the eccentric Californian guitar player Craig T. Cooper, utilises an ambient style that recalls the oversmoked dub of the Upsetter's Black Ark studio at its peak. The track combines a large number of samples from a wide range of sources: a fragment lifted from the chorus of the Average White Band's "Pick up the Pieces" (already a Scottish pastiche of the style of James Brown's JBs) struggles to be heard against a go-go beat, half-audible screams, and a steady, synthetic work-song rhythm reconstructed from the sampled sound of the Godfather's own forceful exhalation. Having stated an angular melody and playfully teased out its inner dynamics, Laws's soprano saxophone embellishes and punctuates the apparent chaos of the rhythm track. His horn is phrased carefully so as to recall a human voice trained and disciplined by the antiphonic rituals of the black church. "Identity" is the product of all these influences. Its title offers an invitation to recognise that unity and sameness can be experienced fleetingly in the relationship between improvisation and the ordered articulation of musical disorder. The chaos which would have torn this fragile rendering of black identity apart is forestalled for the duration of the piece by the insistent thumping of the bass drum's digital pulse on the second and fourth beat of each bar. The producers of the record underscored its political point by pressing it on white vinyl.

It bears repetition that the premium which all these black diaspora styles place on the process of performance is emphasised by their radically unfinished forms—a characteristic which marks them indelibly as the products of slavery.[68] It can be glimpsed in the way that the basic units of commercial consumption in which music is fast frozen and sold have been systematically subverted by the practice of a racial politics that has colonised them and, in the process, accomplished what Baudrillard refers to as the passage from object to event:

> The work of art—a new and triumphant fetish and not a sad alienated one—should work to deconstruct its own traditional aura, its authority and power of illusion, in order to shine resplendent in the pure obscenity of the commodity. It must annihilate itself as familiar object and become monstrously foreign. But this foreignness is not the disquieting strangeness of the repressed or alienated object; this object does not shine from its being haunted or out of some secret dispossession; it glows with a veritable seduction that comes from elsewhere, having exceeded its own form and become pure object, pure event.[69]

From this perspective, the magical process whereby a commodity like a twelve-inch single, released from the belly of the multinational beast, comes to anticipate, even demand, supplementary creative input in the hidden spheres of public political interaction that wait further on up the road seems less mysterious. We do, however, need an enhanced understanding of "consumption" that can illuminate its inner workings and the relationships between rootedness and displacement, locality and dissemination that lend them vitality in this countercultural setting. The twelve-inch single appeared as a market innovation during the late seventies. It was part of the record companies' response to the demands placed upon them by the dance subcultures congealed around the black genres—reggae and rhythm and blues. Those demands were met halfway by the creation of a new type of musical product which could maximise their own economic opportunities, but this had other unintended consequences. The additional time and increased volume made possible by the introduction of this format became powerful factors impelling restless subcultural creativity forwards. Once dubbing, scratching, and mixing appeared as new elements in the deconstructive and reconstructive scheme that joined production and consumption together, twelve-inch releases began to include a number of different mixes of the same song, supposedly for different locations or purposes. A dance mix, a radio mix, an a capella mix, a dub mix, a jazz mix, a bass mix, and so on. On the most elementary level, these plural forms make the abstract concept of a changing same a living, familiar reality. Record companies like this arrangement because it is cheaper for them to go on playing around with the same old song than to record additional material, but different creative possibilities open out from it. The relationship of the listener to the text is changed by the proliferation of different versions. Which one is the original? How does the memory of one version transform the way in which subsequent versions are heard and understood? The components of one mix separated and broken down can be more easily borrowed and blended to create further permutations of meaning. The twelve-inch single release of LL Cool J's rhythm and blues–hip hop hybrid hit "Round the Way Girl" came in five different versions: the LP cut, built around a sample from the Mary Jane Girls' 1983 Motown pop soul hit "All Night Long," and several remixes that extended and transformed the meaning of the original rap and this first sample by annexing the rhythmic signature of Gwen McCrae's "Funky Sensation." This funky southern soul record from 1981 was an original B. Boy cut, used by the old-school DJ's and rappers who originated hip hop to make breaks. These borrowings are especially noteworthy because they have been orchestrated in pursuit of a means to signify Cool J's definition of authentic black femininity. The record's mass appeal lay in the fact that his definition of authenticity was measured by vernacular style reviled on the one hand by the Africentrists as preconscious because it didn't conform to the stately postures expected of the African queen and disavowed on the other by the entertainments industry in which bizarre, white-identified standards of feminine beauty have become dominant. To be inauthentic is, in this case at least, to be real:

I want a girl with extensions in her hair
bamboo earrings at least two pair
a Fendi bag and a bad attitude
that's what it takes to put me in a good mood.[70]

The hybridity which is formally intrinsic to hip hop has not been able to prevent that style from being used as an especially potent sign and symbol of racial authenticity. It is significant that when this happens the term "hip hop" is often forsaken in favour of the alternative term "rap," preferred precisely because it is more ethnically marked by African-American influences than the other. These issues can be examined further through the example of Quincy Jones, whose personal narrative of racial uplift has recently become something of a cipher for black creativity in general and black musical genius in particular. The identification of black musical genius constitutes an important cultural narrative. It tells and retells not so much the story of the weak's victory over the strong but the relative powers enjoyed by different types of strength. The story of intuitive black creative development is personalised in the narratives of figures like Jones.[71] It demonstrates the aesthetic and commercial fruits of pain and suffering and has a special significance because musicians have played a disproportionate part in the long struggle to represent black creativity, innovation, and excellence. Jones, an entrepreneur, preeminent music producer, record company executive, arranger of great skill, sometime bebopper, fundraiser for Jesse Jackson's campaigns, and emergent TV magnate, is the latest "role model" figure in a long sequence that descends from slavery and the racially representative heroism of men like Douglass.

Jones is untypical in that he has recently been the subject of a biographical film, "Listen Up: The Many Lives of Quincy Jones," supported by a book, and a CD/Tape sound track and single. In all these interlocking formats "Listen Up" celebrates his life, endurance, and creativity.[72] Most of all, it affirms black participation in the entertainment industry, an involvement that Jones has summed up through a surprising invocation of the British Broadcasting Company's distinctive corporate code: the three E's, "Enlightenment, Education, Entertainment."[73] The process which culminated in this novel commemorative package was clearly encouraged by Jones's growing involvement with television as producer of "The Fresh Prince of Bel Air" and "The Jesse Jackson Show." But it began earlier with the release of his 1990 LP "Back on the Block."[74] This set made use of rap as its means to complete the circle of Jones's own odyssey from poverty on Chicago's South Side through Seattle, New York, Paris, Stockholm, and thence to Los Angeles and mogulhood. The positive value of "Back on the Block" is its powerful and necessary argument for the seams of continuity which lie beneath the generational divisions in African-American musical culture. However, there were other more problematic elements at large in it also. One track, a version of Joseph Zawinul's composition "Birdland," typifies the spirit of the project as a whole by uniting the talents of old- and new-school rappers like Melle Mel, Kool Moe D, Ice T, and Big Daddy Kane with singers and instrumentalists drawn from earlier generations. George Benson, Dizzy Gillespie, Sarah Vaughan, Miles Davis, and Zawinul himself were among those whose vocal and instrumental input was synthesized by Jones into an exhilarating epic statement of the view that hip hop and bebop shared the same fundamental spirit. Jones put it like this: "Hip hop is in many ways the same as Bebop, because it was renegade-type music. It came from a disenfranchised sub-culture that got thrown out of the way. They said, 'We'll make up our own life. We'll have our own language.'"[75]

Rap provided this montage (it is tempting to say mélange) with its articulating and framing principle. Rap was the cultural and political means through which Jones completed his return to the touchstone of authentic black American creativity. Rapping on the record himself in the unlikely persona of "The Dude," he explained that he wanted the project "to incorporate the whole family of black American music . . . everything from Gospel to Jazz that was part of my culture." Brazilian and African musical patterns were annexed by and became continuous with his version of black America's musical heritage. They are linked, says Jones, by the shared "traditions of the African griot storyteller that are continued today by the rappers." The delicate relationship between unity and differentiation gets lost at this point. Old and new, east and west simply dissolve into each other or rather into the receptacle provided for their interaction by the grand narrative of African-American cultural strength and durability. However compelling they may be, Jones's appropriations of Brazilian rhythm and African language become entirely subservient to the need to legitimate African-American particularity. The promise of a truly compound diaspora or even global culture which could shift understanding of black cultural production away from the narrow concerns of ethnic exceptionalism and absolutism recedes rapidly. The potential signified in the inner hybridity of hip hop and the outer syncretism of the musical forms which makes Jones's synthesis plausible comes to an abrupt and premature end. It terminates in a portrait of the boys, back on the block where they ride out the genocidal processes of the inner city through the redemptive power of their authentic racial art.

Young Black Teenagers Then and Now

Quincy Jones tells us that "the times are always contained in the rhythm." Assuming for a moment that most black cultural critics do not want simply to respond to the end of innocent notions of the black subject with festivities—whether they are wakes or baptisms—do we attempt to specify some new conceptions of that subjectivity that are less innocent and less obviously open to the supposed treason which essentialism represents? Or do we cut ourselves off from the world where black identities are made—even required—by the brutal mechanics of racial subordination and the varieties of political agency which strive to answer them?

When I was a child and a young man growing up in London, black music provided me with a means to gain proximity to the sources of feeling from which our local conceptions of blackness were assembled. The Caribbean, Africa, Latin America, and above all black America contributed to our lived sense of a racial self. The urban context in which these forms were encountered cemented their stylistic appeal and facilitated their solicitation of our identification. They were important also as a source for the discourses of blackness with which we located our own struggles and experiences.

Twenty years later, with the sound tracks of my adolescence recirculating in the exhilaratingly damaged form of hip hop, I was walking down a street in New Haven, Connecticut—a black city—looking for a record shop stocked with black music. The desolation, poverty, and misery encountered on that fruitless quest forced me to confront the fact that I had come to America in pursuit of a musical culture that no longer exists. My scepticism about the narrative of family, race, culture, and nation that stretches down the years from Crummell's chilling remarks means that I cannot share in Quincy Jones's mourning over its corpse or his desire to rescue some democratic possibility in the wake of its disappearance. Looking back on the adolescent hours I spent trying to master the technical intricacies of Albert King and Jimi Hendrix, fathom the subtleties of James Jamerson, Larry Graham, or Chuck Rainey, and comprehend how the screams of Sly, James, and Aretha could punctuate and extend their metaphysical modes of address to the black subject, I realise that the most important lesson music still has to teach us is that its inner secrets and its ethnic rules can be taught and learned. The spectral figures of half-known or half-remembered musicians like Bobby Eli, Duck Dunn, Tim Drummond, Andy Newmark, Carol Kaye, John Robinson, and Rod Temperton appeared at my shoulder to nod their mute assent to this verdict. Then they disappeared into the dusk on Dixwell Avenue. Their exemplary contributions to rhythm and blues have left behind a whispered warning that black music cannot be reduced to a fixed dialogue between a thinking racial self and a stable racial community. Apart from anything else, the globalisation of vernacular forms means that our understanding of antiphony will have to change. The calls and responses no longer converge in the tidy patterns of secret, ethnically encoded dialogue. The original call is becoming harder to locate. If we privilege it over the subsequent sounds that compete with one another to make the most appropriate reply, we will have to remember that these communicative gestures are not expressive of an essence that exists outside of the acts which perform them and thereby transmit the structures of racial feeling to wider, as yet uncharted, worlds.

4

"Cheer The Weary Traveller": W. E. B. Du Bois, Germany, and the Politics of (Dis)placement

Race would seem to be a dynamic and not a static conception, and the typical races are continually changing and developing, amalgamating and differentiating . . . we are studying the history of the darker part of the human family, which is separated from the rest of mankind by no absolute physical line and no definite mental characteristics, but which nevertheless forms, as a mass, a series of social groups more or less distinct in history, appearance and in cultural gifts and accomplishment.

> *W. E. B. Du Bois*

It is not culture which binds the peoples who are of partially African origin now scattered throughout the world, but an identity of passions. We share a hatred for the alienation forced upon us by Europeans during the process of colonisation and empire and we are bound by our common suffering more than by our pigmentation. But even this identification is shared by most non-white peoples, and while it has political value of great potency, its cultural value is almost nil.

> *Ralph Ellison*

IN THE SPACE and time that separate Robert Johnson's "Hellhound on My Trail," the Wailers' exhortation to "Keep on Moving," and the more recent Soul II Soul piece with the same name, the expressive cultures of the black Atlantic world have been dominated by a special mood of restlessness. These songs, like so many others in the same intertextual sequence, evoke and affirm a condition in which the negative meanings given to the enforced movement of blacks are somehow transposed. What was initially felt to be a curse—the curse of homelessness or the curse of enforced exile—gets repossessed. It becomes affirmed and is reconstructed as the basis of a privileged standpoint from which certain useful and critical perceptions about the modern world become more likely. It should be obvious that this unusual perspective has been forged out of the experiences of racial subordination. I want to suggest that it also represents a response to the successive displacements, migrations, and journeys (forced and otherwise) which have come to constitute these black cultures' special conditions of existence.

As was suggested in the opening chapter, the appeal to and for roots and rootedness which is another more obvious characteristic of these cultural forms needs to be understood in this context. It is possible to argue that the acquisition of roots became an urgent issue only when diaspora blacks sought to construct a political agenda in which the ideal of rootedness was identified as a prerequisite for the forms of cultural integrity that could guarantee the nationhood and statehood to which they aspired. The need to locate cultural or ethnic roots and then to use the idea of being in touch with them as a means to refigure the cartography of dispersal and exile is perhaps best understood as a simple and direct response to the varieties of racism which have denied the historical character of black experience and the integrity of black cultures.

This chapter seeks to explore these issues by focusing on W. E. B. Du Bois's life and some of his copious writings. This is profitable because in Du Bois's thought the relationship of modern black political theory to European romantic nationalism in general and German nationalism in particular becomes even more explicit than it was in the work of his predecessors—Crummel, Blyden, Delany, and Douglass.

Apart from examining this pivotal relationship, I want to interpret some of Du Bois's writings in the context provided by historical consideration of the movement of blacks outside Africa which Dubois helped to create and shape in the early years of the twentieth century. This necessarily involves analysing the organisational forms, cultural politics, and political cultures created by African diaspora populations in a threefold process of political engagement: first, in active pursuit of self-emancipation from slavery and its attendant horrors; second, towards the acquisition of substantive citizenship denied by slavery; and finally, in pursuit of an autonomous space in the system of formal political relationships that distinguishes occidental modernity. What follows will try to map something of the development of these distinctive forms of political action as they oscillate between two primary tendencies or options. The first involves being a social movement, oriented towards the rational pursuit of a good life, while the second can best be described as accepting the fact that in a racially structured society this movement is going to be somehow anti-social and probably defensive in character. The tension between a politics of fulfilment and a politics of transfiguration suggested in Chapter 1 reappears here in this new guise which is entirely congruent with Du Bois's theory of double consciousness. The pan-African movements founded in the aftermath of slavery brought these two different approaches towards modern black politics together in a synthesis of national and transnational concerns.[1] These movements allow us to see manifestations of the restless black political sensibility that was forced to move to and fro across the Atlantic and crisscross the boundaries of nation states if it was to be at all effective. They have frequently been dominated by the latter project, transfiguration, and its attendant disassociation of black struggles from the supposedly teleological progress of occidental civilisation. Du Bois's writings were instrumental in the development of these movements at several different stages in their unfolding. They can be used to illustrate an ambivalent stance towards the fruits of modernity that can be marked out between these two contrasting responses.

His theory of modernity pursues the sustained and uncompromising interrogation of the concept of progress from the standpoint of the slave, which was the subject of Chapter 2. It has both spatial and temporal aspects but is dominated by the latter, expressed in a strong sense of the novelty of the nineteenth century and in his apprehension of the unique social forces at work in a transformed world constituting unprecedented, symbiotic conceptions of self and society, their democratic potential disfigured by white supremacy:

> The nineteenth was the first century of human sympathy,—the age when half wonderingly we began to descry in others that transfigured spark of divinity which we call Myself; when clodhoppers and peasants, and tramps and thieves, and millionaires and-sometimes-Negroes, became throbbing souls whose warm pulsing life touched us so nearly that we half gasped with surprise, crying, "Thou too! Hast Thou seen Sorrow and the dull waters of hopelessness? Hast Thou known Life?" And then all helplessly we peered into those Otherworlds, and wailed, "O World of Worlds how shall man make you one?"[2]

This analysis was so deeply rooted in the post-slave history of the new world that it became difficult for Du Bois's understanding of modernity to incorporate contemporary Africa. Africa emerged instead as a mythic counterpart to modernity in the Americas—a moral symbol transmitted by exquisite objects seen fleetingly in the African collection at Fisk University but largely disappearing from Du Bois's account, leaving an empty, aching space between his local and global manifestations of racial injustice. However, after responding to Franz Boas's encouragement to study Africa seriously in the first decade of this century, Du Bois began to retell the narrative of western civilisation in systematic ways that emphasised its African origins and expressed a deeper disengagement from modern forms of thought that were discredited by their association with the continuing practice of white supremacy. Du Bois's analysis of modernity also expressed his turn away from the United States. That country ceased to be the locus of his political aspirations once it became clear that the commitments to private rectitude and public reason, for which he had argued so powerfully, would not be sufficient to precipitate the comprehensive reforms demanded by black suffering in the North as well as the South. His fragmentary use of African history to bolster his critiques of America and the West as well as to mark those moments in his own discourse where transcendence of western, racialised truths seemed necessary can be traced back to *The Souls of Black Folk,* the book that made him a leader of black Americans.

The exceptionally fluid political collectivities that emerge under the aegis of early Pan-Africanism are only half grasped by the unsatisfactory term "movement." Exploring them raises its own difficulties. It is necessary, for example, to appreciate that these histories of subversive political organisation cannot be charted satisfactorily either in conventional terms of party, class, ethnic group or through more potent but also more evasive concepts like race and nation. The phenomena we struggle to name as Pan-Africanism, Ethiopianism, Emigrationism, Washingtonism, and Garveyism coexist with these terms but also register deep dissatisfaction with what the more orthodox concepts derived from respectable disciplines can offer black political thought premised on their inadequacy. Successive phases of struggle by blacks in, but not completely of, the West have pushed at the very limits of what Euro-American modernity has delineated as the approved space for politics within its social formations. Conventional ideas of modern citizenship have sometimes been stretched so that they might accommodate black hopes. At other times they have been compressed to the point of implosion by the dead weight of black suffering. This is another way of saying that the specific forms of democracy and mutuality that inhere within the dynamic oppositional structures blacks have created to advance their interests require a different political and philosophical vocabulary from that endorsed by past and present social scientific conventions. Du Bois's work has plenty to offer in this regard. It had been a sense of the need for new analytical languages and procedures that had drawn him away from his initial studies in history and towards psychology and sociology. His eminent status as the first black sociologist and a pioneer of the discipline in America offers another important reason for using his life and work to focus the arguments in this chapter, for his sociology also bears the imprint of his ambivalence. He discussed the appeal of the new discipline in a commentary on the work of Herbert Spencer that begins the chapter "Science and Empire" in *Dusk of Dawn,* one of several autobiographical works:

The biological analogy, the vast generalisations were striking, but actual scientific accomplishment lagged. For me an opportunity seemed to present itself. I could not lull my mind to hypnosis by regarding a phrase like "consciousness of kind" as a scientific law. But turning my gaze from fruitless word-twisting and facing the facts of my own social situation and racial world, I determined to put science into sociology through the study of the condition and problems of my own group. I was going to study the facts, any and all the facts, concerning the American Negro and his plight, and by measurement and comparison and research, work up to any valid generalization which I could.[3]

From Frederick Douglass[4] on down, black writers grappling with the antinomies of modernity turned to the conceptual tools of the social sciences and related disciplines in their attempts to interpret the social relations of racial subordination and to legitimate their strategies for its overcoming. The move towards this type of writing—equally distant from the residual political language of anti-slavery and the morally charged rhetoric of the black church—is a further means to gauge the complexity of their location within and sometimes against the social and moral conventions of western modernity. Though fully accomplished in the niceties of sociological research and theorising, Du Bois deployed these tools selectively and intermittently. The genre of modernist writing he inaugurated in *The Souls of Black Folk* and refined further in his later work, especially *Darkwater*, supplements recognisably sociological writing with personal and public history, fiction, autobiography, ethnography, and poetry. These books produce a self-consciously polyphonic form that was born from the intellectual dilemmas that had grown alongside Du Bois's dissatisfaction with all available scholarly languages. This stylistic innovation is not reducible, as one of his biographers has suggested, to an enduring affection for the essay form as practised by Emerson and Carlyle, Hazlitt and Lamb.[5] I prefer to see its combination of tones and modes of interpellating the reader as a deliberate experiment produced from the realisation that none of these different registers of address could, by itself, convey the intensity of feeling that Du Bois believed the writing of black history and the exploration of racialised experience demanded. This distinct blend was also an important influence on the development of black literary modernism.

There are a number of other reasons for using Du Bois's life and his writings as a means to develop my argument about modernity and to construct an intercultural and anti-ethnocentric account of modern black history and political culture. He too was a black American, but unlike Richard Wright, who is the central subject of the next chapter, he was raised in a tiny New England black community, Great Barrington, Massachusetts. Compared to the South, where Du Bois was to discover and internalise a new way of being black, his northern birthplace was seen by some commentators on his life as an inauthentic and insufficiently black location because of its remoteness from the institution of slavery. The problems of racialised ontology and identity—the tension between being and becoming black—are therefore deeply inscribed in Du Bois's own life. He was open about the way he had to learn the codes, rhythms, and styles of racialised living for himself when he left the protected but nonetheless segregated environment in which he had grown up and took his place at Fisk University, the Jubilee Singers' alma mater, in Nashville, Tennessee. It was at Fisk that Du Bois first encountered the music which was to play such an important role in his analysis of black culture.

> One unforgettable thing that Fisk University did for me was to guide and enlarge my appreciation of music. In Great Barrington the only music we had was that of the old English hymns, some of them set to German music. The music was often fine, but the words usually illogical or silly . . . Fisk had the tradition of her Jubilee Singers, who once hid in a Brooklyn organ loft, lest pious congregationalists see their black faces before they heard their heavenly voices . . . then the nation listened and the world opened its arms and The Fisk Jubilee Singers literally sang before Kings . . . There I met some of these singers and heard their music.[6]

He incorporated these learning experiences into his work and used the insights they provided into the social construction of black identity as a means to open up the constitution of all racial identities. Some of the more openly and consistently autobiographical writings make clear that Du Bois had self-consciously reconstructed his sense of self and his understanding of community amidst the racially affirmative culture of Fisk University: "So I came to a region where the world was split into white and black halves, and where the darker half was held back by race prejudice and legal bonds, as well as by deep ignorance and dire poverty. But facing this was not a lost group, but at Fisk a microcosm of a world and a civilisation in potentiality. Into this world I leapt with enthusiasm. A new loyalty and allegiance replaced my Americanism: hence-forward I was a Negro."[7] This process of reconstruction and self-discovery was possible only in the protected location provided by an ethnically absolute and racially homogeneous culture. Du Bois recognised this as something that inclined him towards the highly personal form of segregationism that fitted in well with his social awkwardness: "Then of course, when I went South to Fisk, I became a member of a closed racial group with rites and loyalties, with a history and a corporate future, with an art and philosophy. I received these eagerly and expanded them so that when I came to Harvard the theory of race separation was quite in my blood."[8]

Though his ideological outlook changed during his long life from Darwinism through elitism to socialism, from Pan-Africanism through voluntary self-segregation and eventually to official communism, Du Bois was a political activist who managed to combine these oppositional commitments with serious scholarship even when universities snubbed him and ignored his extraordinary productivity. There may be lessons for contemporary political culture in the type of extra-academic, activist intellectual that he was. However, the most conspicuous product of his changing views seems to be a bitter contest over the political complexion of his legacy, which is seen in essentially conservative terms by some commentators and as espousing a radical form of democratic socialism by others.[9]

Du Bois is also appealing and important from the point of view of this book because of his lack of roots and the proliferation of routes in his long nomadic life. He travelled extensively and his life ended in African exile after he took up residence in Ghana and renounced his American citizenship at the age of ninety-five. His accounts of his visits to Africa pose the relationship between American blacks and their estranged homeland with something of the same starkness that was encountered in Martin Delany's trip to Niger Valley. Still further questions about the identity and non-identity of black cultures are raised by the length and complexity of Du Bois's relationships to Europe. For Du Bois, Douglass, and the constellation of other thinkers whose work constitutes an antiphonal dialogue with their writings, nagging anxiety over the inner contradictions of modernity and a radical scepticism towards the ideology of progress with which it is associated are compounded by these experiences of travel both within and away from America. The issues of travel, movement, displacement, and relocation that emerge from Du Bois's work are therefore a primary concern of this chapter.

Modernity, Terror, and Movements

In several respects, what follows will attempt to take the social and political struggles of diaspora blacks on their own problematic terms and try to determine where their distinctive cultural momentum has come from. In particular, taking cues from Du Bois's concept of double consciousness, I will extend his implicit argument that the cultures of diaspora blacks can be profitably interpreted as expressions of and commentaries upon ambivalences generated by modernity and their locations within it.

A profound sense of the way in which modernity frames the complicity of rationality with the practice of white supremacist terror is the initial vehicle for writing this history of ambivalence. It appears at the core of Du Bois's interpretation of modernity, in his positioning of slavery in relation to modern civilisation, and in his emphasis upon the constitutive role of that terror in configuring modern black political cultures: "the characteristic of our age is the contact of European Civilization with the world's undeveloped peoples . . . War, murder, slavery, extermination, and debauchery,—this has again and again been the result of carrying civilization and the blessed gospel to the isles of the sea and the heathen without the law."[10]

His emphasis on terror as a defining feature of slave regimes sanctified by both God and reason is a recurrent theme. His discussion of the place of education in the liberation of blacks opens, for example, by establishing the slave ship as the inaugural location both for his own scepticism and for "the tangle of thought and afterthought" in which the critical ethical and political questions of the age must be decided.[11] The same idea is reworked again, in yet more complex forms, once the temporary gains of Reconstruction are beaten back in the counter-revolutionary carnival of lynching and its related public spectacle of barbarity in the late nineteenth century. These hateful residues of the slave system have turned the South into an "armed camp for intimidating black folk." The significance and functionality of racial terror thus becomes a central preoccupation in Du Bois's indictments and affirmations of modernity. Its importance is conveyed in the link it establishes between *The Souls* and *Dusk of Dawn*, a book produced some thirty-seven years later which makes repeated mention of lynching as a social ritual and means of political administration. In the later volume, Du Bois provided a powerful account of the effect on him of the killing and mutilation of Sam Hose, a Georgia labourer lynched after a fight over money with a plantation owner.[12] Hose's severed knuckles had been placed on public display in the window of a grocery store on Mitchell Street close to Atlanta University where Du Bois was working as a professor of sociology. He summed up the inner transformation wrought by this discovery: "one could not be a calm, cool, and detached scientist while Negroes were lynched, murdered and starved . . ." In order to evaluate this remark, it is essential to appreciate the scale and public significance of lynching as a spectacle during this period. The Hose case points to some of this, but Du Bois emphasised its place as a popular theatre of power in a second case discussed later in the same volume: "A Negro was publicly burned alive in Tennessee under circumstances unusually atrocious. The mobbing and burning were publicly advertised in the press beforehand. Three thousand automobiles brought the audience, including mothers carrying children. Ten Gallons of gasoline were poured over the wretch and he was burned alive, while hundreds fought for bits of his body, clothing and the rope."[13]

Du Bois's sense of the importance of ritual brutality in structuring modern, civilised life in the South was developed both through his arguments for its continuity with patterns of brutality established during slavery and in his fragmentary commentaries on the genocide of Native Americans. He articulates these histories of ethnocidal terror and they become twinned in the ironic account of modernity's failed promises which he constructs from the mobile vantage point afforded by the window of a Jim Crow railway car: "we must hasten on our journey. This that we pass as we near Atlanta is the ancient land of the Cherokees,—that brave Indian nation which strove so long for its fatherland, until Fate and the United States Government drove them beyond the Mississippi."[14] Even with the history of conquest restored to its proper place and a cruel and unusual degree of brutality routinely seen to be operating as a mechanism of political administration, the experience of racial subordination is insufficient to account for the richness and consistency of the defensive and transformational struggles of blacks in the West. Recognising this obliges one to follow Du Bois in asking some simple but awkward questions about precisely what distinguished these particular political forms from other, possibly more familiar ones. For example, it means enquiring into precisely where the self-identity of these international movements against slavery, for citizenship and political autonomy had resided. It requires that we delve into their hidden history and take nothing for granted about the means of their reproduction and transmission in word and in sound. These investigations become more complicated still because answers to such questions cannot always be found in the convenient if misleading records that distinguish the organisation of political struggles that have been conducted according to the principles of bureaucratic rationality. Particularly in the slave period, but also after it, there are few committee minutes, manifestos, or other programmatic documents that aim at setting down these movements' objectives and strategy in transparent form. Their reflexive self-consciousness must be sought elsewhere. Though written traces of it can be found, it is more often likely to be gleaned from sources that are both more imaginative and more ephemeral. Du Bois suggests that it is regularly expressed in cultural rather than formally political practices that are, for reasons connected to the extreme varieties of social subordination practised in the name of race, especially dense and even opaque to outsiders. That density, so necessary to the maintenance of the integrity of the interpretive community of slaves and their descendants, is not constant. It fluctuates as the chemistry of cultural syncretism responds to changes in the political pressure and the economic atmosphere. Once again, *The Souls of Black Folk* can be shown to be an especially important text because of the way that it sensitised blacks to the significance of the vernacular cultures that arose to mediate the enduring effects of terror. The book endorsed this suggestion through its use of black music as a cipher for the ineffable, sublime, pre-discursive and anti-discursive elements in black expressive culture. As I have shown in the previous chapter, music has been regularly employed since *The Souls* to provide a symbol for various different conceptions of black commonality. Du Bois's work initiates this strategy.

The more mystical versions of black communitarianism are frequently heard as part of the argument that an innate or fundamental unity can be found beneath the surface of the irreducible plurality of new world black styles. However, the essential motif for this vision of racial identity has been the sign "Africa" and its associated black nationalisms, which have been extremely important in the conduct of black political culture in the age of imperial power. The history and origins of these often romantic and necessarily exclusivist ideas of national identity, national culture, and national belonging will have to be dealt with in detail elsewhere. As an alternative to these familiar positions, my aim here is to present and defend another more modest conception of connectedness which is governed by the concept of diaspora and its logic of unity and differentiation. Du Bois makes an important contribution to this task that is often overlooked by African-American critics who do not find this aspect of his work to their parochial taste. His writing sometimes operates in a more general, less particularistic tone, and his struggles to validate the concept of an African diaspora as an abstraction should not be read as a signal that smaller, more immediate or local shifts are unimportant to him. Du Bois seems to suggest that paying more careful attention to the inner asymmetry and differentiation of black cultures is the only way to approach the level of connectedness that grand rhetorical theories of racial similarity either invoke or presuppose. It is obvious, though, that attention to these often contradictory local components of blackness can outweigh consideration of the special modalities that connect the lives and experiences of blacks in the western hemisphere whether or not they are directly conscious of it. In other words, it is important, while bearing significant differences in mind, to attempt to specify some of the similarities to be found in diverse black experiences in the modern West. We shall see below that this is what the political aspirations of Pan-Africanism themselves demand. The worth of the diaspora concept is in its attempt to specify differentiation and identity in a way which enables one to think about the issue of racial commonality outside of constricting binary frameworks—especially those that counterpose essentialism and pluralism. *The Souls* was the first place where a diasporic, global perspective on the politics of racism and its overcoming interrupted the smooth flow of African-American exceptionalisms. Du Bois's nationalist impulses coexisted in that book with their transcendence. They grated slowly against each other as he moved beyond simply using European history to generate comparative examples of denied nationality and subordinated ethnic identity as Delany and Crummell had done. Instead of this one-way traffic, a systematic account of the interconnections between Africa, Europe, and the Americas emerged slowly to complicate the exceptionalist narrative of black suffering and self-emancipation in the United States. International slavery provided the rationale for this perspective, but it was associated with Du Bois's desire to demonstrate the internal situation of blacks, firmly locked inside the modern world that their coerced labour had made possible. To this end, he carefully displayed a complete familiarity with the cultural legacy of western civilisation. He claimed access to it as a right for the race as a whole, and produced a text that demonstrated how he regarded this legacy as his own personal property. There were both strategy and sheer bravado in the way he paraded an apparently easy and effortless erudition before his white readers, while using it simultaneously as a polemic against those among his black reading public who followed Booker T. Washington's denial of the fundamental relationship between freedom and education or concurred with his view that higher learning was an absurd distraction from the practical tasks essential to ensuring racial survival and prosperity.

> I sit with Shakespeare and he winces not. Across the color line I move arm in arm with Balzac and Dumas, where smiling men and welcoming women glide in gilded halls. From out of the caves of evening that swing between the strong-limbed earth and the tracery of stars, I summon Aristotle and Aurelius and what soul I will, and they come all graciously with no scorn nor condescension. So wed with Truth, I dwell above the veil. Is this the life you grudge us . . . Are you so afraid lest peering from this high Pisgah, between Philistine and Amalekite, we sight the Promised Land?[15]

Du Bois's image of the Black University is central to this argument. In opposition to Washington's anti-academic emphasis on the technical, vocational, and practical, he defended the ideal of higher learning both as a goal in itself and as the foundation upon which a new educational system must be constructed: "where forsooth, shall we ground knowledge save on the broadest deepest knowledge? The roots of the tree rather than the leaves, are the sources of its life; and from the dawn of history, from Academus to Cambridge, the culture of the University has been the broad foundation-stone on which is built the kindergarten's ABC."[16] This argument about education is one of several ways in which what has been called the "Black Radical Tradition,"[17] a term suggested by Cedric Robinson, can be shown to have interesting cultural correlates in the lifeworlds of black subjects and in the grounded aesthetics which animate their social aspirations to be free and to be themselves. Though the power of Robinson's term is obvious, it is in turns both illuminating and misleading. This is because it can suggest that it is the radical elements of this tradition which are its dominant characteristics (something Du Bois's complex and shifting positions can be used to dispute), and because the idea of tradition can sound too closed, too final, and too antithetical to the subaltern experience of modernity which has partially conditioned the development of these cultural forms. Where the communities of interpretation, needs, and solidarity on which the cultures of the black Atlantic rest become an intellectual and political multiplicity, they assume a fractal form in which the relationship between similarity and difference becomes so complex that it may continually deceive the senses. Our ability to generalise about and compare black cultures is therefore circumscribed by the scale of the analysis being conducted. The perceived contours of these movements vary according to the precise location of the observer. I have suggested in the previous chapter that this diaspora multiplicity is a chaotic, living, disorganic formation. If it can be called a tradition at all, it is a tradition in ceaseless motion—a changing same that strives continually towards a state of self-realisation that continually retreats beyond its grasp. There are, however, three phases in its untidy evolution that can be heuristically identified and that are useful because they correspond loosely to the three-part structure of Du Bois's *The Souls of Black Folk.* The first can be defined by the struggles against the institution of slavery conducted throughout the new world. These were struggles for emancipation from coerced labour, producing commodities for sale on a world market, and the distinctively modern system of colour-coded oppression associated with it. The second is recognisable through the protracted struggles to win human status and the consequent bourgeois rights and liberties for the free black populations of the modernised and industrialised countries in which Liberty, Justice, and Right get marked "For White People Only."[18] These struggles were above all a quest for citizenship, whether conducted in the context of state-managed migrant labour systems or in less formal and less centralised structures of racial subordination. This dynamic is connected both to the political forms that succeed it and to the slavery that preceded it. It draws much of its strength and its symbolic potency from the distinctive and vibrant patterns of collective political action that slavery made possible. The third strand of political struggles can be defined by its pursuit of an independent space in which black community and autonomy can develop at their own pace and in their own direction. This final component encompassed the desire of American and Caribbean blacks to secure an independent African homeland in Liberia and elsewhere. It relates also to the encroachment of European colonisers into the African continent and to the complex political conflicts which grew up around the need to liberate Africa. Though vitally important in its own right, the liberation of Africa also operates as an analog for the acquisition of black autonomy in general. It is typically presented as a homological point of reference by means of which local or even individual progress towards various forms of self-determination could be evaluated against the global dynamics involved.[19]

The unevenness with which battles against racism appear in all these stages is a reminder that the three dimensions do not follow one another in a neat linear sequence. The traces of each become inscribed in the political and cultural imaginaries of the others. Struggles orientated towards particular tactical goals often coexisted and even actively contradicted one another by generating radically different sets of political priorities, alliances, and conceptual agendas. In Du Bois's work, a shifting relationship to the idea of nationality can be used as a rough means to mark out movement from one stage or mood to another. The first is expressed in the need to gain admission to the national community and to American civil and political society, the second in the need to make that national community live up to the promises inherent in its political and judicial rhetoric, and the third in the need either to integrate with or to disassociate from that community once its essentially illusory character had been recognised. At this point, other types of racial association, of a local, urban, or even international nature, can be shown to be more significant than the overdue chance to be an American.

There are other ways in which the non-linear, self-similar pattern of these political conflicts can be periodised. They are, for example, battles over the means of cultural representation available to racially subordinated people who are denied access to particular cultural forms (like literacy) while others (like song) are developed both as a means of transcendence and as a type of compensation for very specific experiences of unfreedom. In the first stage, the population is coerced into illiteracy and held there by terror. In the second, where the door to literacy is not closed by legal sanctions, survival may require the mastery of specially encoded linguistic and verbal expressions in addition to command of the written word.[20] The battle between Du Bois and Washington shows how education emerged as a major focus for political activity. The third stage characteristically involves a deliberate and self-conscious move beyond language in ways that are informed by the social memory of earlier experiences of enforced separation from the world of written communication. A countercultural sense of the inability of mere words to convey certain truths inaugurates a special indictment of modernity's enforced separation of art and life as well as a distinct aesthetic (or anti-aesthetic) standpoint. Music is the best way of examining this final aspect.

Looking at it yet another way, it may be possible to periodise these same three moments in black political culture through the different configuration each gives to the project of liberation and the place of culture within it. Here, the first stage would be identified by the attempt to liberate the body of the slave from a rather deeper experience of reification than anything that can be mapped through the concept of the fetishism of commodities, and the second phase by the liberation of culture, especially language, as a means of social self-creation. Though music plays a significant role in both of the earlier phases, the third can be defined by the project of liberating music from its status as a mere commodity and by the associated desire to use it to demonstrate the reconciliation of art and life, that is, by exploring its pursuit of artistic and even aesthetic experience not just as a form of compensation, paid as the price of an internal exile from modernity, but as the favoured vehicle for communal self-development.

Thinking through *The Souls of Black Folk*

These three interrelated aspects of modern black political culture are expressed forcefully in *The Souls*. This classic canonical work was first published in 1903 when the author was thirty-five and working as a teacher of economics and history at Atlanta University. It was a carefully orchestrated collection of his old and new writings. Nine previously published and slightly rewritten pieces were given an introduction and supplemented by five new essays. The chapters defy easy summary. They range across Du Bois's own life in the North and in the South and include detailed analyses of the social and economic relations in the post-Reconstruction South; there are reflections on the city of Atlanta, the Freedmen's Bureau, the Black Belt, cotton, and Alexander Crummell, as well as a powerful polemic against Booker T. Washington's ideas on the value and quality of education for blacks. One short story is included, and a wistful, elegiac account of the death of Du Bois's son. The collection ends with an essay on the music of the slaves and its significance for black political culture.

Du Bois's approach to analysing the particular, local histories and experiences of American blacks as part of the more general, discontinuous, and sharply differentiated processes that contribute to a diaspora drew its inspiration from some diverse sources. It was conditioned by a well-tuned sense of history which is the obvious product of his encounter with historical materialism. It was also marked by the refined sociological sensibilities that characterise his writing and was parented by a complex understanding of the relationship between race, nation, and culture that was itself shaped by Du Bois's familiarity with German idealism. Of these influences, it was Marxism that fared badly in its translation into the black idiom. It foundered on several other attributes of the distinctive history that Du Bois felt obliged to try and reconstruct as part of his critique of the theory of modernity to which Marxian thinking subscribes. The history of slavery was repeatedly used as a tool to interrogate the assumptions of occidental progress that Marxism shared. As I have already suggested, the central place of racialised and racialising terror in slavery and since was used to query the legitimacy of America's political culture and its claims to rationality. The relationship between modes of production and the structures of the nation state was similarly complicated by showing the internal differentiation of the United States and the transnational character of the slave trade. Du Bois's attention to the specific dynamics of racial subordination and racial identity produced a theory of political agency in which the priority of class relations was refused and the autonomy of cultural and ideological factors from crudely conceived economic determination was demonstrated. These points were clarified in his essay on the travels of the Fisk Jubilee Singers.

The stylistic innovation represented by *The Souls of Black Folk* is expressed in the way the power of music was invoked and musical quotations used to frame and to qualify what the written text could convey. Each chapter was prefaced by two epigraphs. The first was usually[21] drawn from the canon of European literature while the other was a fragment extracted from one of the "sorrow songs" to which the final chapter was entirely devoted.

Whatever terms they use to describe them, most critics agree that the book falls into three fairly discrete sections.[22] Chapters one to three are mostly historical, chapters four to nine are basically sociological in focus, and chapters ten to fourteen leave these fixed perspectives behind to explore the terrains of black art, religion, and cultural expression with a variety of voices including biography, autobiography, and fiction. The book is directed at and expressive of the experience of blacks in America—a people swathed within the folds of the veil of colour. Yet it is also somehow addressed to the worlds beyond that constituency. It speaks directly to white Americans, challenging their sense of colour-coded civilization and national culture, and it is also addressed to a wider transnational community

of readers both in the present and in the future. It aspired to give the particular post-slavery experiences of western blacks a global significance. I
want to focus on this tension in the work through the different ways it
projects or spatialises the contrasting conceptions of race, nation, culture,
and community that Du Bois conjures up. My starting point is the concept
of double consciousness with which *The Souls of Black Folk* commenced
and which supplied the deep structure of its organisational rationale.
Double consciousness was initially used to convey the special difficulties
arising from black internalisation of an American identity: "One ever feels
his twoness,—an American, a Negro; two souls, two thoughts, two unreconciled strivings; two warring ideals in one dark body whose dogged
strength alone keeps it from being torn asunder." However, I want to suggest that Du Bois produced this concept at the junction point of his philosophical and psychological interests not just to express the distinctive
standpoint of black Americans but also to illuminate the experience of
post-slave populations in general. Beyond this, he uses it as a means to
animate a dream of global co-operation among peoples of colour which
came to full fruition only in his later work. This perspective eventually
found its fullest expression in the novel *Dark Princess,* but it erupted periodically into Du Bois's more ethnocentric concerns, appearing oddly, for
example, in the middle of this pan-African reverie from *Dusk of Dawn:*

> As I face Africa, I ask myself: what is it between us that constitutes a
> tie that I can feel better than I can explain? Africa is of course, my
> fatherland. Yet neither my father nor my father's father ever saw Africa
> or knew its meaning or cared overmuch for it. My mother's folk were
> closer and yet their direct connection, in culture and race, became
> tenuous; still my tie to Africa is strong . . . one thing is sure and that
> is the fact that since the fifteenth century these ancestors of mine have
> had a common history, have suffered a common disaster, and have one
> long memory . . . the badge of colour [is] relatively unimportant save
> as a badge; the real essence of this kinship is its social heritage of slav-
> ery; the discrimination and insult; and this heritage binds together not
> simply the children of Africa, but extends through yellow Asia and
> into the South Seas. It is this unity that draws me to Africa.[23]

The duality which Du Bois placed at its intellectual and poetic core was
particularly significant in widening the impact of *The Souls.* Its influence
spread out across the black Atlantic world to directly inspire figures as diverse as Jean Price Mars, Samuel Coleridge Taylor, and Léopold Sédar
Senghor and to indirectly influence many more. Its power is still felt in the

special resonance which the term "soul" continues to enjoy in modern black political discourse and cultural axiology.

Double consciousness emerges from the unhappy symbiosis between three modes of thinking, being, and seeing. The first is racially particularistic, the second nationalistic in that it derives from the nation state in which the ex-slaves but not-yet-citizens find themselves, rather than from their aspiration towards a nation state of their own. The third is diasporic or hemispheric, sometimes global and occasionally universalist. This trio was woven into some unlikely but exquisite patterns in Du Bois's thinking. Things become still more complicated because he self-consciously incorporated his own journeying both inside and outside the veiled world of black America into the narrative structure of the text and the political and cultural critique of the West which it constructed through an extended survey of the post–Civil War history of the American South.

Guided by the apparatus of his pan-Africanism and in explicit opposition to a mode of analysis premised on the fixity of the modern nation state as a receptacle for black cultures, Du Bois developed an approach to comprehending the political and cultural history of blacks in the west which was capable of focusing upon their conspicuous differences from one another and from blacks in Africa—past and present. He refined this perspective in a number of works,[24] but an early expression of it appeared in *The Souls of Black Folk*, where it coexisted uneasily with a rather idealised, volkish conception of African-American exceptionalism that has some contemporary equivalents in Africalogical thought.

The book remains notorious for its elegant, understated insistence that the problem of this century was the problem of "the color-line." This too raises the relationship between nationality and transnational political solidarity. When this claim is made in the introduction and repeated at the beginning and again at the end of the second chapter, the local racism, which deforms the experience of African-Americans and which was articulating the brutal counter-revolution against racial justice in the South that framed and animated Du Bois's project, is described as but one phase in a larger *global* conflict stretching from the United States to Asia, Africa, and the islands of the sea. It was a "phase" in this broader conflict between darker and lighter races of men in these places that "caused the civil war." The challenge for black Americans at the beginning of the new century was therefore to grasp the continuities that linked their present predicament with the special horrors of their past and to connect their contemporary sufferings with the racial subordination inflicted on other peoples of colour by a common foe:

I have seen a land right merry with the sun, where children sing, and rolling hills lie like passioned women wanton with harvest. And there in the King's Highways sat and sits a figure veiled and bowed, by which the traveller's footsteps hasten as they go. On the tainted air broods fear. Three centuries' thought has been the raising and unveiling of that bowed human heart, and now behold a century new for the duty and the deed. The problem of the Twentieth Century is the problem of the color-line.[25]

Sounding a cautionary note against the lure of racial exceptionalism, Du Bois warned his African-American sisters and brothers that the slavery experienced by blacks in the United States, though terrible, was "not the worst slavery in the world, not a slavery that made all of life unbearable, rather a slavery that had here and there something of kindliness, fidelity, happiness . . ."[26] *The Souls of Black Folk* is especially valuable precisely because it crystalises these recurrent tensions between Du Bois's understandable desire to comprehend African-American particularity and a vaguer, more general order of subaltern experience which he described allusively as the "strange meaning of being black at the dawning of the twentieth century." With this in mind, it is significant that the punning title of his book was not ethnically restricted or closed off by a reference to the distinctive American conditions in which it originated. There is a sense in which the blackness invoked there is in a complex, dissonant relationship to the word "folk" which follows it, narrowing the meaning of the title and tying it tightly to a highly specific but also highly mystical and organic conception of community that is not straightforwardly endorsed by the text.

I have already argued that Du Bois's clever statements of his ambivalence towards modernity first appear in his scathing attack on Booker T. Washington. They are elaborated in his next essay: a meditation on the meanings which the concept of Progress can have when approached from the standpoint of the slave. There Du Bois narrates his happy experiences as a schoolteacher in rural Tennessee during the vacations from Fisk University. He encounters rural black folk and wants to celebrate and affirm their "dull and humdrum" rhythm of life, so very different from his own upbringing in New England. Their indifference to the education he offered them emerged as a key problem which he could resolve only on a temporary basis: "I knew that the doubts of the old folks about book learning had conquered again, and so, toiling up the hill, and getting as far into the cabin as possible, I put Cicero 'pro Archia Poeta' into the simplest English with local applications, and usually convinced them—for a week or so."[27]

Their religious appetites also divided them from Du Bois, fragmenting the fragile unity of preacher and teacher who, he tells us, together "embodied once the ideals of this people."[28] He appreciates the role of the church on a general level in providing "the social centre of Negro life in the United States, and the most characteristic expression of African character."[29] But when he found himself in the midst of the Folk his responses became more contradictory. This was precisely because of the anti-modern conservatism that these important social institutions reproduced even while consolidating the "half-awakened common consciousness" produced in this "tiny community" by the effects of hardship and racism, the aftermath of slavery, and the common experiences of "joy and grief at burial birth or wedding." The issue of terror reappears once again in his more detailed chapter on the social and political attributes of black southern Christianity, as an important factor that shaped its healing rituals and provided Du Bois with the key to interpreting them. It was in religious practices that the buried social memory of that original terror had been preserved. It was frequently revisited by ritual means: "As I approached the village and the little plain church . . . A sort of suppressed terror hung in the air and seemed to seize us,—a pythian madness, a demoniac possession, that lent a terrible reality to song and word."[30]

Du Bois situated his nuanced accounts of the continuing slave-like toil of these rural communities in the wider framework supplied by the history of Reconstruction and global capitalist development. The opportunity Reconstruction offered has passed these communities by. Instead new tragedies have been created as the nation blunders into the future "just as though God really were dead." Returning some years later to the rural settlement where he had taught as a young man, Du Bois was forced to confront the way its inhabitants had not been carried forward by the teleological momentum of historical development. Progress, he tells us, speaking of the new building that had replaced the old log schoolhouse he remembered so fondly, "is necessarily ugly." The ironic tone in which he accepts that Progress has touched and transformed the miserable lives of the building's users and their families is less significant than his view that the lives of these black people had been lived according to a special pattern that made the estimation of Progress impossible: "How shall man measure Progress there where the dark faced Josie lies? How many heartfuls of sorrow shall balance a bushel of wheat? How hard a thing is life to the lowly and yet how human and real! And all this life and love and strife and failure,—is it the twilight of nightfall or the flush of some faint-dawning day? Thus sadly musing, I rode to Nashville in the Jim Crow car."[31]

Some indication of the importance of this theme is provided by the way

Du Bois returned to it again on the concluding pages of the book where, in the context of his famous discussion of the "sorrow songs" and their significance for world culture as the precious, redeeming gift of centuries of black suffering, he moved towards a more relativist understanding of culture and ethnicity that could challenge the logic of racial eugenics that he has identified as "the silent growing assumption of the age."

> So wofully [sic] unorganized is sociological knowledge that the meaning of progress, the meaning of "swift" and "slow" in human doing, and the limits of human perfectability, are veiled unanswered sphinxes on the shores of science. Why should Æschylus have sung two thousand years before Shakespeare was born? Why has civilization flourished in Europe, and flickered, flamed, and died in Africa? So long as the world stands meekly dumb before such questions, shall this nation proclaim its ignorance and unhallowed prejudices by denying freedom of opportunity to those who brought the Sorrow Songs to the Seats of the Mighty?[32]

It should be obvious that *The Souls* occupies a special place in the literature of modern black political thought both inside and outside the United States. From within black America, James Weldon Johnson helped to locate it in American political culture by describing the book as "a work which . . . has had a greater effect upon and within the Negro race in America than any other single book published in this country since Uncle Tom's Cabin."[33] Johnson's own writings are themselves testimony to the book's importance. His extraordinary 1912 novel, *The Autobiography of An Ex-Coloured Man,* took its cues from Du Bois's aporetic responses to American modernity and sought to translate that distinctive stance into the literary initiative of a black modernism which, in "striving to break the narrow limits of traditions,"[34] would enable "the future Negro novelist and poet to give the country something new and unknown." Johnson's debts to Du Bois are too many to explore in detail here. He acknowledged the "concentrated force" of Du Bois's ideas in his own autobiography, *Along This Way.* In his novel, Johnson both answered Du Bois's questions and extended his arguments in ways that invite interpretation as generational manifestations of a closed and internally coherent dialogical tradition of racial letters, a reading of their relationship proposed by Robert Stepto.[35] There are many correspondences between the two books. Johnson shared Du Bois's concern with intraracial differences often based on class and his anthropological interest in the religious rituals of rural black populations. He repeatedly pointed out that the roots of European civilisation lay in African sources and made similar points to Du Bois about the social construction and plasticity of black identities: "It is remarkable, after all, what an adaptable creature the Negro is. I have seen the black West Indian gentleman in London, and he is in speech and manners a perfect Englishman. I have seen the natives of Haiti and Martinique in Paris, and they are more Frenchy than a Frenchman. I have no doubt that the Negro would make a good chinaman, with the exception of the pigtail."[36]

Johnson also placed the idea of double consciousness at the centre of his narrative. He rechristened it "dual personality" and made its inner contradiction sharper still by approaching it via the experiences of a protagonist who appreciated Du Bois's book as "a beginning" but who could cross the colour line and pass for a white man whenever he wished. His duality is signfied by the literal doubling involved in being somehow both black and white. This man was also a gifted musician whose capacity as a performer exceeded "mere brilliancy of technique" and was shaped by the awesome knowledge that the sublime songs by means of which he made his living entertaining whites "contain more than mere melody; there is sounded in them that elusive undertone, the note in music that is not heard by the ears."[37] It was entirely in keeping with Du Bois's thematic orientation that a lynching provided Johnson's nameless, picaresque hero with a means to reflect upon his own status, on the centrality of terror in stimulating black creativity and cultural production, and on the failures of modernity in the South. Sensitised to the power of the phatic and the ineffable conjoined in the enduring potency of what I call the slave sublime, Johnson's unhappy protagonist finds the sound track to this ritual barbarity especially disturbing:

> Before noon they brought him in. Two horsemen rode abreast; between them, half dragged, the poor wretch made his way through the dust. His hands were tied behind him, and ropes around his body fastened to the saddle horns of his double guard. The men who at midnight had been stern and silent were now emitting that terror-instilling sound known as the "rebel yell." A space was quickly cleared in the crowd, and a rope placed around his neck, when from somewhere came the suggestion, "Burn him!" . . . *He gave out cries and groans that I shall always hear.* The cries and groans were choked off by the fire and smoke . . . Some of the crowd yelled and cheered.[38] (emphasis added)

He watches this drama passively, unable to avert his eyes. The bitter words spoken after he has witnessed this scene echo Frederick Douglass's diagnosis of the ills of the plantation system uttered half a century earlier and quoted in Chapter 2 above: "The Southern whites are not yet living quite in the present age; many of their general ideas hark back to a former century, some of them to the Dark Ages. In the light of other days they are sometimes magnificent. Today they are often cruel and ludicrous."[39]

Johnson's hero travelled to Europe as both Du Bois and Douglass had done before him. Like them, his consciousness of "race," self, and sociality were profoundly changed by the experience of being outside America. These changes are symbolised in several interesting ways that can be referred to the discussion of authenticity in the previous chapter. Johnson queried the most obvious strategies for specifying the essence of racialised being by making Germany the place where his protagonist's impulses to blend and fuse European "classical" music with the music of the black vernacular were fully articulated. It is only by being outside, far removed from the rootedness which will later appear as the sine qua non of black cultural production, that the ex-coloured man can imagine completing the special creative project that he had only glimpsed while in the United States. The stimulus is supplied by a creative meeting with a white man encountered in European conditions as an equal:

> I went to the piano and played the most intricate rag-time piece I knew. Before there was time for anybody to express an opinion on what I had done, a big bespectacled, bushy-headed man rushed over, and, shoving me out of the chair, exclaimed "Get Up! Get up!" He seated himself at the piano, and, taking the theme of my rag-time, played it through first in straight chords; then developed it through every known musical form. I sat amazed. I had been turning classical music into rag-time, a comparatively easy task; and this man had taken rag-time and made it classic. The thought came across me like a flash—It can be done, why can't I do it? From that moment my mind was made up. I clearly saw the way of carrying out the ambition I had formed when a boy.[40]

The trope of race as family which has supplied the other principal means to signify racial authenticity is also acknowledged in a complex and ambiguous way in the book. Like William Wells Brown's heroine Clotelle, who met her long-lost father in Voltaire's home town, Ferney on the borders of Lake Léman, the soon to be ex-coloured man also encountered an estranged father and sister in Europe. He observed them by chance at the opera house in Paris where all three had fortuitously turned up to hear Faust on the same night. He felt unable to identify himself to them, and in the midst of this genuine family tragedy we are told that "Valentine's love seemed like a mockery." Siting the partial completion of this desirable but impossible familial network in Europe emphasises the perils of rootless cosmopolitanism as well as the absurdity of America's racial codes. The central character's lack of belonging to anyone or any place looks like a curse rather than an opportunity at this point in the text.

These journeys outside the United States are complemented by patterns of travel inside America. If the memory of slavery and the middle passage represents one form of geographical and cultural dislocation and these touristic journeys to Europe stand for a second, freely chosen variety, the figure of the Pullman porter and the chronotope of the train which constitute another link between Du Bois and Johnson exemplify a third and more complex kind of travel experience. Much has been written recently about travel and the politics of location.[41] These themes are important in the study of identities and political cultures because the limits of approaches premised on fixity were reached sometime ago. They are especially important in the history of the black Atlantic, where movement, relocation, displacement, and restlessness are the norms rather than the exceptions and where, as we have already seen, there are long histories of the association of self-exploration with the exploration of new territories and the cultural differences that exist both between and within the groups that get called races. The work of Du Bois and Johnson points towards more fruitful ways of understanding the tension between roots and routes. Their work can be used to identify the folly of assigning uncoerced or recreational travel experiences only to whites while viewing black people's experiences of displacement and relocation exclusively through the very different types of travelling undergone by refugees, migrants, and slaves. The Pullman porter who benefits from the enhanced mobility provided by modern technologies but does so in a subordinate role, managing the travel experiences of others and servicing their needs at the expense of those of his own family, is recognised by both authors as an important symbol of the new opportunities and the new constraints that fell upon blacks in the late nineteenth century.[42] The porters worked in ways that both continued patterns of exploitation established during slavery and anticipated the novel forms of debasement and humiliation associated with contemporary service work. They worked in and around the bodies of whites, and this called for special codes and disciplines. In exchange for their wages they were required to sell something more than their labour power to clients whose expectations included the simulation of caring, intimate acts that appear at the very limits of economic rationality.[43]

We have already seen that the definitive characteristics of this early black modernism are wedded inescapably to the history of the new world in general and of America in particular. It is deeply ironic then that the obsession with black exceptionalism which endows *The Souls* with much of its intellectual drive is itself the obvious product of its author's journeying outside the United States. It gives voice to an understanding of the relationship between race, nationality, and culture which, even if Du Bois acquired it in the United States (and this is debatable), was considerably refined in Germany through an engagement with Hegel and the neo-Hegelian[44] thought that was popular in Berlin while he was studying there. This was not always a comfortable setting for Du Bois. He described the mixture of feelings he encountered listening to the Prussian chauvinism of Heinrich von Trietschke, a living link with the figure of Bismarck and an important architect of late-nineteenth-century German nationalism:

> Africa was left without culture and without history. Even when the matter of mixed races was touched upon their evident and conscious inferiority was mentioned. I can never forget that morning in the class of the great Heinrich Von Trietschke in Berlin . . . his words rushed out in a flood: "Mulattoes," he thundered, "are inferior." I almost felt his eyes boring into me, although probably he had not noticed me. "Sie fuhlen sich niedriger!" "Their actions show it," he asserted. What contradiction could there be to that authoritative dictum?[45]

In spite of his objections to this statement, the influence of these European ways of linking race, nation, culture, and history made a great impression on Du Bois. His own theories of history, racial particularity, culture, and civilisation draw selectively on Hegelian themes, alloying them with an Afro-Asiatic genealogy of civilisation's developmental course. On the most basic level, these influences are visible in Du Bois's attempt to present black Americans as a seventh world-historic people, extending Hegel's list in a rhetorical mode which also betrays his inspiration:

> After the Egyptian and Indian, the Greek and Roman, the Teuton and Mongolian, the Negro is a sort of seventh son, born with a veil, and gifted with second sight in this American world,—a world which yields him no true self consciousness, but only lets him see himself through the revelation of the other world. It is a peculiar sensation, this double consciousness, this sense of always looking at one's self through the eyes of others, of measuring one's soul by the tape of a world that looks on in amused contempt and pity.[46]

It matters little, at this point, whether this "second sight" is a true privilege rather than some sort of disability. Both options are signaled at different points in this passage. What is more significant for present purposes is that Du Bois's list is derived from a reading of Hegel's writings on the philosophy of history and is taken from a text which is also the occasion for Africa's expulsion from the official drama of historical movement.[47] This highly contradictory variety of Hegelianism is itself the site of a contest between Du Bois's biographers over the political drift and ideological implications of his early writings. Du Bois was clearly more comfortable with Hegel's view of the history of the world as "none other than the progress of the consciousness of Freedom" than with his Eurocentrism and identification of history's theatre as "the temperate zone," let alone his collapsing of historical progress into the practical achievements of the Prussian state machine. It is significant that Du Bois's autobiographies are candid about the extent to which his admiration for German nationalism and the achievements of the Prussian state in particular preceded his visit to Germany. It might be worth speculating whether these dreams of order appealed to him precisely because he was an American. Certainly the conception of freedom that guided him was deeply influenced by this body of work. Blacks are continually invited to discover the forms of freedom consequent upon yielding to the organic power of a resolute racial collectivity assured of the historicality *(Geschichtlichkeit)* of its political and philosophical aspirations.

This integral racial culture is something that Du Bois consistently figured in the feminine gender. In this he breaks sharply with the stance of earlier thinkers who had made the integrity of racial culture accessible through an idealised and heroic masculinity. Instead, successive images of the female form embody the harmony, mutuality, and freedom that can be acquired by dissolving individuality into the tides of racial identity. The first of these female figures is the "black, little and lithe body" of his great grandmother Violet. She it was who "crooned a heathen melody to the child between her knees." This bequest was passed on down the generations until it reached Du Bois and gave him his "one direct cultural connection" with Africa. The second female figure is the impossibly beautiful Lena Calhoun, grandmother of Lena Horne, who was a classmate of Du Bois's at Fisk and his first love there. Her beauty, glimpsed on his first happy evening at Fisk, conveyed the promise and pleasure of his cultural rebirth as a "Negro" amidst the unfamiliar racial codes of the Jim Crow South.[48] The third black woman is Du Bois's dead mother, to whom he dedicated his library in a strange ritual ceremony on the occasion of his twenty-fifth birthday, which he celebrated in his Berlin lodgings. The fourth is the image of Africa herself, personified thus after Du Bois's first trip there in the early 1920s: "I believe that the African form in color and curve is the beautifullest thing on earth; the face is not so lovely, though often comely with perfect teeth and shining eyes—but the form of the slim limbs, the muscled torso, the deep full breasts!"[49] A fifth image of black femininity in Du Bois's cultural cosmology is the woman's body he used to personify black cultural creativity in his 1938 book *Black Reconstruction in America*. She appeared in the strange portrait of black music as a woman, "raped and defiled" by the incomprehending attention of whites who listen to it. The femininity of this culture complemented the masculinity of its educated male citizenry to form a familial whole:

> There was joy in the south. It rose like perfume—like a prayer. Men stood quivering. Slim, dark girls, wild and beautiful with wrinkled hair, wept silently; young women, black, tawny, white and golden, lifted shivering hands, and old broken mothers black and gray, raised great voices and shouted to God across the fields, and up to the rocks and the mountains. A great song arose, the loveliest things born this side of the seas. It was a new song. It did not come from Africa, though the dark throb and beat of that Ancient of days was in it and through it. It did not come from white America—never from so pale and thin a thing, however deep these vulgar and surrounding tones had driven. Not in the Indies nor the hot South, the cold East or the heavy West made that music. It was a new song and its deep and plaintive beauty, its great cadences and wild appeal wailed, throbbed and thundered on the world's ears with a message seldom voiced by man. It swelled and blossomed like incense, improvised and born anew out of an age long past, and weaving into its texture the old and new melodies in word and and in thought.
>
> They sneered at it—those white southerners who heard it and never understood. They raped and defiled it—those white northerners who listened without ears. Yet it lived and grew; always it grew and swelled and lived, and its beauty sits today at the right hand of God, as America's one gift to beauty; as slavery's one redemption, distilled from the dross of its dung.[50]

The idealised figuration of racial culture and community through the bodies of black women in Du Bois's non-fiction has to contend with the rather less celebratory images of African-American womanhood that appeared in his novels. The ambiguities which spring up around his presentation of racial culture, kinship, nationality, and community in gendered form are a big problem lying dormant in the critical writing about his work.

In spite of its insights, much of this criticism founders precisely on the problem of how Du Bois comprehends and fixes the cultural and geographical boundaries of the racial community. The double-consciousness effect has had extensive consequences in African-American analyses of Du Bois's work. Writing from an openly radical position, Cornel West locates Du Bois in the all-American landscape provided by a genealogy of pragmatism. For West, Du Bois's work becomes a response to the turn-of-the-century crisis in American pragmatism. His turn away from epistemology-centred scholastic philosophy is read as a manifestation of bluff, no-nonsense Americana in intellectual work which marks Du Bois as the authentic offspring of Emerson, Dewey, and William James. West sees Du Bois's time in Europe mainly as a period in which his anti-imperialism and anti-Americanism developed. He plays down the impact of Hegel on Du Bois but emphasises that *The Souls* was produced at a time when its author was still stressing the "backwardness" of American blacks. According to West, Du Bois felt that their backwardness could be remedied by an elitist and paternalist political agenda that viewed racism as an expression of stupidity and implied that progress, rational social policy, and the Victorian moral virtues advocated by the talented tenth could uplift the black masses. There is much merit in this view. To be sure, Du Bois does "provide American pragmatism with what it lacks."[51] I do not wish to minimise these elements in Du Bois nor to overlook the proximity of his thought to Emerson and other representative American pragmatists. However, I want to suggest that this way of positioning Du Bois's work can lead to the novelty and power of his critique of modernity being overlooked. For example, the ways in which *The Souls* unravels the assumptions of progress and develops a critique of the place it has in the strategy for racial amelioration pass completely unseen. Worse than that, Du Bois's studiously constructed projection of doubleness as insight gets lost. It collapses into a needless affirmation of American intellectual ethnocentrism.[52]

Writing from a more culturally and politically conservative position that pays allegiance to literary criticism in the same way that West signals his disciplinary loyalty to philosophy, Robert Stepto[53] uses the idea of antiphony as a means to delimit the cultural relationships that facilitate the emergence of the racial community. Stepto offers a subtle and perceptive commentary on *The Souls* and, in a brilliant move, places it in what he sees as the symbolic geographical projection of African-American rather than American particularity. He relates this understanding of the racial essence to the work itself and to a frustratingly organic and seamless conception of the culturally specific and spatially mediated linkages it establishes between body, place, kinship, and community.[54] For Stepto, *The Souls* is a poetics of race and place. It becomes a "cultural immersion ritual" in which Du Bois, the New England black, finds and reconstructs himself anew in the southern black belt. Du Bois's book is seen as a performance which needs to be appreciated in the intertextual and intracultural context supplied by Douglass, Weldon Johnson, Washington, and others. Stepto is also right in emphasising the pronounced spatial turn in the book. His understanding of the call-and-response ritual in which *The Souls* is located is bolstered theoretically by Victor Turner's notions of ritual topography.[55] With this support, he identifies a vernacular landscape which his authors traverse with varying degrees of difficulty. Stepto appreciates Du Bois's concern with the value of movement, relocation, and displacement, a theme that is underscored by the emergence of the train, the Jim Crow car, and the Pullman porter as key tropes. However, I think he is mistaken in reading the book primarily as a process of immersion into a closed ethnic culture. His racially conservative culturalism leads him to misinterpret the meaning of Du Bois's interest in the pleasures and dangers of displacement. He superimposes the borders of Du Bois's landscape onto the internal frontiers of America and thereby closes down the side of Du Bois which is not concerned with inspecting the viscera of Afro-American particularity. From this perspective it is also harder to account for the transcendent quality of the book's final third—the last five chapters, which Stepto identifies as a phase of ascent—the final component in its North/South/North triptych, which in my view offers a means to read it as a narrative of emergence from rather than immersion in racial particularity.

Looking at this final section of the book in less ethnocentric ways requires paying attention to a number of themes touched on above which reach a crescendo in these last pages. The closing chapters confirm the transformation and fragmentation of the integral racial self—accompanied by and expressed in the accounts of Du Bois's journey to the South and his travels there. More important, this part of the book can be read as a bid to escape not just from the South or even from America but from the closed codes of *any* constricting or absolutist understanding of ethnicity. This is most powerfully conveyed in Du Bois's account of his infant son's death—a chapter routinely overlooked by critics. In this moving essay he deploys the racially particular as a deliberate tactic for seizing hold of the universal tragedy involved in parental grief. This is done partly in order to demonstrate the extent of black humanity everywhere denied by the absurdities of racial domination. But Du Bois turns once again to the experiential rift that divided the black elite from ordinary black folk. His lament comes embellished by an exploration of the stress experienced by black intellectuals who strive to live up to the demands placed upon them by a racial counterculture which requires that they cultivate the capacity to live with death and see it as a release—a welcome chance to acquire the substantive freedoms unsullied by white hostility and worldly indifference to black suffering: "Not dead, not dead, but escaped; not bond but free."[56]

Du Bois's open discussion of his mixed feelings about fatherhood and his absence of spontaneous affection towards the child he learns to love via his feelings for its mother could be used to institute a very different discourse on black masculinity than is usually evident in nationalist political culture. The organicity and homology of race, nation, patriarchal family, and integral male identity are suddenly interrupted by a tragedy that could have provided them with their most glorious hour. This suffering has no redemptive moment. Du Bois's presentation of Alexander Crummell as a surrogate father in the chapter which follows points to the conspicuous power of a non-biological kinship and shares something of the same bitter spirit. Crummell was yet another Atlantic nomad, but what Du Bois calls his "weird pilgrimage" ended in a return to and reconciliation with America after years spent in England and Africa.[57] This destination also throws the boundaries of the racial family/nation into question. "Of the Coming of John," the bleak short story which precedes Du Bois's final chapter on the sorrow songs, is notable for its troubling insistence that in the extreme conditions under which black Americans live, the education necessary to their advancement brings unhappiness to those who experience its benefits. This is an unhappiness, however, that they will not forgo, because it brings both personal and social insight. This solitary piece of fiction also attends to differences of class and culture that could be found inside the racial group. It offers a warning to members of the intellectual elite that they must be cautious and respectful of the different sensibilities and priorities of those people in their own communities whom they hope, in turn, to elevate.

These communities have a special and sometimes unreasonable investment in the privileged status of the elite few, but this token elevation may be more significant as a symbol for the possibility of change than as a concrete means to bring reforms about. The conservatism of the rural black folk becomes entirely understandable as we see John's inability to speak their language and lack of ease in the world he left seven years earlier to go and study in the North. He returns to take charge of the local school, but this return to his roots generates nothing but misery and chaos for everyone involved. John meets his death at the hands of a lynch mob after intervening to protect his younger sister's virtue against the lascivious actions of another John, a white boyhood playmate who is also the son of the judge who rules the segregated community with a rod of iron. The story unconvincingly transposes some of Du Bois's own experiences in Berlin onto his protagonist's discovery of Wagner's music in a New York concert hall where he had also encountered his white namesake. Black John turns "his closed eyes toward the sea" before accepting the attentions of the mob that has come to take his life. He softly hums the song of the bride from *Lohengrin* in German in a scene that should constitute a powerful obstacle to the more ethnocentric appropriations of Du Bois's legacy. Taken together these chapters constitute a catalogue of ambivalence and frustration with the veil of racial consciousness. They comprise an early statement of the transgressive rejection of both American and African-American nationalisms that gets completed in Du Bois's second novel, *Dark Princess.* The value of this reading of *The Souls* is underscored in the way the book ends—on a deliberately restless note with a muted appropriation of the sorrow song: "Cheer the Weary Traveller." "And the traveller girds himself, and sets his face towards the Morning, and goes his way."[58] The direction of this journey, as these words make clear, is neither north nor south but eastward.

I want to conclude this chapter by exploring the shape these arguments over identity and particularity take in *Dark Princess,* the 1928 "romance" that Du Bois described as his favourite book. *Dark Princess* was the subject of a long-forgotten tirade from Wyndham Lewis, who used it in *Paleface,* alongside consideration of work by other African-American writers, to open his examination of the ethical issues arising from racial interaction, whiteness, and the philosophy of the melting pot.[59] However, this was not sufficient to secure its place in the canon of black modernism. It sold poorly on publication and is also often passed over silently or condemned by African-American critics. Francis Broderick sets out the coordinates of a generally dismissive orthodoxy: "Du Bois' handling of the material ranged from photographic realism so precise that a reviewer for the Chicago Defender obligingly identified one character, to personal fantasy so obtuse as to be meaningful only to the author."[60] Arnold Rampersad is hardly more sympathetic: "This queer combination of outright propaganda and Arabian tale, of social realism and quaint romance, is a challenge to the casual reader."[61]

The book is divided into four parts: The Exile, The Pullman Porter, The Chicago Politician, and The Maharajah of Bwodpur, expressing different phases in the life of Mathew Towns, its medical student hero. The narrative opens with a transatlantic crossing. Mathew is fleeing to Europe, having been unable, like Martin Delany, Du Bois's predecessor at Harvard, to complete his training in medicine at a white institution. It is not long before he becomes the proto-typical black flaneur sipping his tea on the Unter den Linden. Roused into action by the need to protect a beautiful "coloured" woman from the uncivil attentions of an uncouth white American, Mathew meets and falls in love with Princess Kautilya of

Bwodpur. She invites him to a dinner with a committee of representatives drawn from the "Darker Peoples" of the world. They are planning an anti-imperialist realignment in global power and have been discussing whether black Americans are really capable of joining them in this enterprise. The only African representative at the table is an Egyptian who is sceptical of their right to join. He dismisses black Americans as having mixed blood, only to be rebuked by the Princess, who explains to him the derivation of Indian civilisation from African sources "as our black and curly haired Lord Buddha testifies in a hundred places."[62] After an urbane discussion of Kandinsky, Picasso, Matisse, Schonberg, Proust, Croce and, much to the surprise of Wyndham Lewis, vorticism, Mathew silences the doubters with a clock-stopping rendition of "Go Down Moses"; we learn later that this is the moment when the Princess begins to reciprocate his love.

> *Go Down Moses!*
> *Way down into Egypts land,*
> *Tell Old Pharoah*
> *To let my people go!*

He stopped as quickly as he had begun, ashamed, and beads of sweat gathered on his forehead. Still there was silence—silence almost breathless. The voice of a Chinese woman broke it. "It was an American slave song! I know it. How—how wonderful." A chorus of approval poured out, led by the Egyptian.[63]

Mathew's modern, democratic ways do not endear him to the more aristocratic members of this international, anti-imperialist coalition. Their hatred of the West is often closely associated with the defence of traditions menaced by modernity, and they do not take kindly either to the Princess's proto-feminism or to her Bolshevik inclinations. Though they try to prevent it, she gives Mathew a mission on behalf of the committee. He must return to America and establish links with a black political underground there that is moving towards a carefully planned uprising. He must also send regular bulletins of his impressions and recommendations regarding the fitness of black Americans to join their more esteemed brothers and sisters in racial subordination. He returns to the United States as a stowaway, working his passage in a multi-ethnic but racially stratified crew. In New York, he becomes a Pullman porter because it affords "the best opportunity to see and know the Negroes of this land" and then makes contact with Manuel Perigua, the Garveyesque leader of a black organisation committed to answer white supremacy with a racialised counter-terror of its own:

"Know how to stop lynching?" he whispered.

"why—no,—except—"

"We know. Dynamite. Dynamite for every lynching mob."[64]

Mathew is unsympathetic to these strategies but, after he is caught up in a Richard Wright–style incident with an unclothed white woman who accuses him of sexual harassment in her sleeping compartment, a fellow porter is lynched in his stead. He descends into bitterness and agrees to cooperate in the destruction of a trainload of Ku Klux Klansmen on their way to a convention, only to discover that his beloved Princess is a passenger on the same train. The slaughter is averted, but Mathew, whose role in the plot remains mysterious and ill-defined, receives a ten-year sentence for conspiracy. He is pardoned after three years when his case becomes of interest to the Chicago political machine managed by Sara Andrews, the devious, elegant, near-white beauty for whom "this world-tangle of races is a lustful scramble for place and power and show." He marries her and she orchestrates a glittering political career for him. He gradually grows tired of the corruption of this world in a way that gives important clues towards Du Bois's own struggles to differentiate the good from the beautiful:

> revolt stirred within him against this political game he was playing. It was not moral revolt. It was esthetic disquiet. No, the revolt slowly gathering in Mathew's soul against the political game was not moral; it was not that he discerned anything practical for him in uplift or reform, or felt any new revulsion against political methods in themselves as long as power was power and facts, facts. His revolt was against things unsuitable, ill adjusted in bad taste; the illogical lack of fundamental harmony; the unnecessary dirt and waste—the ugliness of it all—that revolted him.[65]

Mathew searches in vain for some cultural and emotional authenticity in this insubstantial, depthless world. He takes refuge in the art and music that his uncultivated, power-hungry, and money-grabbing wife cannot fathom. His retreat from the pursuit of money and power is confirmed when the Princess makes a redemptive reappearance in his life. She has been broadening her queenly education by working as a sexually harassed maid, waitress, and tobacco roller in Virginia. Now she is a senior official in the box makers' union. She has been organising the sweated labour on the Lower East Side. The couple set up an idyllic home together in an attic nest. Mathew discovers that the dignity of hard physical toil which has done so much to improve Kautilya can work wonders for him too, particularly when combined with regular visits to the art gallery. Kautilya has been socialising with Mathew's mother. It is through their relationship that the first hints of an American reconciliation of Africa and Asia are projected: "Oh, Mathew, you have a wonderful mother. Have you seen her hands? Have you seen the gnarled and knotty glory of her hands? . . . Your mother is Kali, the Black One; wife of Siva, Mother of the World!"[66] Their love blossoms. They take pleasure in each other's bodies. He goes to work. She cooks curry. Their transgressive love does not find favour with the local children, who express their displeasure at race mixing in the neighbourhood with stones and jeers. The lovebirds listen to Beethoven, Dvorak. "They had their benediction of music—the overture to Wilhelm Tell, which seemed to picture their lives. Together they hummed the sweet lilt of the music after the storm." Kautilya tells Mathew of her privileged life in the colonial world, of the English nanny she loved and her proposal of marriage from Captain the Honourable Malcolm-Fortescue Dodd. She explains her royal obligations and duties and tells her lover the story of her little kingdom in a way that makes its battles continuous with the struggles of black Americans to which she has now made a contribution. They are happy until "the long straight path of renunciation" leads them in different directions. Kautilya insists that Mathew has obligations to Sara. He should offer her another chance to love him in his new guise of manual labourer. The Princess must return to her kingdom, where harsh decisions in the de-colonisation struggles await her along with the duty to find a suitable husband. They part and continue their intimacy by letter. Mathew's ascetic life continues until he is summoned to attend her court, reconstituted without ill effects on American soil in Prince James County, Virginia.

Mathew arrives by plane for what he fails to realise until the last minute is his own wedding. The representatives of the coloured races of the world are in attendance, though the proceedings are dominated by the presence of the messianic child that links their histories and can therefore lead them forward in the next generation of conflicts against the global forces of white supremacy. The couple are married at dawn. Mathew's mother looks on and a down-home black preacher reads from the seventh chapter of Revelation.

> He saw her afar; standing at the gate there at the end of the long path home, and by the old black tree—her tall and slender form like a swaying willow. She was dressed in the eastern style, royal in colouring, with no concession to Europe. As he neared, he sensed the flash of great jewels nestling on her neck and arms; a king's ransom lay between the naked beauty of her breasts; blood rubies weighed down her ears, and about the slim brown gold of her waist ran a girdle

such as emperors fight for. Slowly all the wealth of silk, gold, and jew-
els revealed itself as he came near and hesitated for words; then suddenly he sensed a little bundle on her outstretched arms. He dragged
his startled eyes down from her face and saw a child—a naked baby
that lay upon her hands like a palpitating bauble of gold, asleep.[67]

There are several serious points to be sifted from this extravagance. The
conclusion of *Dark Princess* is important to the politics of the black Atlantic in numerous ways. Read as a beginning rather than an ending, it offers
an image of hybridity and intermixture that is especially valuable because
it gives no ground to the suggestion that cultural fusion involves betrayal,
loss, corruption, or dilution. The startling portrait of procreation—cultural formation and transformation—is constructed so that the integrity
of both its tributaries remains uncompromised by their confluence. This is
not the fusion of two purified essences but rather a meeting of two heterogeneous multiplicities that in yielding themselves up to each other create
something durable and entirely appropriate to troubled anti-colonial
times. On one side, with the preacher's benediction, the intellectual and
the wizened old woman who bore him become ethnic associates representing a black America that can blend with Asia without betraying its African
origins. On the other, an equally hetero-cultural, composite India arises
from Du Bois's montage of ethnic and religious groups. It is the internal
differentiation of these multiplicities, their irreducible complexity, which
sanctions the new association made concrete in the appearance of the messianic boy-child. This is also interesting because it anticipates and affirms a
global political relationship that would flourish in Martin Luther King's
appropriation of Gandhi's concepts and methods in the elaboration of his
mass, non-violent populism in the years after Du Bois's death. This link
between anti-colonial politics and the development of African-American
political culture is an important one that stretches back into the early years
of the twentieth century when Du Bois and Gandhi (at that time a lawyer
in South Africa) took their places alongside Annie Besant, Georg Simmel,
Werner Sombart, and Ferdinand Thonnies at the 1911 Universal Races
Congress in London. This is a history we would do well to recover and
reassess today when the overriding appeal of "ethnic" sameness has become an obstacle to living with difference. Though we may baulk at Kautilya's naive enthusiasms for the Japanese aristocracy as a vehicle for the
democratic hopes of the world's non-white masses, this intercultural, transnational anti-imperialist alliance was not something that Du Bois plucked
out of the air. The book expresses the upsurge of anti-imperial struggles
during the 1920s. Mary White Ovington suggested in 1928 that it was at

the same London conference that Du Bois glimpsed the woman who would supply the prototype for the fictional Kautilya.[68] These transnational political linkages and the responses to them, from critics who resent the intrusion of global concerns into their ethnically cleansed canon-building operations, will be explored again in a different context in the next chapter.

5

"Without the Consolation of Tears": Richard Wright, France, and the Ambivalence of Community

I have no race except that which is forced upon me. I have no country except that to which I'm obliged to belong. I have no traditions. I'm free. I have only the future.
Richard Wright

Someone, someday, should do a study in depth of the role of the American Negro in the mind and life of Europe, and the extraordinary perils, different from those of America but not less grave, which the American Negro encounters in the Old World.
James Baldwin

. . . each of Wright's works contains what Baudelaire would have called "a double simultaneous postulation"; each word refers to two contexts; two forces are applied simultaneously to each phrase and determine the incomparable tension of his tale. Had he spoken to the whites alone, he might have turned out to be more prolix, more didactic and more abusive; to the negroes alone, still more elliptical, more of a confederate, and more elegiac. In the first case, his work might have come close to satire; in the second, to prophetic lamentations. Jeremiah spoke only to the Jews. But Wright, a writer for a split public, has been able both to maintain and go beyond this split. He has made it the pretext for a work of art.
Jean Paul Sartre

RICHARD WRIGHT was the first black writer to be put forward as a major figure in world literature. He received a Guggenheim Fellowship in 1939 and, following the publication of *Native Son* in 1940 and *Black Boy* five years later, he was certainly the most famous black author in the world. His work enjoyed a global reading public of an unprecedented size for a black author. It was translated into numerous languages[1] and took the experience of racial subordination in the southern United States to a mass black readership inside and outside America.[2] These achievements are all the more extraordinary because they took place during a period when the injustices and political administration by racial terror explored in his work were gravely embarrassing to the American government, both in its anti-Nazi posture and in its later dealings with the emergent politics of anti-colonial liberation.

Wright's success can also be shown to mark important changes in the cultural politics and the political economy of publishing black authors. On the one hand, his relationship with the Book-of-the-Month Club, which published *Native Son,* was an entirely new phenomenon for a black writer approaching the cultural mainstream of American society. On the other hand, his work occupied a central place in the radical political culture of the international communist movement. It was the latter force that was responsible for introducing it into Europe via underground, anti-fascist organisations which resisted the ultra-right in France and Italy.[3]

Wright's historical importance is also bound up with his role in developing, both directly and indirectly, the talents of a cadre of young writers who built their successes on his own.[4] He was in a sense a new kind of black author, one whose open political affiliations and demands and fearless projection of anger released new creative possibilities and changed the terms in which the racial politics of literary expression were articulated. For these and many other reasons, Wright's work provides a useful opportunity to extend our consideration of issues arising from the relationship of blacks to western modernity. Through him we can explore, in George Kent's memorable phrase, "blackness and the adventure of western culture."[5] Wright's writing itself, his international career as a public figure, his political trajectory, and the intense debates that they all generated raise a number of the themes that have already been examined in the work of others and in different historical circumstances: the problem of ethnic and racial identity and their limits, the significance of black dissidence within the West, the development of black politics, and the political and philosophical character of black culture.

Wright's intellectual legacy is especially interesting because it has been so routinely misunderstood. The depth of his philosophical interests has been either overlooked or misconceived by the almost exclusively literary enquiries that have dominated analysis of his writing. The relationship of "The Negro" to western civilisation was something that exercised him greatly, particularly during the last years of his life. And Wright is fascinating above all because, in his life and work, the tension between the claims of racial particularity on one side and the appeal of those modern universals that appear to transcend race on the other arises in the sharpest possible form. Wright's sense of this opposition and the conflicting forms of identity to which it gives rise adds another notch of complexity and bitterness to formulations of double consciousness.

Wright's understanding of the forms of black consciousness that grew unseen *within* the western world developed alongside a gradual change in his thinking whereby a sense of the urgency of anti-colonial political struggle displaced an earlier exclusive interest in the liberation of African-Americans from their particular economic exploitation and political oppression. This enthusiasm for an emergent, global, anti-imperialist and anti-racist[6] politics need not be seen as a simple substitute for Wright's commitment to the struggles of blacks in America. He strives to link it with the black American vernacular in a number of ways. This connection is established, for example, in the humorous discussion of the colour of interplanetary travellers that appears at the beginning of *The Outsider.* A debate over whether visitors to earth from Mars are black leads one of Wright's Chicagoan characters into a powerful commentary on modern racism that is inseparable from a decidedly anti-ethnocentric statement of the potential unity of peoples of colour on the earth:

> For four hundred years these white folks done made everybody on earth feel like they ain't human, like they're outsiders. They done kicked 'em around and called 'em names . . . What's a Chinese to a white man? Chink-Chink Chinaman with pigtails down his back and he ain't fit for nothing but to cook and wash clothes. What's a Hindu to a white man? A nigger who's in love with ghosts and kisses cows. What's a black man to a white man? An ape made by God to cut wood and draw water, and always with a yen to rape white girls. A Mexican? A greasy, stinking rascal who ought to be worked to death and then shot. A Jew? a Christ killer, a cheat, a rat. A Japanese? A monkey with a yellow skin . . . Now our colored brothers are visiting us from Mars and Jupiter and the white folks is sweating in a panic.[7]

The same basic point was conveyed again, this time in a tone more remote from Wright's residual communism, in a letter he sent to Pandit Nehru in 1950: "The changing physical structure of the world as well as the historical development of modern society demand that the peoples of the world become aware of their common identity and interests. The situation of oppressed people the world over is universally the same and their solidarity is essential, not only in opposing oppression but also in fighting for human progress."[8]

We shall discover below that Wright's understanding of human progress was rather different from that to which Du Bois had subscribed. His sceptical, Nietzschean inclinations contrast sharply with the older man's Marxian attachment to the pursuit of social perfectibility by transparent, scrupulously rationalist means. These utopian visions of a world beyond the grasp of distinctions based on colour recur and supply an index for evaluating what substantive progress might be. Wright would see this world of racial solidarity and anti-imperialist common identity powerfully prefigured in the conference of twenty-nine Asian and African nations convened at Bandung in 1955.

> Living for centuries under Western rule, [the delegates] had become filled with a deep sense of how greatly they differed from one another. But now face to face, their ideological defences dropped . . . They began to sense their combined strength; they began to taste blood . . . They could now feel that their white enemy was far, far away . . . Day after day dun coloured Trotskyites consorted with dark Moslems, yellow Indo-Chinese hobnobbed with brown Indonesians, black Africans mingled with swarthy Arabs, tan Burmese associated with dark brown Hindus, dusky nationalists palled around with yellow communists, and Socialists talked to Buddhists. But they all had the same background colonial experience of subjection, of colour consciousness, and they found that ideology was not needed to define their relations . . . Racial realities have a strange logic of their own.[9]

Never tempted by the lure of facile political analyses, even in the reconfigured nationalist mode that buffered the diplomatic critique of official communism that he made while still a party member, Wright saw the Negro as "America's metaphor,"[10] a historical and social construction which was intimately related to the institution of racial slavery and which corresponded to no fixed cultural or biological attributes common to blacks: "Truly, you must know that the word Negro in America means something not racial or biological, but something *purely social,* something made in the United States"[11] (emphasis added). This simple insight, expressed repeatedly in what we might today recognise as an anti-essentialist conception of racial identity, is something that has confounded and perplexed many of Wright's American critics. The distinction he draws between "the social" and "the racial" has proved to be an embarrassment for some commentators, especially those who have sought to position him at the head of the official pantheon of twentieth-century African-American letters. Wright's deliberately provocative anti-essentialism, which was refined later during his travels in Africa, would trigger a bitter debate over racial identity and its boundaries at the first conference of black artists and writers hosted by the journal *Présence Africaine* in Paris in 1956. However, these themes go back to his earliest non-fiction work:

> The word "Negro," the term by which, orally or in print, we black folk in the United States are usually designated, is not really a name

at all nor a description, but a psychological island whose objective form is the most unanimous fiat in all American history; a fiat buttressed by popular and national tradition . . . This island, within whose confines we live, is anchored in the feelings of millions of people, and is situated in the midst of the sea of white faces we meet each day; and by and large, as three hundred years of time has borne our nation into the twentieth century, its rocky boundaries have remained unyielding to the waves of our hope that dash against it.[12]

Wright left America in 1947 and was based in Europe for the final years of his life. Apart from this complete relocation, he was also a traveller. Three books of reflexive travel writing are another important, though regularly ignored, part of his intellectual bequest to contemporary cultural criticism. They have not, however, fared well either with the black American reading public, who looked in vain for a reflection of their experiences in works that must have seemed esoteric, or with those critics whose interest in Wright is defined primarily by his fiction and secondarily by his autobiographical works. His turn towards a style of writing that formalised his self-exploration and his estrangement from the world by deploying the traveller's guise has even been dismissed by his principal biographer as "merely good journalism" though "a good read."[13] Even George Kent, an insightful and often brilliant commentator on Wright, ridiculed these books by saying that "the personality behind the print ranges from that of a bright, but somewhat snippish Western tourist to that of a Western schoolmarm."[14] I will try to demonstrate that, on the contrary, Wright's life bears witness to the value of critical perceptions that could only have been gained through the restlessness, even homelessness, that he sometimes manages to make into an analytic opportunity.

Bearing in mind Ralph Ellison's endorsement of Heraclitus's axiom "Geography is fate"[15] as well as his revelation that Wright had told him in 1956 "Really, Ralph after I broke with the Communist Party I had nowhere else to go,"[16] I want to make some claims for the value of these travel books which offer much more than a series of failed attempts to make the condition of chronic rootlessness habitable. Without necessarily accepting any of Wright's conclusions, it seems possible to view this body of work as an extended exercise in intercultural hermeneutics which has important effects upon Wright's theories about "race," modernity, identity, and their interrelation. In the case of the most controversial volume, *Black Power*, he produced a deliberate, if ultimately unsuccessful, attempt to articulate his critical self-understanding with the difficult work of accessible political, sociological, and historical analysis.

Like Du Bois, Douglass, Wells Barnett, and the rest of his African-American antecedents, Wright began his travels within the borders of the United States. He spent time in Africa, Spain, Asia, and Central and South America before his premature death in Paris in 1960. Three of his major journeys, to revolutionary Ghana, to Franco's Spain, and to Indonesia, are extensively "theorised" in published accounts of his intellectual and political development. Writing through and about these journeys provided him with ample opportunities for reflection on various historical, strategic, and philosophical problems and became incorporated into his metacommentary on the value of western civilisation, the relation of tradition to modernity, and the class divisions forced upon colonial peoples by the bloody, terroristic processes of imperial rule.

Wright is important to the overall argument of this book because his life constitutes another fragmentary part of the history of the international social and political movement known hazily and inadequately by the label Pan-Africanism. This movement, like the anti-slavery organising on which it was built, challenges our understanding of modern politics precisely because it overflows from the confining structures of the nation state and comprehensively queries the priority routinely attached to those structures in historical and sociological explanations of social and cultural change. I have already mentioned that Wright was actively involved in *Présence Africaine*, the journal that attempted to bring together the thinking of Africans and Africanists with that of American, Caribbean, and European blacks at least so that their similarities and differences might be systematically explored.

Wright is an exemplary figure in weighing the black responses to modernity because he was a sophisticated and perceptive critic of Marxism and of the communist movement of his time. His critique was initially conducted from within the party and developed further outside the organisation. His selective appropriation of Marxist analytical tools combined with an uncompromising denunciation of the Leninist Party as an organisational structure animated by the will to power[17] contributed much to his sceptical evaluation of the possibility of social perfectibility and progress—at least in the overdeveloped countries. The ambiguities that stem from Wright's uncomfortable position—inside but not organically of the West—become unbearable in *Black Power*, his study of Ghana during Nkrumah's revolutionary government, and in the other works where he spelled out his understanding of the relationship between precapitalist, traditional societies and the dynamic, imperial structures of technological and philosophical modernity.

These parts of Wright's oeuvre sold poorly even while he was alive and are seldom read these days. The works which made his name as a writer were marketed primarily as literary expositions of American racism. They revealed its wholly unforeseen inscription within the depths of a black inner life hitherto undreamt of by white America. Though mainly fictional, these works— *Uncle Tom's Children, Native Son,* and *Black Boy,* as well as numerous short stories—derived some of their special cultural authority and a good deal of their literary status in the white world from what was perceived to be the unchallengeable racial authenticity of their Mississippian author.[18] In his psychological portrait of African-American leaders, Allison Davis points out that Wright, the son of sharecroppers, had not spent a full year in school by the age of thirteen.[19] Largely self-taught, he was a beneficiary of the informal educational structures that bolstered the Communist Party and later of the guidance provided by academics like Louis Wirth and Horace Cayton who became his friends while he was living in Chicago. Wright would later supply a memorable foreword to Cayton and St. Clair Drake's classic sociological study of the South Side ghetto, *Black Metropolis.*[20]

Wright's literary celebrity identified him immediately as a representative of his race and thus as an advocate for the immiserated Negroes whose society he had himself partially escaped. The literary richness of his early writings must have been all the more perplexing to literary critics when it was appreciated that their author was a refugee from the South's black peasantry who had enjoyed little formal education. Wright's success certainly posed new problems of cultural value and aesthetic judgement for modern American letters. His exploration of black consciousness demanded the elevation of race to the status of an interpretive device if his work was even to be credibly denounced. The hollow promises of an inclusive Americanism were exposed and, more important, the experiential, cognitive, moral, and cultural gulf that divided black and white America from each other was continually brought to mind. Two problems become impacted together here: the issue of Wright's racial typicality as a means for locating and interpreting his work—this was proposed by those who shared his racial community as well as those who did not—and, secondly, the changes in thinking about race that must have followed the acceptance of such an unexpected and unqualified person as the source of carefully crafted, modernist literature of this type. The shock to the American literary establishment must have been no less than that felt by Phyllis Wheatley's startled inquisitors that fateful day in Boston[21] when the power of imaginative writing was first enlisted in order to demonstrate and validate the humanity of black authors. Indeed, if Wheatley's volume represented the beginning of a process in which the attributes of universal humanity for which the production of imaginative literature was emblematic were seen to be within the grasp of Negroes, then *Native Son* was a sign that this phase was at an end. The *Book-of-the-Month Club News* announced that Wright's book was "quite as human as it is Negro" and explained that the author of *Native Son* had broadened "a tale of crude violence" into a "Human tragedy."

Wright first discussed the historical and social location of his own work within the context of a wider analysis of the role and direction of black writing in his celebrated 1937 essay "Blueprint for Negro Writing." He returned to this topic from a slightly different perspective some years later in a lecture on the position of Negro literature in the United States which eventually became a chapter in *White Man Listen!*, the book of essays constructed from his lectures that was published in 1957. In the earlier text, the author explored his relation to the idea of his own racial typicality and avoided the too simple polarisation between racial particularity and human universality through a thoughtful and non-reductive version of historical materialism. This identified the social and economic conditions in which particular styles of black writing grew and then employed a discussion of the differences between them to illuminate the order of political and aesthetic conflicts to be found *within* the "national" community of American Negroes. At this point, Wright only implies what would later become one of his favourite themes, namely that differences between the groups we know as races are associated with the repression of differences within those races. Literary and other cultural forms thus provide him with a chance to comprehend how a race may differ from itself. Notions of typicality and racial representativeness in aesthetic and political judgement are rejected because they arrest the play of these differences.

These abstract problems rapidly became concrete obstacles for Wright. The jacket of the first edition of *Native Son* announced that his novel was "the finest as yet written by an American Negro . . . a novel which only a Negro could have written; whose theme is the mind of the Negro we see every day." This faint praise points to how the problem of judging the quality of a book by a black author according to debased Jim Crow standards of literary quality became connected in Wright's thinking to the autonomy of white readers and critics and their scope for misreading a racially encoded text, consciously and unconsciously misrecognising its arguments and misinterpreting its consequences for their lives. He was especially horrified at the possibility that his mass white readership might discover deep pleasures in the image of blacks as victims of racism or, more simply, that they might be completely comfortable with the representations of black pain and suffering which inevitably flowed from attempts to deal seriously with the systematic operation of racism in American society. Wright discussed this problem in another essay which now regularly serves as an introduction to *Native Son*. In this piece, "How Bigger Was Born," he presented part of his motivation in writing *Native Son* as the desire to find an answer to the pernicious effects of the portrait of blacks as victims which had emerged unwittingly from his first published volume, *Uncle Tom's Children:* "When the reviews of that book began to appear, I realized that I had made an awfully naive mistake. I found that I had written a book which even bankers' daughters could read and weep over and feel good about. I swore to myself that if I ever wrote another book no one would weep over it; that it would be so hard and deep that they would have to face it without the consolation of tears. It was this that made me get to work in dead earnest."[22] Wright's image of this ideal misreader as a white woman raises the complicated issue of his misogyny, to which I will return below. The desire to present blacks in a role other than that of the victim is something that links Wright's output beneath his ideological shifts and the profound changes in his philosophical perspective. Even when exploring the depths of that spontaneous "nihilism" which he felt to be modern American racism's most significant contribution to black culture, his focus remained on the scope for agency which blacks enjoyed even in the most restricted conditions. As his elegiac collaboration with the photographer Edwin Rosskam, *Twelve Million Black Voices*, shows, this was sometimes at odds with his Marxism and with the equally deterministic social psychology that grew from his interest in psychiatry and psychoanalysis.

Like that of many of the black American writers who followed in his wake, Richard Wright's creative development was boosted and transformed by the decision to relocate himself far away from the United States. This relocation contributes much to the presentation of the links between the struggles against racial subordination inside America and wider, global dimensions of political antagonism: anti-fascism, anti-imperialism, and political and economic emancipation from colonial domination. This is an extremely complicated part of Wright's thinking and is not, as some critics have suggested, a situation in which, under the lingering influence of his Marxist training, the lives of black Americans become emblematic of the struggles of exploited and oppressed human beings in general. Wright's work in fiction, cultural criticism, autobiography, and his more eclectic styles of writing presents an elaborate body of philosophically informed reflection on the character of western civilisation and the place of racism within it. This inquiry is mediated by his political concerns and by his grasp of the history of black subordination in the new world. It generates and tests out a nuanced and sophisticated theory of modernity in which some, though not all, of the claims of African-American particularity are publicly renounced. It bears repetition that his distinctive perspective was decisively shaped by lengthy involvement in the official communist movement, by the interests in sociology and psychoanalysis which developed while he lived in Chicago and New York, and by the intellectual milieu of life in Paris where he made a new home for the last thirteen years of his life. This body of reflection upon modernity and its racial antinomies was filtered through the mesh provided by his combination of fervent anti-communism and passionate anti-capitalism. This blend perplexed the agents of the American state delegated to monitor Wright's political activities in Europe and still confounds some of his readers today.[23]

Racial Writing and Racial Criticism

Wright was born in Mississippi in 1908. He left school in 1925 and moved north, first to Memphis and then to Chicago, where he worked among other things as a postal clerk, a dishwasher, and a burial society premium collector. His career as a writer developed initially within the John Reed Clubs, cultural organisations of the Communist Party,[24] to which he remained loyal for a further decade. He eventually abandoned his communism after a series of bitter disagreements which saw him denounced as a Trotskyist and an intellectual.[25] His move to Europe after the 1939–1945 war was at the instigation of Gertrude Stein, who met Wright and his family on their arrival in Paris at the Gare du Nord.

The range and diversity of Wright's work are overshadowed by the fortifications which critics have placed between the work he produced in America and the supposedly inferior products of his European exile. He wrote thirteen books in all, of which four were published while he was resident in America; a fifth, *Lawd Today,* written there during the 1930s, was not published until several years after his death. He wrote three more novels, *Savage Holiday, The Outsider,* and *The Long Dream;* three travel books, *Pagan Spain, Black Power,* and *The Color Curtain; White Man Listen!,* a book of essays originally given as lectures; and *Eight Men,* a diverse collection of short pieces connected only by a tentative exploration of black masculinity. All of these were written or assembled for publication in Europe. Critical writing about Wright has been dominated by work on the first four books: *Uncle Tom's Children, Native Son, Twelve Million Black Voices,* and *Black Boy.* Of these, *Twelve Million Black Voices* has received the most cursory treatment.[26] *Lawd Today,* Wright's interesting first novel, has recently been republished and rehabilitated by Arnold Rampersad, who proclaims it superior to the later, flawed fiction that was produced in Eu-

rope, dealt erroneously with the experience of white characters, and succumbed to the alien influences of Freudianism and Existentialism:

> While it is certainly flawed, the tale is also quite possibly the second
> most important novel written by Wright, and it is clearly inferior only
> to the landmark *Native Son* (1940) among his novels. Far less grand
> in theme than *The Outsider* (1953), it is also less bleak and didactic
> than that existentialist story. Certainly it is more compelling than *Sav-
> age Holiday* (1954), Wright's somewhat thin and improbable ac-
> counting, according to the Freudian scheme, of a lonely white man
> (there are no blacks in the novel) driven to psychopathic murder. And
> although conspicuously less rich in characterisation and plot, at least
> in a conventional sense, than *The Long Dream* (1957), *Lawd Today*
> is nevertheless a more exuberant and spontaneous, as well as a more
> decisively motivated, piece of fiction than the last novel published in
> Wright's lifetime.[27]

Rampersad's remarks typify the critical consensus established around
Wright's books. The consensus stipulates that as far as his art was concerned, the move to Europe was disastrous. This argument takes several
forms and has to be considered carefully. It dismisses Wright's entitlement
to hold a view of modernity at all and has grave implications for how we
place his work in debates over black modernism(s). It is claimed that after
moving to France Wright's work was corrupted by his dabbling in philosophical modes of thought entirely alien to his African-American history
and vernacular style. Secondly, it is argued that the interest in psychiatry
and psychoanalysis which had, in any case, preceded his transatlantic move
got out of control in the European milieu. Third, it is suggested that, once
resident in Europe, Wright was simply too remote from the vital folk
sources which made his early work so uniquely powerful. Wright can be
condemned on these grounds while still being applauded for having produced the most vivid accounts of life in the Jim Crow South and for offering literary insights into the wretched existence of Chicago's new black
population. His eventual betrayal of the African-American vernacular is
then all the more profound and comprehensive because of his erstwhile
closeness to the Folk whose sentimental representation supplies the yard-
stick against which authentic racial culture is evaluated. This reverence for
the Folk bears the clear imprint of European romanticism absorbed into
black intellectual life by various routes.[28] In an influential study of the folk
roots of African-American poetry, Bernard Bell has shown how organicist
Herderian notions about the value of folk art and its relationship to other

kinds of cultural production came to dominate criticism of black art and literature and to be an important element within the tenets of nineteenth- and twentieth-century black nationalism.[29] Wright has been a victim of this approach to axiology and aesthetics. He was always deeply ambivalent both about the Folk and about all forms of popular culture, in which he observed the effects of racism as well as the dazzling capacity for creative improvisation in the face of adversity. This ambivalence is evident in his approach to music, to the church, and to the forms of verbal play which he identified as characteristically black. Ellison questions Wright's ethnic credentials by disclosing that he "knew very little about Jazz and didn't even know how to dance."[30] However, Wright would write blues lyrics[31] and make a recording with Paul Robeson, Count Basie, Jimmy Rushing, and others under the direction of John Hammond. He also wrote LP sleeve notes for the work of artists like Quincy Jones, Louis Jordan, and Big Bill Broonzy and even attempted a brief, psychoanalytic interpretation of the "devil songs" that he regarded as "a form of exuberantly melancholy folk song that has circled the globe" in a tantalising introduction he wrote to Paul Oliver's *The Meaning of the Blues*[32] in 1959.

Wright's affirmative claims for the blues and the vernacular culture from which they spring were spelled out more clearly in the discussion of the blues that arose midway through his essay "The Literature of The Negro in The United States." There, Wright linked the blues and the improvised oral poetry he called the Dirty Dozens. He presented them as "the apex of sensual despair" and pondered the "strange and emotional joy found in contemplating the blackest aspects of life." This pun around the word "blackest" introduced another typical piece of Wright's humour: "what the psychoanalysts call ambivalence is put forward by illiterate Negroes in terms that would have shocked Dr. Freud." Dismissing interpretations of the Dozens that focus on their risqué quality, Wright defended them as a coherent assault on God and rationality that had been produced directly from the characteristically modern experience of plantation slavery:

The Dirty Dozens extol incest, celebrate homosexuality; even God's ability to create a rational world is naively but scornfully doubted . . . This is not atheism; this is beyond atheism; these people do not walk and talk with God they walk and talk about Him. The seduction of virgins is celebrated with amoral delight . . . That white men who claimed that they followed the precepts of Christ should have been guilty of so much cruelty forced some nameless black bard to utter:
　　Our father, who art in heaven
　　White man owe me 'leven and pay me seven,

Thy kingdom come thy will be done
And ef I hadn't tuck that, I wouldn't got none.[33]

At other points Wright was much more harsh in his judgement of this
mode of cultural expression. He denounced it for its affirmation of "a protracted inability to act . . . a fear of acting"[34] and identified its primary motivation in guilt. When Wright was in this mood, music was nothing more
than a projection of hurt in which blacks attempted to prepare some "compensatory nourishment for themselves."[35] Clearly speaking for this side of
his creator's response to the music, one of Wright's characters described
the rebel art of blue-jazz as "The scornful gesture of men turned ecstatic
in their state of rejection; . . . a musical language of the satisfiedly amoral,
the boastings of the contentedly criminal."[36] This jazz was endowed with
"the frightened ecstasy of the unrepentant."[37] It offered an emotional
home to those who obtained pleasure from its "rhythmic flauntings of
guilty feelings, the syncopated outpourings of frightened joy existing in
guises forbidden and despised by others."[38]

Wright may have been too harsh on this profane culture, but he was even
more uncompromising when he turned to the sacred elements in the black
expressive tradition. Here the links with his own early life as a Seventh-Day
Adventist may be easier to behold. He argued that the power of the church
was a strongly gender-specific and unremittingly conservative factor which
maintained the social and psychological machinery of racial subordination:

> A song ended and a young black girl tossed back her head and closed
> her eyes and broke plaintively into another hymn:
>
> *Glad glad, glad, oh, so glad*
> *I got Jesus in my soul . . .*
>
> Those few words were all she sang, but what her words did not say,
> her emotions said as she repeated the lines, varying the mood and
> tempo, making her tone express meanings which her conscious mind
> did not know. Another woman melted her voice with the girl's and
> then an old man's voice merged with that of the two women. Soon
> the entire congregation was singing . . . They're wrong, he whispered
> in the lyric darkness. He felt that their search for a happiness they
> could never find made them feel that they had committed some
> dreadful offence which they could not remember or understand . . .
> Why was this sense of guilt so seemingly innate, so easy to come by,
> to think, to feel so verily physical?[39]

These observations are not to be interpreted, as has sometimes been suggested, as simply either a hatred of self or a hatred of other blacks. The

dominant sentiment they convey is a strong sense of the toll that racism took upon the psychological and social attributes of blacks forced to live under the coercive, sometimes terroristic, social relations that are licensed by the notion of racial difference. The patterns of internal repression, guilt, misery, and desperation established under the social discipline of slavery endure even though the political and economic order that created them has been partially transformed. Wright was making the still heretical argument that the effects of racism on black people were not generated by the leviathan machine of white supremacy alone. He was suggesting that blacks should bear some measure of responsibility for the evil and destructive things that we do to one another, that racism should not provide an alibi for the anti-social aspects of our communal life.

Wright's Theory of Modernity

In an essay on the development of black studies as a coherent academic project, C. L. R. James tells a revealing anecdote concerning his friendship with Wright. Having gone to the French countryside to spend the weekend with the Wright family, James was ushered into their house and shown numerous volumes of Kierkegaard on a bookshelf. Wright pointed to the shelf, saying, "Look here Nello, you see those books there? . . . Everything that he writes in those books I knew before I had them." James suggests that Wright's apparently intuitive foreknowledge of the issues raised by Kierkegaard was not intuitive at all. It was an elementary product of his historical experiences as a black growing up in the United States between the wars: "What [Dick] was telling me was that he was a black man in the United States and that gave him an insight into what today is the universal opinion and attitude of the *modern* personality" (emphasis added). James characteristically concludes that "What there was in Dick's life, what there was in the experience of a black man in the United States in the 1930s that made him understand everything that Kierkegaard had written before he had read it . . . is something that . . . has to be studied."[40] In this observation, James proposes precisely what *The Outsider* demands and initiates in fictional form, namely, analysis of the place and experience of blacks within the modern world. In Wright's mature position, the Negro is no longer just America's metaphor but rather a central symbol in the psychological, cultural, and political systems of the West as a whole. The image of the Negro and the idea of "race" which it helps to found are living components of a western sensibility that extends beyond national boundaries, linking America to Europe and its empires. The transmutation of the African into the Negro is shown to be central to western civilisation, especially to the primitive, irrational, and mystical elements in European culture that Wright would seek to explore in *Pagan Spain,* his study of Franco and Spanish fascism.

Kierkegaard was not the only European philosopher whose work Wright would recognise as somehow connected to the standpoint of dislocation associated with black experiences of modernity. This is not the place to speculate over why Wright might have found Husserl's theory of subjectivity attractive. However, the latter's almost Baconian fervour for the uniqueness of Europe and its civilisation is something that influenced Wright, who went so far as to have his copies of *Phenomenology* and *Ideas*[41] rebound in hard-wearing black leather so that he could carry them around in his pockets while completing *The Outsider* in Paris during 1947. More than any other book of Wright's, *The Outsider* elaborates a view of blackness and the relational ideologies of race and racism which support it, not as fixed and stable historical identities to be celebrated, overcome, or even deconstructed, but as metaphysical conditions of the modern world's existence that arise with, and perhaps out of, the overcoming of religious morality. The book represents Wright's first attempt to account for the correspondences and connections which joined the everyday lifeworld of African-Americans to the visceral anxieties precipitated in modern European philosophy and letters by the collapse of religious sensibility in general and the experience of twentieth-century life in particular.

For Wright the decisive break in western consciousness which modernity identifies was defined by the collapse of a religious understanding of the world. He held this view consistently. It spans his fiction, his journalism, and his works of theory and cultural criticism, and it partially explains his great interest in Nietzsche—another obvious illustration of significant correspondences he saw between the vernacular culture of black people in the United States and the sometimes esoteric products of European philosophising. He used Nietzsche mainly to bolster his sense of the affirmative power of nihilistic cultural forms like the Dirty Dozens and to replace a theory of racial subordination centred on ideology with one that was rooted in historical psychology or at least in a more psychological approach to consciousness and power than Wright's Marxian training could have supported: "The black man's is a strange situation; it is a perspective, an angle of vision held by oppressed people; it is an outlook of people looking upward from below. It is what Nietzsche once called a 'frog's perspective.' Oppression oppresses, and this is the consciousness of black men who have been oppressed for centuries,—oppressed so long that their oppression has become a tradition, in fact a kind of culture."[42] Wright glossed the key concept of a frog's perspective and used it to give the notion of double consciousness an explicitly psychoanalytic dimension:

> "Frog Perspectives." This is a phrase that I've borrowed from Nietzsche to describe someone looking from below upward, a sense of someone who feels himself lower than others. The concept of distance involved here is not physical; it is psychological. It involves a situation in which for moral or social reasons, a person or a group feels that there is another person or group above it. Yet physically they all live on the same general, material plane. A certain degree of hate combined with love (ambivalence) is always involved in this looking from below upward and the object against which the subject is measuring himself undergoes constant change. He loves the object because he would like to resemble it; he hates the object because his chances of resembling it are remote, slight.[43]

Wright's black subject is internally divided by cultural affiliation, citizenship, and the demands of national and racial identity. Yet the process of internal conflict that Du Bois described as the joining of "two warring souls in one black body" is taken further so that its unconscious aspects become more significant. It acquires an ethno-psychiatric flavour specific to colonial and semi-colonial social life. Wright's understanding of the distinctive standpoint of blacks within the modern world did, however, correspond to Du Bois's description of a constitutive double consciousness in other ways. Having taken on the Nietzschean idea of perspectival ways of knowing, Wright referred to it typically as "double vision"[44] rather than double consciousness. Like Du Bois, he was clear that this special condition is neither simply a disability nor a consistent privilege. He returned to its inner ambivalences in both his fiction and his theoretical writings. His opinion of this sensitised state shifted constantly as he argued against different positions held by thinkers still enmeshed in the manichean logic of western colour consciousness and as his political focus moved away from exclusive concern with American racial politics and towards an interest in the geo-politics of (anti)imperialism and the place of various different racisms within the structures of imperial rule. As with the plight of the westernised elite in countries subjected to colonial domination, Wright regarded this double vision as something internal to the West. It provided him with a chance to observe and describe "A fight of the West with itself, a fight that the West blunderingly began, and the West does not to this day realize that it is the sole responsible agent, the sole instigator."[45]

In another essay where the doubling effect of double consciousness was

also referred to as a splitting process, Wright located its origins in two connected but still independent historical conditions: being a product of western civilisation and having a racial identity "deeply conditioned" by and
"organically born of" that civilisation. It is interesting that he expressed
this dissident consciousness of the West in temporal terms. Claiming, in
effect, that even split subjectivity carried some significant advantages: "I've
tried to lead you back to my angle of vision slowly . . . My point of view is
a Western one, but a Western one that conflicts at several vital points with
the present, dominant outlook of the West. Am I ahead of or behind the
West? My personal judgement is that I'm ahead. And I do not say that
boastfully; such a judgement is implied by the very nature of those Western
values that I hold dear."[46]

In several essays and almost every book, Wright turned back to this
problem of his own hybrid identity as a modern man. In *Pagan Spain,* a
book devoted to an enquiry into the residually prerational, pagan, or traditional components of European experience, Wright was confronted by the
enduring hold of religious belief on Spanish society and culture. He tried
to demonstrate how this retention of religion was articulated to the practice of fascism which periodically interrupted his own text in the form of
lengthy passages quoted from a Falangist catechism for young women.
Facing this disjuncture between the traditional and the modern, the author
suddenly obtained an important insight into his own place caught somewhere between the promises and the curses of occidental modernity. He
realised for the first time that the step from tradition to modernity did not
parallel the distinction between primitive and civilised, or even the opposition between black and white:

> To be a functioning and organic part of something is to be almost
> unconscious of it. I was a part, intimate and inseparable, of the West-
> ern world, but I seldom had had to account for my Westernnness, had
> rarely found myself in situations which had challenged me to do so.
> (Even in Asia and Africa I had always known where my world ended
> and theirs began. But Spain was baffling; it looked and seemed West-
> ern, but did not act or feel Western) . . . what did being Western
> mean? . . . Was being Western something so absolutely different from
> Spanish life and civilization as to be of another genus? Or was that
> difference a mere nuance, an angle of vision, a point of view? It was
> not my task to define the totality of the contents of Western civilisa-
> tion; I was interested only in that aspect of it that engaged my atten-
> tion in relation to Spain . . . Spain was a holy nation, a sacred state—

a state as sacred and as irrational as the sacred state of the Akan in the African jungle.[47]

Here is an opportunity to focus on two related issues that are highlighted by Wright's exploration of distinctively modern experience. First, there is his response to and analysis of the cultural and political flux of modernity. Amidst this turbulence, racism can provide a momentary stabilising force for the white rulers who employ it to secure their precarious position. Racial subordination is integral to the processes of development and social and technological progress known as modernisation. It can therefore propel into modernity some of the very people it helps to dominate. Second, this discussion supplies a key to the manner in which the forms and themes of modernist aesthetics and politics are themselves adapted and transformed by Wright's own politically engaged mode of racial writing. These two concerns are most gracefully synthesised in Wright's final published novel, *The Long Dream,* which remains his most complete attempt to produce a philosophical novel in the black idiom and will be discussed below. But first, we must examine *The Outsider,* an earlier book that shared many of the same aspirations and themes. It was published in 1953, seven years after Wright had begun his exile in Paris. As its title suggests, *The Outsider* was shaped by a developing philosophical interest in the existentialism which he claimed was already a systematic part of his racialised outlook on life as a black Mississippian. It is mistaken to accept the charge made by some African-American critics that the book presents only a pseudo-European desire to escape from the restrictions of racial writing and deal with broader, grander, and less particularistic themes. Its weighty intellectual concerns were not, after all, a new departure for Wright, whose attempts to move beyond the constraining forces of economistic Marxism and the artistic conventions of "Negro Literature" had preceded his move to Europe by many years. Both these intentions had been clearly signalled when *Native Son* was originally published. In that text, through the personality and murderous actions of Bigger Thomas, Wright had tried to illuminate the formation of a new kind of urban working-class man, equally ripe for the appeal of either communist or fascist politics. Bigger, the product of an entropic society—"an American product, a native son of this land [who] carried within him the potentialities of either Communism or Fascism"—provided a strikingly different image of the proletariat from that enshrined within the Stalinist orthodoxy of the American Communist Party, which Wright had joined in the early 1930s and which he had intermittently attacked. The same point was made less cryptically in his foreword to *Black Metropolis:* "Do not hold a light attitude toward the slums of Chicago's South Side. Remember that Hitler came out of such a slum. Remember that Chicago could be the Vienna of American Fascism! Out of these mucky slums can come ideas quickening life or hastening death, giving us peace or carrying us toward another war."[48]

In the assertive yet despairing violence through which Bigger effectively created himself as a subject, it is possible to detect the first stirring of *The Outsider*'s main protagonist, Cross Damon, a man who, Wright informs us, acts "individually just as modern man lives in the mass each day,"[49] and who defiantly reminds another character that "Negroes can be fascists too."[50] Bigger Thomas, the protagonist of *Native Son,* had been drawn unconsciously to the existential dimension of his barbarous acts. However, in Cross, Wright created a character who, released from the earlier book's obligation to try and make Stalinism intelligible, could opt to embrace the moral and political implications of his anti-social inclinations, a man who, in a striking prefiguration of themes named routinely these days as post-modern, "had had no party, no myths, no tradition, no race, no soil, no culture, and no ideas—except perhaps the idea that ideas in themselves were, at best dubious."[51]

Another of Wright's carefully dislocated heroes, Freddie Daniels, in his unpublished novel "The Man Who Lived Underground," faced similar dilemmas to Bigger and Cross in equally bleak circumstances. Falsely accused of a murder, he escapes from police custody and hides in the gloomy depths of the municipal sewers, where the existential dimensions of his wretched metropolitan life confront him with a new clarity which had not been possible while he dwelt above the ground. Like *Native Son, The Outsider,* and *The Long Dream,* this story situates the philosophical and political problems of black America in the provocative progression from a mode of literary realism defined by race to a metaphysics of modernity in which notions of racial particularity appear trivial and inconsequential.

The violent actions which propel all these misanthropic narratives to their desolate conclusions are a further unifying motif which is more than the simple product of Wright's daemonic personal anger or supposed psychological derangement. *The Outsider* is marked from end to end by his resolution to write a powerful, unassimilable prose which could be read only "without the consolation of tears." This goal radiates from each uncomfortable image and pattern of apparently nihilistic interaction. It is Wright's studied political and intellectual answer to the problems posed for the black artist by the commodification and sale of their work to large white audiences and to the competing needs and demands of a plural reading public fractured along the experiential fault lines of gender, race, and class.

The Outsider's significant continuities with Wright's earlier work should not detract from its status as his most ambitious literary attempt to defeat the culture which shaped him. The book was the last place where his political commitments around race and his desire to reveal the philosophical depth of black experience lay unreconciled. These two powerful obligations sit side by side in the text. The book is also notable because it comprises his final and most considered words on the vexed relationship between the oppression of blacks and liberatory projects conducted under the banner of Marxism. It is therefore particularly significant that the book grew in step with his expanding sense that the racial subordination which qualified the claims of American civilisation was only one part of the historical process which had formed him. According to his biographers, the book took coherent shape only after he left the United States, a move which he described as being of the most profound significance for his development as a writer of fiction and as a political philosopher: "The break from the U.S. was more than a geographical change. It was a break with my former attitudes as a Negro and a Communist—an attempt to think over and redefine my attitudes and my thinking. I was trying to grapple with the big problem—the problem and meaning of Western civilisation as a whole and the relation of Negroes and other minority groups to it."[52] Despite the clarity with which this important claim is stated, very little has been written about the character and development of the black modernist perspective implicit in these words. The critical inquiry into the problem and meaning of western civilisation as a whole to which Wright aspired has been completely overlooked in favour of a dubious preoccupation with the "raw, phallic realism and naturalism" that supposedly defines his work. In order to better appreciate *The Outsider*'s complexities and its author's political and philosophical ambitions, it may be helpful to specify some of the features which contribute to his distinctive visions of modernity, modernisation, and modernism. All are mediated by the historical memory of slavery and the order of racial terror that succeeded it in the South. As elsewhere in Wright's work, *The Outsider* defines modernity as a period and a region characterised by the collapse of old myths. This insight provides the context for Wright's discussion of both fascism and communism, equivalents in that both are "political expressions of the twentieth century's atheistic way of life":[53]

"I admit they are different," Cross conceded. "But the degree of the difference is not worth arguing about. Fascists operate from a narrow, limited basis; they preach nationality, race, soil and blood, folk feeling and other rot to capture men's hearts. What makes one man a Fascist and another a Communist might be found in the degree to which they are integrated with their culture. The more alienated a man is the more he'd lean toward Communism . . ."[54]

An uncompromising challenge to the universal and positivistic pretensions of Stalin's dialectical materialism is woven together with an indictment of the vanguard party. This is integrated with a more general critical discussion of historical materialism as a sociological method and a philosophical orientation. This exchange reaches a crescendo in the lengthy confrontation between Cross and the party leadership that comes towards the end of *The Outsider*'s fourth book. This angry debate repays careful study. In it Wright goes far beyond simply attacking the party's methods and procedures. The substance of his wrath was directed not only at the "Jealous Rebels" who sought to use this particular ideology for their own cynical purposes but at the whole fiction of democratic representation and at the idea of political parties per se. This critique is further fuelled by Wright's belief in the ephemeral nature of the open, democratic forms of modern political culture. He feared that these institutions comprised nothing more than a sentimental interlude preceding the establishment of even more barbaric, absolutist, post-political regimes: "Communism and Fascism are but the political expressions of the twentieth century's atheistic way of life . . . the future will reveal many, many more of these absolutistic systems, whose brutality and rigor will make the present day systems seem like summer outings."[55] Cross's dialogue with the Communists he loathes conveys the idea that Marxism is a useful starting point but little else. His polemical outbursts derive their power from the suggestion that, in the twentieth century, western political life, which had been changed once by the advent of modernity, underwent a further transformation. It was no longer dominated by the desire "to make the ideas of Mill and Hume and Locke good for all people, at all times, everywhere."[56] Marxism was not equipped to respond to the profound changes heralded by the rise of fascism and consolidated by other cultural and technological developments:

> Communication, inventions, radio, television, movies, atomic energy, by annihilating distance and space and the atmosphere of mystery and romance, create the conditions for the creation of organizations reflecting the total and absolute in modern life. Commercial advertising, cheapening and devaluing our notions of the human personality, develops and perfects techniques that can be used by political leaders who want to enthrone the total and the absolute in modern life.[57]

Elsewhere, Wright was to call Marx's doctrine "but a transitory make-shift pending a more accurate diagnosis" while he identified communism as nothing more than "a painful compromise containing a definition of man by sheer default."[58] The intensity with which this debate flares up inside *The Outsider* is more than just important evidence that Wright's stormy involvement with the party and its literary front organisations was both longer and more complex than his avowedly autobiographical writings admit. Though from the beginning his independence of mind attracted suspicion and charges of intellectualism and Trotskyism, he had been hailed as the organisation's most distinguished proletarian author. Parts, though by no means all, of his writing had been identified as the perfect embodiment of the hard-boiled style of class-conscious fiction demanded under the leadership of Earl Browder and the cultural dictates of Mike Gold. Wright's steady disenchantment with the organisation he supported between 1934 and 1942 evolved in a period[59] when important political and theoretical issues were thought to hang on the ability of black Americans to progress from racial to class-based forms of social solidarity and political organisation. The task of developing a pure class sentiment posed a series of complex questions about the relation of race to class and of literature to politics which Wright had tried to answer in "Blueprint for Negro Writing."[60] Examining the issue of class differences within the race, he had argued on that occasion that the backward and narcissistic aesthetic strategies of the black middle class could be overcome by a new perspective which sought its inspiration in the black vernacular and derived its political momentum from the struggles of the urban black poor. In contrast to what he saw as the ornamental writing produced from liaisons between "inferiority complexed Negro geniuses and burnt out white Bohemians with money" and the literature which was content to be "the voice of the educated Negro pleading with white America for justice," Wright defined a mode of cultural production which not only derived its inspiration from the consciousness and political action of ordinary black people but also identified them as a significant reading public: "An emphasis upon tendency and experiment, a view of society as something becoming rather than something fixed and admired is the one which points the way for Negro writers to stand shoulder to shoulder with Negro workers in mood and outlook."[61]

The model of literary modernism which this text constructs is supported by another sketchy account of modernity and of the dissident black presences within it. Wright described a "whole" autonomous, black culture irreducible to the effects of slavery and racial subordination which had "for good or ill" clarified the consciousness of blacks and created emotional

attitudes and psychological characteristics associated with particular notions of freedom and a characteristic understanding of subjectivity. This
"racial wisdom" was produced from and during slavery. It is largely reproduced by the black church but also in the profane folklore which answers
its authoritarian power. In Wright's hands, the profane nihilistic stance exemplified in the Dozens tested Herderian elevation of folk-cultural forms
to the limit. Though defined against the world of formal politics from
which blacks were (and in Wright's time remained) excluded, this culture
promoted specific forms of identity, strategies for survival, and distinct
conceptions of social change.

> It was . . . in a folklore moulded out of rigourous and inhuman condi-
> tions of life that the Negro achieved his most indigenous and com-
> plete expression. Blues, spirituals, and folk tales recounted from
> mouth to mouth; the whispered words of a black mother to a black
> daughter on the ways of men; the confidential wisdom of a black fa-
> ther to his black son; the swapping of sex experiences on street corners
> from boy to boy in the deepest vernacular; work songs sung under
> blazing suns—all these formed the channels through which the racial
> wisdom flowed.[62]

The privilege accorded to music and talk about sex in this account of authentic racial culture should underscore the argument about the discourse
of racial authenticity outlined above in Chapter 3. Wright saw the unwrit-
ten and unrecognised culture of the "Negro masses" in bitter opposition
to the "parasitic and mannered outpourings" that sprung from the pens of
the sons and daughters of a rising Negro bourgeoisie. In this conflict, he
took the side of the vernacular and then attempted to reinvent a conception of black nationalism which could be adequate to defending that controversial and necessarily nihilistic allegiance. It was a nationalism that
could address the manifest fracturing of national unity revealed by the
transformation of rural peasants into something like an urban proletariat.
It was a popular nationalism that retained a class-specific character. It thus
aspired to be more than an inverted image or "reflex expression" of the
exclusionary power of institutionalised white supremacy. Wright's popular
nationalism was the repository of a revolutionary, anti-capitalist politics potentially capable of transforming American society. He described it as "a
nationalism whose reason for being lies in the simple fact of self-possession
and in the consciousness of the interdependence of people in modern society," and he identified the opportunity which black writers had now acquired as their chance to create values by which their race "is to struggle,
live and die."

Though Wright's residual debt to the intellectual architecture of economistic Marxism is still sometimes visible, he confirmed the anti-ideological character of the operation which he favoured in significant, but oblique, references to "theory" and "perspective." These concepts were introduced in contrast to the trivial potency of mere isms:

> What vision must Negro writers have before their eyes . . . What angle of vision can show them all the forces of modern society in process, . . . Must they believe in some "ism"? They may feel that only dupes believe in isms; they feel with some measure of justification that another commitment means only another disillusionment. But anyone destitute of a theory about the meaning, structure and direction of modern society is a lost victim in a world he cannot understand or control.[63]

In Wright's careful usage, "theory" and political ideology might overlap but they were not the same thing. After his painful break with the party he would explain how the former could be undermined and even destroyed by an excess of the latter. In a discussion of the writer's craft which followed the above passage, he made his critique even more overt when he rejected the demand that a politicised black art should carry a great load of didactic material. He warned that a surplus of vulgar or too simple political ideology had disastrous effects upon artistic sense: "The relationship between reality and the artistic image is not always simple and direct . . . Image and emotion possess a logic of their own."

When Wright returned to these problems twenty years later in *White Man Listen!* he would be even more remotely connected to the Marxian thinking which was a scar left by his years as a communist. The later text offers a more satisfactory and more elegant synthesis of themes culled from the work of Marx, Freud, and Nietzsche but filtered through and reconstituted by his political and philosophical commitments to the history of blacks inside the West. More significantly, at this stage he renamed the two contradictory streams he had noted coexisting inside black cultural expression. Though their class character was essentially unchanged, they were no longer to be described as simply bourgeois and proletarian but rather as "The Narcissistic Level" and "The Forms of Things Unknown." Wright's interest remained focused upon the African-American, urban vernacular, and he offered a complex and sympathetic exploration of its significance which undermines the suggestion that he was remote from or even contemptuous of black culture. As we have already seen, the standard examples of music and sexuality were the means through which his argument about intraracial division would unfold.

The Outsider was certainly the most portentous of several of Wright's texts to treat on these themes. It repeated his frequent suggestion that the secular character of modernity was what distinguished it and ruptured it from its prehistory. He made this observation while noting that this state of affairs poses a number of special problems for people who entered the shrine of western culture through the portals of its churches and who have appropriated its religious ideology as a bulwark for the defence of their political and cultural autonomy during slavery and since.

Wright's enhanced sense of the importance of psychology enabled him to refine this argument considerably. He insisted, against the assumptions of economistic Marxism ritually spouted by his communist characters, that for the "twentieth-century westerners who have outlived the faith of their fathers" the essence of life is no longer straightforwardly material. It has become essentially psychological: "men may take power with arms, but their keeping of it is by other means." This view of the increasing importance of psychological aspects of domination, and of psychology and psychoanalysis as analytical and political tools in the service of black liberation, is associated with Wright's simultaneous alarm at and fascination with the development of mass society and its accompanying politico-cultural forms. It was also shaped by his practical involvement in the struggle to provide independent psychiatric resources to the black community in Harlem and by his close association with Dr. Frederic Wertham, a Bavarian-born psychiatrist who had been teaching at Johns Hopkins University.[64] Wright made use of psychology and psychoanalysis in a number of ways, but they are most prominent in his distinctive adaptation of analyses of colonial societies to the experience of black Americans. Inspired, above all, by the work of Octave Mannoni,[65] which he acknowledged later in an epigraph to part two of *The Long Dream,* Wright tried to demonstrate that in either location the relationship between oppressor and the oppressed could generate specific forms of mental illness in both groups. He seems to have found Mannoni's residually Hegelian insistence on the interdependency of coloniser and colonised especially suggestive. His extension of this argument and its transfer into the analysis of African-American experience is a notable feature of all the later fiction. In *The Outsider,* Cross becomes an important vehicle for his author's own urgent, Freudian questioning: "Aren't all cultures and civilizations just screens which men have used to divide themselves, to put between that part of themselves which they are afraid of and that part of themselves they want to preserve?"[66]

Wright's attempts to incorporate elements of Freudian theory into the critique of modernity expressed by *The Outsider* provide further keys to the character of Cross, whose nihilism is eventually condemned for its mistaken belief that the "restless, floating demon" of desire is itself the authentic core of reality. It is this that enables District Attorney Eli Houston to unravel Cross's crimes: "desire is what snared you my boy. You felt that what obstructed desire could be killed; what annoyed, could be gotten rid of . . ."[67]

The novel's philosophical content attracted adverse critical comment from reviewers. Wright's relationship to the work of Heidegger, Husserl, Kierkegaard, and Nietzsche was more complex than many critics seem to appreciate. It is worth repeating that he was not straining to validate African-American experience in their European terms but rather demonstrating how the everyday experience of blacks in the United States enabled them to see with a special clarity of vision—a dreadful objectivity—the same constellation of problems which these existentialist authors had identified in more exalted settings. In a book that was uncomfortable with its editor's attempts to turn it into a murder mystery, the work of these writers also became a carefully deployed clue to Cross's crimes.[68] This points to another feature of Wright's ambiguous relationship to literary modernism, namely the populist impulse inherent in his adaptation of the genre of detective fiction. The effect of this ploy is to demystify some of the preoccupations and themes of high modernism by transposing them into an accessible register which confounds the European distinction between high and vernacular cultural forms and demonstrates yet again the correspondence between the everyday lifeworld of urban black Americans and the existential anxieties of the European savant.

Wright emphasised that his protagonist in this book could have come from any racial group. The distinctive outlook signalled in his hybrid name—which combines an acknowledgement of Judeo-Christian morality with its Nietzschean overcoming—marks Cross Damon, far more than either Bigger Thomas or Freddie Daniels before him, as a representative figure. His god-like feelings may exist beyond the orbit of racial identity, but in spite of these inclinations Cross remained shackled by and to the voiceless, bestial condition of America's urban blacks. Through his desperate actions, he was obliged to articulate some of the feelings that they experienced without always being able to express.

> He sensed how Negroes had been made to live in but not of the land of their birth, how the injunctions of an alien christianity and the strictures of white laws had evoked in them the very longings and desires that that religion and law had been designed to stifle.[69]

> He tramped grimly past towering Negro churches from whose doorways rolled softly, almost apologetically, the plaintive spirituals of his people. How lucky they were, those black worshippers, to be able to feel lonely together! What fantastic blessings were theirs to be able to express their sense of abandonment in a manner that bound them in unison![70]

These passages are important because it has sometimes been overlooked, in the dazzle of its philosophical pretensions, that *The Outsider* manages to remain a book about the experience and effects of racial subordination. The narrative develops explicitly through the history and culture of black America even where these are dismissed or, like the black church, belittled as a pathetic salve with which the oppressed have attempted to repair the misery of their lives in the pools of human degradation that America's metropolitan centres have become. Wright identified the growth of urban life with the process of industrial development which he described as a kind of war against all mankind. The great industrial cities created a cultural environment which nurtured a whole caste of men like Cross. It was the anonymity provided by the metropolis which gave him the opportunity to re-create himself in a new persona and set out on his picaresque journey. Chance encounters in the new public spaces created by networks of transportation prove decisive, not only in allowing him to affect his own death but also in bringing him into contact with his nemesis, the disabled district attorney Eli Houston.

It bears repetition that Wright did not see this destructive pattern of modern experience as unique to blacks, though, for a variety of reasons, he felt that blacks encountered its effects at a special intensity. Cross was the product of Wright's own urgent obligation to attempt to speak for the black masses deprived of public speech, "to be a witness to their living." The words which he hurled into the void that was the horror of modern life, his critique of European ideology and culture in its religious and critical communist forms, is a critique that arose from their special history in the modern world. It originated in slavery and stood at the centre of a space unevenly triangulated by industrialisation, capitalism, and the institution of democratic government. Like double vision, this critique has been the product of blacks' peculiar journey from racial slavery to Jim Crow citizenship, from southern shack to metropolitan tenement block. Cross expressed their predicament and their desires, and Wright shared much with him. But Cross is not Wright's only voice in the novel, and in the end his nihilistic stance is dealt with harshly. It is rejected for its inhumanity, a failing that is identified by Eli Houston, the law officer who untangles Cross's bloody crimes: "You were so inhuman that I wouldn't have believed it unless I had seen it. Many sociologists say that the American Negro hasn't had time to become completely adjusted to our mores, that the life of the family of the Western world hasn't had time to sink in. But with you, you're adjusted and more. You've grown up and beyond our rituals."[71]

Wright's desire to criticise and experiment with European philosophy can itself be read as a modernist violation of the literary codes and expectations surrounding Negro literature which his own work had helped to establish. *The Outsider* was condemned for these transgressive ambitions. Some critics attacked Wright's misguided experimenting with intellectual traditions outside his actual experience and cited the text as the proof that his creative powers were in decline. Others argued that his gifts as a story-teller had been effectively smothered by his philosophical erudition. These points have been echoed by more recent critical voices. Michel Fabre, whose sympathetic biography of Wright contains a detailed summary of all the contemporary reviews of the book, criticised its didactic, "professorial" aspects and suggested that it lacked a "coherent symbolism." Charles Davis dismissed the book as "essentially an intriguing philosophical exercise," and, from a different political angle, Amiri Baraka described Wright's "aspi-rant intellectualism" as his "undoing" and his political outlook in exile as "petit Bourgeois individualism."[72] To varying degrees, these mistaken ver-dicts on the book endorse a view of Wright in Paris as a remote and deraci-nated writer. He was, this argument runs, led astray from the realistic and naturalistic styles of fiction to which his experiences in the segregated South gave rise by the heady influences of friends like Sartre and others like Blanchot, Mannoni, and Bataille,[73] whose inappropriately cosmopolitan outlooks poured their corrosive influences on his precious and authentic Negro sensibility. For many African-American critics it seems that Wright's most attractive face was the one James Baldwin had recognised immedi-ately as that of a "Mississippi Picanniny."[74] The question of why this side of Wright should be the most appealing deserves to be answered at length. There is a further suggestion, shared by both those who exalt and those who have execrated Wright as a protest writer, that he should have been content to remain confined within the intellectual ghetto to which Negro literary expression is still too frequently consigned. His desires—to escape the ideological and cultural legacies of Americanism; to learn the philo-sophical languages of literary and philosophical modernism even if only to demonstrate the commonplace nature of their truths; and to seek complex answers to the questions which racial and national identities could only obscure—all point to the enduring value of his radical view of modernity for the contemporary analyst of the black diaspora.

Masculinity, Misogyny, and the Limits of Racial Community

Contemporary critical writing about the aesthetic and political traditions of African-American literature has been dominated by a simplistic and overpolarised approach to fictional representations of the conflict between men and women. These discussions have raged with special ferocity around Richard Wright's literary legacy. This is because the very quality of racial authenticity prized in his early writings was thought to be inseparable from a hatred of women that some critics have found conveyed by the violence and contempt of Wright's male characters.[75] One of the ways in which *The Outsider* produces the effect of racial authenticity that Wright was so keen to deconstruct is through the bleak view of relationships between black women and men it presents, especially in the first book, "Dread." If Sarah Hunter, the wise wife of Bob the Pullman porter, provides something of an exception to these tendencies, Cross's dismal relationships with his wife, his mother, his girlfriend, and his children are all detailed representations of a black man's inability to form emotional attachments to those who are closest to him. These failures may or may not echo aspects of the author's own life, though it is probably significant that Cross is attracted to the white woman artist who becomes a vehicle for Wright's discussion of the problems of artistic form. In the "seemingly disassociated" shapes of her non-objective painting, Cross finds a half-articulate response to the crises of modern living which is almost congruent with his own. The intimacy between them leads her to suicide.

It is important to appreciate that the violence of Wright's characters is not a simple product of their maleness. Violence articulates blackness to a distinct mode of lived masculinity, but it is also a factor in what distinguishes blacks from whites. It mediates racial differences and maintains the boundary between racially segregated, non-synchronous communities. This enabled Wright to see a connection between life in the South and conflictual colonial settings in which the social worlds of the coloniser and the colonised intersected only in the police station. For Wright, violence coloured black social life as a whole. It was internalised and reproduced in the most intimate relationships. This meant that black women could also be violent and that other kinds of brutality were integral to Wright's view of the relationship between black parents and their children. Ralph Ellison is convincing when, in his reading of *Black Boy*, the first segment of Wright's life story, he argues that Wright connected the reproduction of this violence to culturally specific nurturing practices that could, in turn, be traced back to the impact of racial terror on the institution of the black family in the South:

One of the Southern Negro family's methods of protecting the child is the severe beating—a homeopathic dose of the violence generated by black white relationships. Such beatings as Wright's were administered for the child's own good; a good which the child resisted, thus giving family relationships an undercurrent of fear and hostility, which differs qualitatively from that found in patriarchal middle class families, because here the severe beating is administered by the mother, leaving the child no parental sanctuary. He must ever embrace violence along with maternal tenderness, or reject, in his helpless way, the mother.[76]

This insight is valuable in making sense of Wright's work whether or not it contributes anything to understanding Wright himself or to building a materialist theory of the psychological birth and object choices of the black subject. It is cited here neither to excuse Wright's sexist attitude to women nor to legitimate the abusive patterns of nurturing to which black families—like families in general—regularly give rise. The key point is that Wright connected the violence found in the private, domestic sphere to the ritual, public brutality that was a means of political administration in the South. This public terror did more than help create conditions in which private violence could thrive. It was shadowed by the domestic authoritarianism and violence which it also required if the racially coercive social order was to function smoothly. Both varieties of brutality were shaped by the active residues of slave society in which lines between public and private became hard to draw. Wright treated so extensively upon the routine violence between blacks and whites as well as within the black community that James Baldwin used a discussion of his work to illustrate a more general observation about the place of violence in black literature: "In most novels written by Negroes . . . there is a great space where sex ought to be; and what usually fills this space is violence."[77] This became an orthodox critical line in discussions of Wright's fiction for many years.

Rather like the contradictory presentation of black music and vernacular culture examined above, Wright's sense of the significance of violence in black social life was a site of his irreducible ambivalence towards the idea of a closed racial community and the ideology of family that helped to reproduce it. This can be missed when the theme of violence is too swiftly monopolised by discussion of the complex and contradictory feelings that we can name as Wright's misogyny. The complicated term "misogyny" brings together a number of issues that should be clearly differentiated before we can comprehend their association. It has been used to illuminate the powerful critique of the family that emerges from both Wright's fiction and his autobiographical works, particularly *Black Boy*. It is required to interpret events like Bigger's horrible murder of his girlfriend Bessie in *Native Son*, which provides a notorious example of how Wright saw his female characters and their fates. It has also been used to connect these representations with accounts of Wright's own bad relations with the black women who were his collaborators and his kin.[78] While leaving the question of Wright's own views of women open, I want to suggest that attempts to make sense of the complex misogyny in his work should include less straightforward issues such as recognition of the important differences in his presentation of black and white women. They should also be able to connect that uneven misogyny to his path-breaking inauguration of a critical discourse on the construction of black masculinity as well as to the few tantalising feminist and proto-feminist statements sprinkled around his work.[79] For example, Wright began his speech to the first *Présence Africaine* Congress by lamenting the absence of women from that event:

> I don't know how many of you have noticed it [but] there have been no women functioning vitally and responsibly from this platform [and] helping to mold and mobilize our thoughts. This is not a criticism of the conference, it is not a criticism of anyone, it is a criticism that I heap on ourselves collectively. When and if we hold another conference—and I hope we will—I hope there shall be an effective utilization of Negro womanhood in the world to help us mobilize and pool our forces. Perhaps some hangover of influence from the past has colored our attitude, or perhaps this was an oversight. In our struggle for freedom, against great odds, we cannot afford to ignore one half of our manpower, that is the force of women and their active collaboration. Black men will not be free until their women are free.[80]

These words alone suggest that Wright may have been too simplistically denounced as a macho figure whose deep hatred of women also expressed his profound, though sometimes repressed, distaste for all other blacks. This crude and inadequate account of Wright's misogyny has a second aspect. This sees him dismissed[81] repeatedly as the purveyor of a crude, protest-oriented fiction that not only refuses to validate the dynamic, vital qualities of black culture but denies artistic and political legitimacy to the affirmative literary enterprises which are today endowed with feminine qualities. Wright is then positioned at one wing of the great family of African-American letters while Zora Neale Hurston, the woman identified as his cultural and political opposite, is placed at the other. Her folksy and assertively feminine perspective is thought to indicate the direction of a more positive counterpart to the overpoliticised and rugged masculinity of Wright's more pessimistic and more self-consciously modernist work. Her conservatism answers his misguided bolshevism, her exaggerated respect for the authentic voice of rural black folk is interpreted as a welcome antidote to his contemptuous presentation of the bestial, desperate experiences involved in being black in some metropolitan hovel. Wright's celebrated 1937 review of Hurston's *Their Eyes Were Watching God*[82] has become a key document in sustaining this conflict. In it, Wright attacked what he saw as the unseriousness and emptiness of vapid fiction content to exist in the "safe and narrow orbit in which America likes to see the Negro live: between laughter and tears." His unfavourable verdict on Hurston has been frequently cited as the warrant for today's fashionable but unhelpful polarisation which inhibits adequate analysis of either writer. However, the intellectual justification for identifying Wright personally with the woman-slaying exploits of the protagonists of *Native Son* and *Savage Holiday* has simply not been provided.

Those who take this line on Wright have little to say about *Eight Men*, his anthology of pieces loosely connected by the theme of black masculinity. They do not discuss the possibility that this valuable little book might reveal something of Wright's ideas about gender relations in general and about manliness and black masculinity in particular. But there is in *Eight Men* a discourse on black masculinity and male sexuality which should, at the very least, complicate the conventional account of these provocative themes in Wright's work. The material collected in the anthology is linked by his emergent understanding of the junction point of blackness and masculinity. Of the eight pieces, "Man of All Work" and "Man, God Ain't like That" were originally written as radio plays, while "The Man Who Went to Chicago" is more straightforwardly autobiographical, continuing the narrative of *Black Boy*. Several of the other stories are truncated versions of longer pieces that were first conceived long before *Eight Men* was eventually published in 1961. "The Man Who Saw a Flood," for example, goes back to a story called "Silt" published in *New Masses* by Wright as far back as 1937, and "The Man Who Was Almost a Man" resembles a similarly titled story that was published in *Harper's Bazaar* in January 1940. It can be traced back even further to *Tarbaby's Dawn*, a novel that Wright had started in the early thirties. "The Man Who Lived Underground," arguably Wright's most accomplished piece of short fiction, is but one section from a complete novel that was rejected as too short by Harper and Brothers in 1942. This diversity of forms offers a challenge to the reader who would make sense of the collection as a unified whole, connected by more than the sheer force of its author's personality. It requires that close attention be given to the origins of each piece and to the history of Wright's plan to bring them together in this way. Some of the stories had been published in an earlier, Italian volume called *Five Men*. However, the immediate impetus for the larger project which would eventually become *Eight Men* came later, at a time when, according to Constance Webb's biography, Wright was in a degree of financial difficulty and his relations with his editors and agent were not as harmonious as they had once been. Following the publication of *The Long Dream* to very mixed reviews, Wright's status as a commodity on the international literary market was also said to have suffered. The toll which this difficult period took from Wright has led one recent commentator[83] to query the author's commitment to the *Eight Men* project and to ask whether, if "left to himself," he would ever have selected this combination of texts. Wright's failure to complete an introduction to the volume which could have articulated his own conception of its thematic unity is seen as an important sign that its contents were indeed divergent if not fundamentally incongruent with one another. The book is then written off as a desperate commercial manoeuvre intended to revive his flagging career. The fact that Wright appears to have cut two pieces, "Man and Boy" and "Leader Man," from the original ten-story anthology at the instigation of his agent, Paul Reynolds, is read as another sinister comment on the lowly status of a final product born of cynicism and financial desperation. Whatever the reasons for the non-appearance of Wright's own introduction, the contemporary state of black literature and literary criticism demands that we inquire more deeply into the coherence of *Eight Men*. I want to suggest that it does have a unity and that, as its title suggests, its contents are unified through the bond of masculinity that links the eight protagonists.

The collection begins with a story that offers a deeply ironic commentary on the relationship between manliness and the acquisition of a gun. What variety of masculinity demands a firearm as its confirmation? asks Wright, and he ties Dave's desperate desire to possess a revolver to the peculiar psychological setting in which he has come to consciousness of himself as a black man distinct from the black women around him and from the white men who administer the social and political relations of the Jim Crow South. At no point does Wright seek to celebrate or affirm Dave's association of his manhood with the power to take life. The tone of the piece is determinedly critical, seeking to problematise the cluster of associations from which Dave's doomed pursuit of the gun proceeds.

"The Man Who Lived Underground" is a much more complex piece, originally conceived in the period between *Twelve Million Black Voices* and *Black Boy*. Wright identified its significance for his own development by describing it as the first time he had tried to go beyond stories in black and white. The tale is especially notable for its rendering of the themes and preoccupations of aesthetic modernism—recast audaciously in a populist format. The product of a culture stressed by the brute violence and arbitrariness of racism, the protagonist, Freddie Daniels, acquires a measure of the intuitive nihilism that so fascinated Wright. However, despite his radical isolation and the beleaguered nature of his predicament, he is shown to be a family man concerned for the welfare of his immediate kin if not for the condition of the broader racial community from which he is deeply alienated. According to Michel Fabre, the relationship of Daniels to his family is given even greater prominence in the long opening section of the original novella which remains unpublished and inaccessible. In this introductory section, Daniels's wife is apparently about to give birth when he is detained by the police and forced into a confession. He escapes from the maternity hospital and flees into the sewer. His excessive concern for his wife and child serves to emphasise his distance from the other black people around him. This estrangement, visible later on in the narrative in Daniels's secret observation of the black church and its rituals, has also been described as a further illustration of Wright's fundamental distaste for the world view of his racial peers. It is possible to construct a more profound interpretation of that scene in which the impossible memory of slavery itself is what has conditioned the congregation's collective guilt and their fruitless pursuit of happiness.

"Big Black Good Man" is one of several stories in the collection which are saturated in a brand of humour that contradicts Wright's later reputation as an abstract and overly academic writer. The story, set in Copenhagen on a rainy August night, explores how racist ideologies distort social interaction and generate cross-cultural misunderstandings. Its central joke is supplied by the evident discontinuity which cultural differences introduce between the contrasting modes of masculinity enjoyed by the story's two central characters. The white man, Olaf Jenson, thinks that the huge nameless black man who comes to the hotel where he works as a night porter is about to strangle him. The black seafarer is, in fact, only measuring Olaf's collar-size for a gift of shirts that he brings on his next visit. Tom, the man at the centre of "The Man Who Saw a Flood," is another conscientious husband and father locked into a system of racial subordination and economic exploitation that he cannot control and that strictly qualifies the type of man he is able to be. This theme is explored further in "Man of All Work," where humour again plays an important and quite unexpected role in demonstrating the ways in which racism partially determines the content of black gender roles and the interrelation of sexual and labour exploitation. Carl, the hero, is yet another responsible family man, giving his young baby its night-time feeds and nursing his sick wife. He does not need to take somebody else's life in order to discover the emotional co-ordinates which will enable him to orient his own. Under pressure of poverty, he decides to dress up in his wife's clothes and take up the post of cook, housekeeper, and nanny in the wealthy home of the white Fairchild family. He is sexually harassed by the husband and then shot by the wife, who is angry at her lascivious spouse. The crisis in which cross-dressed Carl confronts a naked white woman raises a number of themes that are familiar in Wright's work, though they are resolved in this case without the usual catastrophe. "Man God Ain't like That" deals with the murder of a white man rather than the murder of a white woman and is concerned not with differentiation along gender lines but with the ability of the colonised to distinguish the coloniser from the deity. This time, Wright's murderer evades punishment and the author is clearly less con-cerned with the violence intrinsic to neo-colonial relationships than with the psychological condition of the African neo-proletariat of Paris, adrift in that metropolis without the cultural equipment necessary to interpret the experience correctly.

The capacity of racial groups to live side by side yet non-synchronously and with antagonistic conceptions of what constitutes social reality links this story to the one which follows it. Both focus on "the million psycho-logical miles" that subdivide the world into overlapping black and white constituencies. This tale presents another of Wright's attempts to fathom the outlook of the Africans whose culture he had found so opaque while writing *Black Power*. The confluence of race, sexuality, and gender also emerges again with renewed force in the penultimate piece, "The Man Who Killed a Shadow," a short story written early in Wright's Parisian exile. It is a difficult text for those who would seek to defend Wright from oversimple accusations of woman hating. Like "The Man Who Lived Un-derground" and indeed *Native Son*, it is squarely based on testimony and trial records scrupulously collated from a real criminal case—the trial of Julius Fisher, a black janitor at the Washington National Cathedral sen-tenced to the electric chair in 1944 for the murder of a librarian, Catherine Cooper Reardon. Wright's imaginative appropriation of their tragic story is notable for its striking inversion of the racist mythology that designates the black man as a sexual predator and assailant, for it is the white woman who takes that aggressive role on this occasion. The story is another un-even attempt to portray the distinctively psycho-sexual dynamics of racial antagonism.

The final story in *Eight Men*, "The Man Who Went to Chicago," is a small portion of Wright's autobiography. His publisher's rather arbitrary decision to end the narrative of *Black Boy* with the journey northward left a large amount of material unpublished. Wright used some of it in "I Tried to Be a Communist," his contribution to *The God That Failed*. The full text of the second part was eventually published separately as *American Hunger*. Wright's inclusion of an autobiographical statement at the end of an anthology of fiction is a strategy that needs to be explained. The continuity of fiction with autobiography and the articulation of personal history within imaginative writing are important cultural and aesthetic motifs in African-American letters. But Wright's concluding story serves not simply to position the author in relation to the text as a whole but to accentuate his view of a racial community more marked by its internal conflicts and hostilities than by any ideas of mutuality or fellow feeling. The depressing account of exploitative and abusive relationships between the male agents of the Negro burial society and the impoverished women from whom they collect premiums provides a good example of Wright's unsentimental preparedness to air the race's dirty linen in public. The fact that he disclosed his own participation in this horrible system damns him in the eyes of those who crave pastoral representations of black social life. However, his own behaviour is discussed in a tone of bewilderment and shame. The proto-feminist undertones in this should not be misread as yet another outpouring of his racial self-hatred: "Some of the agents were vicious; if they had claims to pay to a sick black woman and if the woman was able to have sex relations with them, they would insist upon it, using the claims money as a bribe. If the woman refused, they would report to the office that the woman was a malingerer. The average black woman would submit because she needed the money badly."[84]

If the relationships between black women and black men were bad, the interaction between black men was scarcely better. The piece concludes with Wright's numbingly bleak account of his experiences working with three other black men as an orderly in a medical research institute connected to one of the largest and wealthiest hospitals in Chicago. Two new themes relevant to Wright's commentary on modernity emerge from this episode. The first is the exclusion of blacks from the practices of this modern, scientific institution and its regime of knowledge. The second is Wright's growing sense that the black workers in this secular temple are in many respects closer to the animals experimented upon in the laboratory than to the white doctors who supervise the research:

My interest in what was happening in the institute amused the three other Negroes with whom I worked. They had no curiosity about "White Folks' Things," while I wanted to know if the dogs being treated for diabetes were getting well; if the rats and mice in which

cancer had been induced showed any signs of responding to treatment. I wanted to know the principle that lay behind the Ascheim-
Zondek tests that were made with rabbits, the Wasserman tests that
were made with the guinea pigs. But when I asked a timid question I
found that even Jewish doctors had learned to imitate the sadistic
method of humbling a Negro that the others had cultivated.

"If you know too much, boy, your brains might explode," a doctor
said one day.[85]

In this setting, Wright describes a feud between two of his co-workers,
Brand and Cooke. He introduces the chronic conflict between these men
as a moving symbol of the difficulties involved in maintaining genuine intimacy between blacks: "Perhaps Brand and Cooke, lacking interests that
could absorb them, fuming like children over trifles, simply invented their
hate of each other in order to have something to feel deeply about. Or
perhaps there was in them a vague tension stemming from their chronically
frustrating way of life, a pain whose cause they did not know; and, like
those de-vocalised dogs they would whirl and snap at the air when their
old pain struck them."[86] An explosive physical confrontation between these
two puts this small racial community in jeopardy when it leads to the near
destruction of the lab where they work. In another display of the sense of
humour that Wright is not supposed to have had, he assesses the consequences for scientific knowledge brought about by the random redistribu-
tion of the animals the men had previously sorted into specific categories
for the purposes of medical research. The half-conscious state on which
the order of racial domination has come to rely is shown to have grave
effects on the dominant as well as the subordinate participants when the
doctors engaged in research fail to notice that the animals have been
moved around.

Perhaps black artists experience community through a special paradox.
It affords them certain protections and compensations yet it is also a source
of constraint. It provides them with an imaginative entitlement to elaborate the consciousness of racial adversity while limiting them as artists to
the the exploration of that adversity. The striking images of intraracial antagonism in "The Man Who Went to Chicago" present the inescapable
conclusion that in the conditions of extreme privation and stress which
define the limits of the modern world for blacks, racial identity guarantees
nothing in terms of solidarity or fraternal association. That is still a message
which must be given serious consideration.

Of all Wright's texts, it is *Pagan Spain* which is most directly concerned with questions of women's social subordination. But his most developed and sustained treatment of the issue of black masculinity appears in his last published novel,[87] *The Long Dream,* a book which has been overlooked and one which can be viewed as his most complete and successful attempt to write a philosophical novel in the black idiom.

Wright has been attacked for his seeming inability to present a living, functioning black community in his work. *Native Son, The Outsider,* and even *Lawd Today* all disappoint the illegitimate demand for positive images of black sociality which he took pleasure in repudiating. Where community appears, it is usually conflict ridden, as in the hospital lab. People are bound to each other by virtue of the deep disagreements that constantly embarrass the claims of any common racial culture. However, *The Long Dream* presented Wright's portrait of a total, dynamic, black community. The price of this brief organic and systematic image was dearly bought by Wright's deep fascination with its economic, sexual, and cultural stratification. The book is a bildungsroman centred on the life of Rex "Fishbelly" Tucker. We see him growing into manhood through a variety of interactions with his parents, peers, and different adults and institutions, both black and white. Wright rendered Fishbelly's southern community without making any concessions to the pressures to produce a pastoral view. The homophobia, misogyny, and other anti-social attributes of black life were once again uncovered in a manner that must have won Wright few friends and brought forward the accusation of betrayal as well as the suggestion that he was out of touch with changing patterns of life in the South. Not all of these negative social traits were directly traceable to the effects of racism. There is nothing automatic about the choices that his characters make to reproduce social arrangements that work against their own interests. There is always scope for reflexivity and opportunities for black political agency. Several scenes in which Fishbelly and his teenage buddies torment Aggie West, an effeminate boy who is the church pianist and whom they believe to be homosexual, typify Wright's determination to undo the codes and conventions of positive writing which suggests that feelings of racial community and identity are spontaneously produced:

> "Move on, queer Nigger!" Zeke screamed. "Shove off!"
>
> Aggie's lips parted, but he did not move or speak. Nervous hysteria made Sam advance and snatch the baseball bat out of Fishbelly's hand. Lifting the bat, Sam lashed Aggie across the chest. Tony, Zeke and Fishbelly kicked, slapped and punched Aggie . . .
>
> "I tried to kill 'im," Tony spoke through clenched teeth . . .

"Hell, mebbe we oughtn't t've done that." Tony was regretful . . .
"We treat 'im like the white folks treat us," Zeke mumbled with a
self-accusative laugh.
"Never thought of that," Sam admitted frowning.[88]

Much of the book is occupied with an exploration of the relationship
between Fishbelly and his undertaker father, Tyree. Tyree is one of two
prominent black citizens who exercise control over the ghetto in formal
collaboration with a body of corrupt local whites who share the profits
from their illicit schemes and manipulate the local system of criminal justice to maintain this arrangement. The book's central philosophical and
psychological dynamics are constituted via Wright's interest in the master/
slave struggle which I explored in Chapter 2 through the writings of Frederick Douglass. In Wright's perspective this relationship is widened and
socialised. Its dialectic of dependency and recognition is shown to be the
continuing basis of social and economic life in the segregated South. Tyree
acts out the rituals of dependency which whites have been trained to expect
from him and others like him, but he does this in order to manipulate
them. The scope he enjoys to master them cannot match the power of the
institutional order that they control, but it is certainly significant. He is
an exceptional performer in the roles that subservience requires, so skilled
indeed that his son initially misinterprets these performances of racial sub-
alternity:

> Fishbelly understood now; his father was paying humble deference to
> the white man and his "acting" was so flawless, so seemingly effortless
> that Fishbelly was stupefied. This was a father whom he had never
> known, a father whom he loathed and did not want to know. Tyree
> entered the room and looked at him with the eyes of a stranger, then
> turned to watch the retreating white man. When the white man had
> turned a corner in the corridor, Fishbelly saw a change engulf his fa-
> ther's face and body: Tyree's knees lost their bent posture, his back
> straightened, his arms fell normally to his sides, and that distracted,
> foolish, noncommital expression vanished and he reached out and
> crushed Fishbelly to him.[89]

The paternal relationship at the centre of the book is reproduced at all
other levels of the racial hierarchy which governs their town. Armed with
a psychological theory derived from his reading of Mannoni as well as his
Kojèvian understanding of Hegel, Wright emphasises the filial aspects of
Tyree's relationship to the white authority figures who are his partners in
the bar and brothel that he operates. This relationship is not just one in

which the blacks are infantilised by those who dominate them but rather one in which they act out the role of infant as a means to draw certain useful responses from their white rulers. Tyree's performances work because he is able to manipulate the split self which has been at the core of our investigation into Wright's approach to modernity. The performed role of racial subservience becomes a weapon in Tyree's hands; "the harpoon of his emotional claims" sunk "into the white man's heart."[90] The capacity to draw this volatile compassion from the whites is something that Wright traces explicitly back to the master/slave relationship which lived on as a central structuring feature of social life in Mississippi:

> With all the strength of his being, the slave was fighting the master. Fishbelly saw that the terrible stare in the chief's eyes was so evenly divided between hate and pity that he did not know what the chief would do; the chief could just have easily drawn his gun and shot Tyree as he could have embraced him . . . Tyree began timing his moves; he hung his head, his lowered eyes watching the emotionally wrought-up white man like a cat following the scurryings of a cornered mouse. The chief turned, not looking at anything or anybody. Fishbelly knew that Tyree was weighing whether to act further; then he sniffled and remained silent.[91]

These performances induce an ambivalence in the whites they are aimed at which parallels the attraction and repulsion that the blacks feel for whites and whiteness and culminates in a peculiar symbiosis. Wright was not suggesting that blacks were equally responsible with whites for this state of affairs, but he underscored the extent to which their fates, like their histories, were interlinked. This was further explored through one critical episode in Tyree's induction of his son into the distinctive rhythms of black male adulthood. Chris, a young black man whom Tyree has looked up to, is lynched as a result of his apparently consensual involvement with a white woman. Tyree, in his role as the town's undertaker, discusses the meaning of this ritual terror with his partner in corruption, the local doctor. Together the two older men try to propel the boy into emotional and psychological majority through a grisly confrontation with the mutilated corpse. This is the first of Fishbelly's several formative encounters with death:

> "The genitalia are gone," the doctor intoned.
> Fishbelly saw a dark coagulated blot in a gaping hole between the thighs and, with defensive reflex, he lowered his hands nervously to his groin . . .
> "Killing him wasn't enough. They had to mutilate 'im. You'd think

that disgust would've made them leave that part of the black boy alone
. . . No! To get the chance to mutilate 'im was part of why they killed
'im. And you can bet a lot of white women were watching eagerly
when they did it . . ."

"You have to be terribly attracted to a person, almost in love with
'im to mangle 'im in this manner. They hate us, Tyree, but they love
us too; in a perverted sort of way, they love us—"[92]

Analysis of Wright's legacy has been impoverished as a result of his being
overidentified with the same narrow definitions of racialised cultural expression that he struggled to overturn. The part of his work which resists
assimilation to the great ethnocentric canon of African-American literature
have been left unread, and much of it is now out of print. On either side
of the Atlantic, historians of European literature and philosophy have
shown little interest in his work or in its relationship to those European
writers and schools of expression with whom he interacted. For example,
Simone de Beauvoir may have acknowledged the impact of his understanding of race and racism on her capacity to conceive *The Second Sex,* but the
implications of this connection for contemporary politics remains unex-
plored and undervalued.[93] Historians of ideas and movements have generally preferred to stay within the boundaries of nationality and ethnicity and
have shown little enthusiasm for connecting the life of one movement with
that of another. What would it mean to read Wright intertextually with
Genet, Beauvoir, Sartre, and the other Parisians with whom he was in dialogue?

Examining his route from the particular to the general, from America
to Europe and Africa, would certainly get us out of a position where we
have to choose between the unsatisfactory alternatives of Eurocentrism
and black nationalism. The first ignores Wright, the second says that everything that happened to him after he left America is worthless for the
schemes of black liberation. Wright was neither an affiliate of western
metaphysics who just happened to be black nor an ethnic African-
American whose essential African identity asserted itself to animate his
comprehensive critique of western radicalism. Perhaps more than any other
writer he showed how modernity was both the period and the region in
which black politics grew. His work articulates simultaneously an affirmation and a negation of the western civilisation that formed him. It remains
the most powerful expression of the insider-outsider duality which we have
traced down the years from slavery.

6

"Not a Story to Pass On": Living Memory and the Slave Sublime

Slavery was a terrible thing, but when black people in America finally got out from under that crushing system, they were stronger. They knew what it was to have your spirit crippled by people who are controlling your life. They were never going to let that happen again. I admire that kind of strength. People who have it take a stand and put their blood and soul into what they believe.

> *Michael Jackson*

To articulate the past historically does not mean to recognise it "the way it really was." It means to seize hold of a memory as it flashes up in a moment of danger. Historical materialism wishes to retain that image of the past which unexpectedly appears to man singled out by history at a moment of danger. The danger affects both the content of the tradition and its receivers. The same threat hangs over both: that of becoming a tool of the ruling classes. In every era the attempt must be made anew to wrest tradition away from a conformism that is about to overpower it. The Messiah comes not only as the redeemer, he comes as the subduer of Antichrist. Only that historian will have the gift of fanning the spark of hope in the past who is firmly convinced that even the dead will not be safe from the enemy if he wins. And this enemy has not ceased to be victorious.

> *Walter Benjamin*

THE IDEA OF tradition has a strange, mesmeric power in black political discourse. Considering its special force and usage seems an appropriate operation with which to begin the end of a book about blacks and modernity. Tradition crops up frequently in the cultural criticism that has cultivated a dialogue with black political discourse. It operates as a means to assert the close kinship of cultural forms and practices generated from the irrepressible diversity of black experience. This suggests that, in the hands of some black intellectuals and artists at least, the pursuit of social and political autonomy has turned away from the promise of modernity and found new expression in a complex term that is often understood to be modernity's antithesis. This can be explained partly through the threat which the maelstrom of modernity poses to the stability and coherence of the racial self. That self can be safely cultivated and remain secure behind the closed shutters of black particularity while the storms rage outside. We have already examined the work of several black writers who held out against this form of retreat and opted instead to embrace the fragmentation of self (doubling and splitting) which modernity seems to promote. However, this option is less fashionable these days. Appeals to the notion of purity as the basis of racial solidarity are more popular. These appeals are often anchored in ideas of invariant tradition and provisioned equally by positivistic certainty and an idea of politics as a therapeutic activity. The first aim of this chapter is to rethink the concept of tradition so that it can no longer function as modernity's polar opposite. This necessitates a brief discussion of the idea of Africentricity,[1] which may be useful in developing communal discipline and individual self-worth and even in galvanising black communities to resist the encroachments of crack cocaine, but which supplies a poor basis for the writing of cultural history and the calculation of political choices. The Africentric project has an absolute and perverse reliance on a model of the thinking, knowing racial subject which is a long way away from the double consciousness that fascinated black modernists. Its European, Cartesian outlines remain visible beneath a new lick of Kemetic paint: "Afrocentricity is African genius and African values created, recreated, reconstructed, and derived from our history and experiences in our best interests . . . It is an uncovering of one's true self, it is the pinpointing of one's centre, and it is the clarity and focus through which black people *must* see the world in order to escalate"[2] (emphasis added).

The idea of tradition gets understandably invoked to underscore the historical continuities, subcultural conversations, intertextual and intercultural cross-fertilisations which make the notion of a distinctive and self-conscious black culture appear plausible. This usage is important and inescapable because racisms work insidiously and consistently to deny both historicity and cultural integrity to the artistic and cultural fruits of black life. The discourse of tradition is thus frequently articulated within the critiques of modernity produced by blacks in the West. It is certainly audible inside the racialised countercultures to which modernity gave birth. However, the idea of tradition is often also the culmination, or centre-piece, of a rhetorical gesture that asserts the legitimacy of a black political culture locked in a defensive posture against the unjust powers of white supremacy. This gesture sets tradition and modernity against each other as simple polar alternatives as starkly differentiated and oppositional as the signs black and white. In these conditions, where obsessions with origin and myth can rule contemporary political concerns and the fine grain of history, the idea of tradition can constitute a refuge. It provides a temporary home in which shelter and consolation from the vicious forces that threaten the racial community (imagined or otherwise) can be found. It is interesting that in this understanding of the position of blacks in the modern, western world, the door to tradition remains wedged open not by the memory of modern racial slavery but in spite of it. Slavery is the site of black victimage and thus of tradition's intended erasure. When the emphasis shifts towards the elements of invariant tradition that heroically survive slavery, any desire to remember slavery itself becomes something of an obstacle. It seems as if the complexity of slavery and its location within modernity has to be actively forgotten if a clear orientation to tradition and thus to the present circumstances of blacks is to be acquired. Rebel MC's moving assertion in his track "Soul Rebel" that "there's more than just slavery to the history, we have dignity"[3] typifies the best of these revisionist impulses. However, there is a danger that, apart from the archaeology of traditional survivals, slavery becomes a cluster of negative associations that are best left behind. The history of the plantations and sugar mills supposedly offers little that is valuable when compared to the ornate conceptions of African antiquity against which they are unfavourably compared. Blacks are urged, if not to forget the slave experience which appears as an aberration from the story of greatness told in African history, then to replace it at the centre of our thinking with a mystical and ruthlessly positive notion of Africa that is indifferent to intraracial variation and is frozen at the point where blacks boarded the ships that would carry them into the woes and horrors of the middle passage. Asante dismisses the idea of racial identity as a locally specific, social, and historical construction by associating it with the outmoded and pejorative term "Negro":

> One cannot study Africans in the United States or Brazil or Jamaica without some appreciation for the historical and cultural significance of Africa as source and origin. A reactionary posture which claims Africology as "African Slave Studies" is rejected outright because it disconnects the African in America from thousands of years of history and tradition. Thus, if one concentrates on studying Africans in the inner cities of the Northeast United States, which is reasonable, it must be done with the idea in the back of the mind that one is studying African people, not "made-in-America Negroes" without historical depth.[4]

Worse than this, black people are urged to find psychological and philosophical nourishment in the narrative of Africa expressed in rewritten accounts of civilisation's development from its African sources or the spurious security of knowing that our melanin provides us with a measure of biological superiority.[5]

Slavery, which is so deeply embedded in modernity, gets forgotten and the duration of a black civilisation anterior to modernity is invoked in its place: "Our anteriority is only significant because it re-affirms for us that if we once organized complex civilizations all over the continent of Africa, we can take those traditions and generate more advanced ideas."[6] This statement, also taken from the revised edition of *Afrocentricity,* is striking both for its tacit acceptance of the idea of progress and for the easy, instrumental relationship with tradition which it suggests. This gesture minimises the difficulties involved in locating tradition let alone transforming it. It is routinely complemented by the argument that the unique civilisation to which the West lays claim is itself the product of African civilisation. Cheik Anta Diop, George James, and others have demonstrated the power of these claims which even in their crudest form have the virtue of demystifying and rejecting "European particularism" dressed up "as universal."[7] A discussion of the extent to which these historiographical and linguistic claims can be substantiated would be a distraction here. The difficulties involved in projecting the typologies of modern racism back into a past where they are wholly irrelevant can be illustrated through the problems that arise in attempts to name the Egyptians black according to contemporary definitions rather than seeing them as one African people among many others. Martin Bernal's detailed reconstruction of the Hellenistic cults which articulated racism and anti-Semitism into nineteenth-century scholarship is a rare exception in a literature where some Africentric thinkers have come to share the historical assumptions and techniques of eighteenth-century racial metaphysics with their opponents.

Dealing equally with the significance of roots and routes, as I proposed in Chapter 1, should undermine the purified appeal of either Africentrism or the Eurocentrisms it struggles to answer. This book has been more concerned with the flows, exchanges, and in-between elements that call the very desire to be centred into question. By seeking to problematise the relationship between tradition and modernity, this chapter turns attention toward the particular conceptions of time that emerge in black political culture from Delany on. The desire to bring a new historicity into black political culture is more important than the vehicles that have been chosen to bring this end about.

The Africentric movement appears to rely upon a linear idea of time[8] that is enclosed at each end by the grand narrative of African advancement. This is momentarily interrupted by slavery and colonialism, which make no substantial impact upon African tradition or the capacity of black intellectuals to align themselves with it. The anteriority of African civilisation to western civilisation is asserted not in order to escape this linear time but in order to claim it and thus subordinate its narrative of civilisation to a different set of political interests without even attempting to change the terms themselves. The logic and categories of racial metaphysics are undisturbed but the relationship between the terms is inverted. Blacks become dominant by virtue of either biology or culture; whites are allocated a subordinate role. The desperate manner in which this inversion proceeds betrays it as merely another symptom of white supremacy's continuing power.

The idea of ready access to and command of tradition—sometimes ancient, always anti-modern—has become essential to the disciplinary mechanisms that today's stern traditionalists seek to exercise over diverse processes of black cultural production. Tradition provides the critical bond between the local attributes of cultural forms and styles and their African origins. The intervening history in which tradition and modernity come together, interact, and conflict is set aside along with the consequent implications of this process for the mediation of African purity. Tradition thus becomes the means to demonstrate the contiguity of selected contemporary phenomena with an African past that shaped them but which they no longer recognise and only slightly resemble. Africa is retained as one special measure of their authenticity. The enthusiasm for tradition therefore expresses not so much the ambivalence of blacks towards modernity, but the fallout from modernity's protracted ambivalence towards the blacks who haunt its dreams of ordered civilisation.

These features in the use of the term "tradition" take it outside of the erratic flows of history. In the work of some African-American writers, they sometimes sanction a crucial and regrettable slippage from the vernacular and the popular to the provincial and the parochial. In this sense what is known as Africentricity might be more properly called Americocentricity. Its proponents frequently struggle to place their histories onto a bigger diaspora web[9] but have no inhibitions about claiming a special status for their particular version of African culture.[10] It might be possible to demonstrate that the trope of family which is such a recurrent feature of their discourse is itself a characteristically American means for comprehending the limits and dynamics of racial community.[11]

In the light of these problems, this concluding chapter tries to integrate the *spatial* focus on the diaspora idea that has dominated earlier sections of this book with the diaspora temporality and historicity, memory and narrativity that are the articulating principles of the black political countercultures that grew inside modernity in a distinctive relationship of antagonistic indebtedness. It proceeds by querying the importance that has become attached to the idea of tradition in this area of cultural critique, history, and politics. In moving toward a different and more modest for-

mulation of tradition, it asks initially whether the premium placed on duration and generation can itself be read as a response to the turbulent patterns of modern social life that have taken blacks from Africa via slavery
into an incompletely realised democracy that racialises and thus frequently
withholds the loudly proclaimed benefits of modern citizenship.

In the previous chapter, we encountered Richard Wright emphasising
that tradition "is no longer a guide" for the creative aspirations of black
artists. The idea that there might be a single, straight road from tradition
to modernity was both repudiated and rehabilitated by Wright. His confusion is symptomatic of more than his own ambivalence towards modernity
and the precise sense of modernity's aporias that we have already seen gov-
erning the radical political movements in which he located himself. For
him, in America or Europe, modernity emerged at best as a fleeting respite
from the barbarity that is endemic to human civilisation. This barbarity is
underlined not only by slavery but by the brutal and unjust social order of
the Jim Crow South where he grew up. However, as his grasp of the fatal
complicity of technology and imperialism evolved in conjunction with his
involvement with Africa and anti-colonial struggles, Wright's position
shifted in that he grew to identify the forces of tradition explicitly as an
enemy. They fetter black progress towards the limited, unjust, and incomplete democracy that may be the best outcome currently available. The
West is bound to pursue new modes of unfreedom, and, recognising the
dangers involved, Wright urged the "developing countries" to experiment
with their history and autonomy and undertake a gamble against making
the same catastrophic mistakes that had emerged from modernisation elsewhere. The open letter to Kwame Nkrumah which concludes his important and neglected book *Black Power* is a piece of writing that seems
to re-engage with the issues of tradition and modernity that aroused his
nineteenth-century predecessors. However, Wright's observations are
made from an irreversibly post-colonial vantage point:

> Above all feel free to improvise! The political cat can be skinned in
> many fashions; the building of that bridge between tribal man and the
> twentieth century can be done in a score of ways . . . AFRICAN LIFE
> MUST BE MILITARISED!
>   . . . not for war, but for peace; not for destruction but for service;
> not for aggression, but for production; not for despotism, but to free
> minds from mumbo jumbo.[12]

Similarly sceptical views of the value of the premodern can be glimpsed
periodically in the work of the other writers, artists, and cultural activists
whose work this book has cited or examined. But their distaste for the
"mumbo jumbo" of traditional societies is complex and contradictory.

Some nineteenth-century thinkers saw a means to redeem Africa through colonisation. Their love of English was profound and their ambivalence about the African's capacity for civilisation merits extended consideration. Some romanticised Africa as a homeland and a source of Negro sensibility, others didn't. Any scepticism born from their reflections on African barbarism can be matched precisely to the enthusiasms which other "new world" blacks have shown for the stable forms of social life that are identified with the image of the premodern African idyll. These responses to Africa transcode a debate about the value of western modernity that stretches down the years from Delany's railway-building schemes through Crummell's and Blyden's activities in Liberia via Du Bois and Wright in Ghana to contemporary disputes over the contending values of traditional and universal cultures.

In recent years the affirmative, pro-traditional side of this dispute has extended into the active reinvention of the rituals and rites of lost African traditions. African names are acquired and African garments are worn. It can be argued in support of these practices that the bodily fruits of imagined African sensibility can provide a bulwark against the corrosive effects of racism, poverty, and immiseration on individuals and communities. But it is deeply significant that ideas about masculinity, femininity, and sexuality are so prominent in this redemptive journey back to Africa. In a discussion of Kwanzaa, the invented traditional ritual substitute for Christmas, Dr. Maulana Karenga, an important architect of this political position, presents its value through the ideas of rescue and reconstruction: "As cultural nationalists, we believe that you must rescue and reconstruct African history and culture to re-vitalize African culture today . . . Kwanzaa became a way of doing just that. I wanted to stress the need for a reorientation of values, to borrow the collective life-affirming ones from our past and use them to enrich our present."[13]

This rescuing and reconstructive consciousness reaches it highest point of expression so far in Shahrazad Ali's best-selling book *The Blackman's Guide to Understanding the Blackwoman*, where the reconstruction of an appropriately gendered self becomes the sine qua non of communal rehabilitation:

> When the Blackwoman accepts her rightful place as queen of the universe and mother of civilization the Blackman will regenerate his powers that have been lost to him for over 400 years directly. The Blackwoman should not mimic the ideas and attitudes of Western civilization. The whiteman clearly understands that the preservation of the family order is what allows him to rule the world. This fact is not hidden knowledge. When the standards that preserve civilization

are disregarded the result is a do-your-own-thing reckless and disorganized existence.[14]

Similar ideas about the interrelationship of time, generation, authenticity, and political authority animate the belief that the contemporary political and economic crises of blacks in the West are basically crises of self-belief and racial identity. They can be rectified by therapeutic strategies that find their ready equivalent in Delany's proposals for racial uplift. These crises are most intensely lived in the area of gender relations where the symbolic reconstruction of community is projected onto an image of the ideal heterosexual couple. The patriarchal family is the preferred institution capable of reproducing the traditional roles, cultures, and sensibilities that can solve this state of affairs.[15] However, where it is not thought to be reconstructable, the same ideas underpin controversial policy proposals like the demand for special schools in which black boys, under the guidance of "positive male role models,"[16] can receive the culturally appropriate forms of education that will equip them for life as fine, upstanding specimens of black manhood, "the true backbone of the people," capable of leading the community to its rightful position. The integrity of the race is thus made interchangeable with the integrity of black masculinity, which must be regenerated at all costs. This results in a situation where the social and economic crises of entire communities become most easily intelligible to those they engulf as a protracted crisis of masculinity.[17] Without wanting to undermine struggles over the meaning of black masculinity and its sometimes destructive and anti-communitarian consequences, it seems important to reckon with the limitations of a perspective which seeks to restore masculinity rather than work carefully towards something like its transcendence. There is a notable though often inarticulate tension between therapeutic tactics like Ali's that are premised on the regeneration or recovery of tradition and their global circulation through the most sophisticated means that technological postmodernity can furnish. This is especially obvious where transnational entertainment corporations unwittingly supply a vehicle for circulating these ideas in the form of black popular music. These means of distribution are capable of dissolving distance and creating new and unpredictable forms of identification and cultural affinity between groups that dwell far apart. The transformation of cultural space and the subordination of distance are only two factors that contribute to a parallel change in the significance of appeals to tradition, time, and history. In particular, the invocation of tradition becomes both more desperate and more politically charged as the sheer irrepressible heterology of black cultures becomes harder to avoid.

For those of us endeavouring to make sense of these questions from black Atlantic rather than African-American perspectives, it is particularly important that this problem of tradition, modernity, and their respective temporalities was directly confronted in the political activities around the journal *Présence Africaine*. Its formation in 1947 was an important moment in the developing awareness of the African diaspora as a transnational and intercultural multiplicity. The journal sought to synchronise the activities of Africanists and Africans with blacks from the western hemisphere in a new and potent anti-imperialist configuration. It was especially central to their second Congress of Negro Writers and Artists, held in Rome in 1959 but planned and organised from Paris.[18] The central themes of this conference were the unity of "Negro Culture" and the creative political responsibilities which fell upon the caste of black intellectuals responsible for both demonstrating and reproducing that unity. The proposed plan of the event (which bears Richard Wright's characteristic imprint) and its published proceedings[19] demonstrate that the unity of culture was not thought to be guaranteed by the enduring force of a common African heritage. That heritage was to be acknowledged wherever it could be identified and is explored in the conference proceedings across a number of different disciplines—from palaeontology to theology—but other discontinuous and contemporary dimensions of the looked-for "racial" unity were also specified. The "Colonial experience" was, for example, identified as an additional source of cultural synthesis and convergence. This key term was used broadly so as to include slavery, colonialism, racial discrimination, and the rise of national(ist) consciousness(es) charged with colonialism's negation. Lastly, the technological economic, political, and cultural dynamics of modernisation were identified by the conference planners as factors that were fostering the unity of black cultures by forcing them to conform to a particular rhythm of living.

Rough as it is, this threefold model seems to me to be significantly in advance of some of the contemporary approaches to the same problem of calculating the unity and diversity of black cultures. These days, the power of the African heritage is frequently asserted as if interpretation were unnecessary and translation redundant. The different flavour of the event in Rome was conveyed in the remarks given at its opening session by Alioune Diop, the Senegalese who is regularly identified as having initiated the *Présence Africaine* project. He began by exploring the significance of the congress's location for the meaning of the event:

If it be true that we can bring out the features of our personality only through a dialogue with the West, what better representative spokesman for the West could we find than Paris or Rome? . . . These cities are responsible for that image of man which presided over the construction of the world; not necessarily man as he should be, but such as he is, portrayed in the beliefs of those who rule the world. It is according to definitions, principles and objectives of Western Culture that our lives are evaluated and controlled. We have every reason to pay attention to the evolution of Western Culture and to its inner laws. Ought we not then to seek, before the eyes of these cultural authorities, to uncover and set free the original outline and the inherent driving force of our personality?

We are scattered over the four corners of the world, according to the dictates of Western hegemony . . . The effect of an African presence in the world will be to increase the wealth of human awareness and . . . to foster man's sensibility with richer and more human values, rhythms and themes . . .[20]

The ambivalence towards the West which these words convey is easier to bring into focus than the way that they communicate a tension around the teleology of black experience and the registering of time itself. Diaspora time is not, it would seem, African time. The words "original" and "inherent" belong to one cultural field while "evolution" and "scattered" operate in a different plane. Bringing them together requires a stereoscopic sensibility adequate to building a dialogue with the West: within and without.

What's the Time? Nation Time!

Habermas is suggestive in initiating his enquiries into the philosophical discourse of modernity with an examination of its specific consciousness of time.[21] Of course, the concepts of modernisation and modernity raise the problem of time and time-consciousness directly if only because the issue of where it might be possible to identify a line between the present and the past which constitutes it becomes an integral part of enlightenment understanding of progress and social development. Fredric Jameson usefully complicates this further with his observation that a fascination with the workings of existential time and deep memory are a definitive characteristic of the high modern.[22] Perhaps, one day, theories of black literary modernism will have to reckon with the issues of urban synchronicity, memory, and identity transcoded from Joyce's Dublin to Wright's Chicago in the novel *Lawd Today*. While the emphasis falls on modernity as a context for the elaboration of black political culture, it is more important to reckon with the tension between temporalities that leads intellectuals to try to press original African time into the service of their attempts to come to terms with diaspora space and its dynamics of differentiation.

This genealogy of black intellectuals' attempts at rewriting modernity has required me to operate a more ambitious understanding of modernity than the minimal definition that identifies the term simply with the consciousness of the novelty of the present. It is worth emphasising that part of the overall argument of this book is that much of the material discussed here does not fit unambiguously into a time-consciousness derived from and punctuated exclusively by changes in the public, urban worlds of London, Berlin, and Paris. Writers, particularly those closest to the slave experience, repudiated the heroic narrative of western civilisation and used a philosophically informed approach to slavery in order to undermine the monumental time that supports it. Whatever their disagreements about the teleology of black emancipation, Du Bois, Douglass, Wright, and the rest shared a sense that the modern world was fragmented along axes constituted by racial conflict and could accommodate non-synchronous, heterocultural modes of social life in close proximity. Their conceptions of modernity were periodised differently. They were founded on the catastrophic rupture of the middle passage rather than the dream of revolutionary transformation. They were punctuated by the processes of acculturation and terror that followed that catastrophe and by the countercultural aspirations towards freedom, citizenship, and autonomy that developed after it among slaves and their descendants.

In the work of those thinkers and in the black vernacular that surrounds and sometimes threatens to engulf it, temporality and history are marked out publicly in ritualised ways that constitute communities of sentiment and interpretation. The manner in which different sets of ideas about the relationship of past and present, living and dead, traditional and modern, coexist and conflict is another pointer to the problems with modernity that I have tried to suspend while using the concept heuristically and testing it against the content of its black countercultures. I have probably reached the point at which this conflict over modernity can no longer be held outside my text. The redefinition of tradition towards which this chapter is moving also requires a shift in understanding modernity. To put it another way, it matters a great deal whether modern racial slavery is identified as a repository in which the consciousness of traditional culture could be secreted and condensed into ever more potent forms or seen alternatively as the site of premodern tradition's most comprehensive erasure. Similarly, it matters whether modern rationality sanctions or subverts the unfreedoms of the slave system it helped to sanction. These problems are even more pronounced because arguments over where the line between past and present can be drawn continue to be a source of fundamental and valuable tensions inside black cultures. The idea of diaspora might itself be understood as a response to these promptings—a utopian eruption of space into the linear temporal order of modern black politics which enforces the obligation that space and time must be considered relationally in their interarticulation with racialised being. This can be illuminated by going back momentarily to what I described at the end of Chapter 2 as the turn towards death, which appeared again in the exploration of Du Bois's *The Souls of Black Folk*. It ushers in the vital questions of what is viable and what is not, where new beginnings have been identified and consequently where new modes of recollection are deemed to be necessary. The relationship between tradition, modernity, temporality, and social memory is the theme which organises the remainder of this chapter.

The turn towards death also points to the ways in which black cultural forms have hosted and even cultivated a dynamic rapport with the presence of death and suffering. This has generated specific modes of expression and some vernacular philosophical preoccupations that are absolutely antagonistic to the enlightenment assumptions with which they have had to compete for the attention of the black public. We will explore below some additional examples of how that rapport with death emerges continually in the literature and expressive cultures of the black Atlantic. It is integral, for example, to the narratives of loss, exile, and journeying which, like particular elements of musical performance, serve a mnemonic function: directing the consciousness of the group back to significant, nodal points in its common history and its social memory. The telling and retelling of these stories plays a special role, organising the consciousness of the "racial" group socially and striking the important balance between inside and outside activity—the different practices, cognitive, habitual, and performative, that are required to invent, maintain, and renew identity. These have constituted the black Atlantic as a non-traditional tradition, an irreducibly modern, ex-centric, unstable, and asymmetrical cultural ensemble that cannot be apprehended through the manichean logic of binary coding. Even when the network used to communicate its volatile contents has been an adjunct to the sale of black popular music, there is a direct relationship between the community of listeners constructed in the course of using that musical culture and the constitution of a tradition that is redefined here as the living memory of the changing same.[23]

The term "tradition" is now being used neither to identify a lost past nor to name a culture of compensation that would restore access to it. It does not stand in opposition to modernity, nor should it conjure up wholesome images of Africa that can be contrasted with the corrosive, aphasic

power of the post-slave history of the Americas and the extended Caribbean. We have already seen in Chapter 3 that the circulation and mutation
of music across the black Atlantic explodes the dualistic structure which
puts Africa, authenticity, purity, and origin in crude opposition to the
Americas, hybridity, creolisation, and rootlessness. There has been (at
least) a two-way traffic between African cultural forms and the political
cultures of diaspora blacks over a long period. We could shift here from
the chronotope of the road to the chronotope of the crossroads in order
better to appreciate intercultural details like those revealed by James
Brown's description of the elements that he recognised as his own in the
music of West African musicians during the 1960s:

> While we were in Lagos we visited Fela Ransome Kuti's club the Afro
> Spot, to hear him and his band. He'd come to hear us, and we came
> to hear him. I think when he started as a musician he was playing a
> kind of music they call Highlife, but by this time he was developing
> Afro-beat out of African music and funk. He was kind of like the Afri-
> can James Brown. His band had strong rhythm; I think Clyde picked
> up on it in his drumming, and Bootsy dug it too. Some of the ideas
> my band was getting from that band had come from me in the first
> place, but that was okay with me. It made the music that much
> stronger.[24]

The mutation of jazz and African-American cultural style in the town-
ships of South Africa and the syncretised evolution of Caribbean and British reggae music and Rastafari culture in Zimbabwe could be used to supply further evidence.[25] Bearing in mind the significance of the Jubilee
Singers and their odyssey, it is also important to recall the adventures of
Orpheus Myron McAdoo's spin-off from the original group: his Virginia
Jubilee Singers toured extensively in South Africa for five years between
1890 and 1898.[26] Additional examples can be provided by the impact, on
what is thought of as authentic African culture, of music played by the
slaves who returned to Nigeria from Brazil in the 1840s.[27] All of them are
untidy elements in a story of hybridisation and intermixture that inevitably
disappoints the desire for cultural and therefore racial purity, whatever its
source. With these and other illustrations in mind, it may make sense to
try and reserve the idea of tradition for the nameless, evasive, minimal qualities that make these diaspora conversations possible. This would involve
keeping the term as a way to speak about the apparently magical processes
of connectedness that arise as much from the transformation of Africa by
diaspora cultures as from the affiliation of diaspora cultures to Africa and
the traces of Africa that those diaspora cultures enclose.

It is most appropriate that music supplies the best illustrations of these complex dynamics because, in this vernacular, listening to music is not associated with passivity. The most enduring Africanism of all is not therefore specifiable as the content of black Atlantic cultures. It can be seen instead not just in the central place that all these cultures give to music use and music making, but in the ubiquity of antiphonal,[28] social forms that underpin and enclose the plurality of black cultures in the western hemisphere. A relationship of identity is enacted in the way that the performer dissolves into the crowd. Together, they collaborate in a creative process governed by formal and informal, democratic rules. The performer takes on a communicative role comparable to the role of the storyteller which Walter Benjamin mourns because it has departed from a social order that organises its remembrance in novel ways premised on the fact that the gift for listening is lost and the community of listeners has disappeared.[29]

These rescuing interventions into vernacular culture are orchestrated in active, dynamic processes. Whether sacred or profane, the use of music provides the most important locations in which these rituals take place. The church and its secular equivalents nurtured a caste of performers capable of dramatising them and the identity-giving model of democracy/community that has become the valuable intersubjective resource that I call the ethics of antiphony.

Stories are told, both with and without music. More important than their content is the fact that during the process of performance the dramatic power of narrative as a form is celebrated. The simple *content* of the stories is dominated by the ritual act of story-telling itself. This involves a very particular use of language and a special cultural dynamics. Here we have to deal with the dramaturgy of performing these stories and the rituals that structure their reception. They were, of course, initially stories taken from the Bible. Stories of slavery and escape from bondage blasted out of their former place in the continuum of history by Africans and then reaccentuated as an integral part of their struggles in the West. Both story-telling and music-making contributed to an alternative public sphere, and this in turn provided the context in which the particular styles of autobiographical self-dramatisation and public self-construction have been formed and circulated as an integral component of insubordinate racial countercultures. It may be secondary to the antiphonic rituals which constitute community and make the claims of closed tradition seem plausible, but the content of the stories is still significant precisely because it turns so sharply away from the commemoration of slavery itself. The status of this social story-telling activity has changed as the novel has become a more important genre, reducing the power of autobiography and altering the idea of tradition as the relationship between orality and literacy has itself been transformed.

The stories of escape from slavery, the redemptive power of suffering, and the triumphs of the weak over the strong that dominated respectable black cultural production during the nineteenth century gave way gradually to a different variety of story altogether. Comprehending this change requires more than an account of the rise of the novel and the use made of that form by black writers whose command of it demanded an acknowledgement of their imaginative humanity. The power of the text was qualified and contextualised by the emergence of a more significant counterpower in the medium of black popular culture, what we can call, following Houston A. Baker, Jr., the tactics of sound developed as a form of black metacommunication in a cultural repertoire increasingly dominated by music, dance, and performance.

Love Wars and Sexual Healing: A Displaced Poetics of Subordination

The history of these expressive cultures in the black Atlantic is too huge to be captured here in a few—inevitably general—sentences. Instead, I want to explore the fact that the stories which constitute these communities of interpretation and sentiment are not usually commentaries on the experience of social subordination. I want to turn away from analysis of the recognisably political discourse enunciated by this vernacular culture[30] and address instead the fact that the stories which dominate black popular culture are usually love stories or more appropriately love and loss stories. That they assume this form is all the more striking because the new genre seems to express a cultural decision not to transmit details of the ordeal of slavery openly in story and song. Yet these narratives of love and loss systematically transcode other forms of yearning and mourning associated with histories of dispersal and exile and the remembrance of unspeakable terror.

Watching and taking pleasure in the way that African-American and Caribbean singers could win over London crowds and dissolve the distance and difference that diaspora makes through the mimetic representation of an essential black sexuality which knew no borders led me to the puzzle that was briefly introduced in Chapter 3 above. In the context of a discussion of racial authenticity I suggested that some of the most powerful components of what we experience as racial identity are regularly and frequently drawn from deeply held gender identities, particular ideas about sexuality and a dogged belief that experiencing the conflict between men and women at a special pitch is itself expressive of racial difference. This is not the only source of ideas about black subjectivity but it is often the most powerful one. However tendentious it may sound, I believe that it regularly outweighs the significance of racism and its centripetal effects on the constitution of racial communities. In his discussion of the blues, Charles Keil quotes Al Hibbler's definition of the experiential attributes of black male creativity in this musical milieu. Hibbler's list contains three items, offered, we are told, in the order of importance: "having been hurt by a woman, being brought up in that old time religion and knowing what that slavery shit is all about."[31] Keil struggles to account for the priority given to injuries won in the love wars between black men and women in this exposition of the capacity to perform rhythm and blues. The vigour with which this combatively profane art treats upon the themes of guilt, suffering, and reconciliation supplies further clues confirming that it is more than a theodicy. It can be interpreted instead both as a process of identity construction and as an affirmation of racialised being at its most intensely felt. It specifies the boundaries not of community but of sameness by introducing a syncopated temporality—a different rhythm of living and being in which "the night time is the right time" and, as both George Clinton and James Brown have put it, "everything is on The One."[32] Ralph Ellison describes the effects of this temporal disjunction thus: "Invisibility, let me explain, gives one a slightly different sense of time, you're never quite on the beat. Sometimes you're ahead and sometimes behind. Instead of the swift and imperceptible flowing of time, you are aware of its nodes, those points where time stands still or from which it leaps ahead. And you slip into the breaks and look around."[33]

A precious sense of black particularity gets constructed from several interlocking themes that culminate in this unexpected time signature. They supply the accents, rests, breaks, *and* tones that make the performance of racial identity possible. The most obvious is a discourse on the process of racial subordination itself, what might be called a discourse on The Other. I have analysed this elsewhere as both a response to racism and an instance of the anti-capitalist character of modern black politics.[34] My argument here, which is best understood as a complement to the earlier discussion, suggests a different emphasis: it requires attention to the discourse of The Same—a homology—which, coexisting with its more recognisably political counterpart, helps to fix and to stabilise the boundaries of the closed racial community. Together they draw the line between past and present which is so important in black expressive cultures. They skirt the sterile opposition between tradition and modernity by asserting the irreducible priority of the present. That priority is then employed to cultivate a sense of agency which is elaborated in the sacred rituals of the black church and its profane equivalents which sprang up where an extremely specific form of the opposition between public and private cut through the slave quarters. The profane, some would say nihilistic, aspects of the black vernacular are especially valuable because they have supplied a means to think black sociality outside of patterns derived from either family- or church-based forms of kinship and community. They build on the old patterns of talk about sex, sexuality, and gender-based antagonisms that Richard Wright identified as "the forms of things unknown." This profane dialogue between and about black women and men[35] operates by strict genre rules. It establishes the priority of the personal, intimate, and non-work rhythm of everyday living and uses that focus to institute a community or constituency of active listeners that is scarcely distinguishable in its effects from the more saintly one which the church supplies. The sacred and the profane come together in musical events where their differences dissolve into the sublime and the ineffable. The link between this music and distinct conceptions of time that have a special political and philosophical significance is well made by James Baldwin: "Music is our witness, and our ally. The beat is the confession which recognises, changes and conquers time. Then, history becomes a garment we can wear and share, and not a cloak in which to hide; and time becomes a friend."[36]

It seems important to emphasise that the power of music and sound are receding not just relative to the power of the text and the performer but also as the relentless power of visual cultures expands. The emergent culture of the black image offers no comparable experience of performance with which to focus the pivotal ethical relationship between performer and crowd, participant and community. But this music and its broken rhythm of life are important for another reason. The love stories they enclose are a place in which the black vernacular has been able to preserve and cultivate both the distinctive rapport with the presence of death which derives from slavery and a related ontological state that I want to call the condition of being in pain. Being in pain encompasses both a radical, personalised enregistration of time and a diachronic understanding of language whose most enduring effects are the games black people in all western cultures play with names and naming. It is what Wright struggled to describe when, in his lecture on Negro literature in the United States, he spoke of a "tradition of bitterness . . . so complex, [which] was to assume such a tight, organic form that most white people would think upon examining it, that most Negroes had embedded in their flesh and bones some peculiar propensity towards lamenting and complaining."[37]

Examples of being in pain drawn from black music are simply too numerous to explore. Robert Johnson's "When You Got a Good Friend" and Billie Holiday's "God Bless the Child" spring immediately to mind along with the secret aesthetic codes that govern the pleasures of listening to Miles Davis play or Donny Hathaway and Esther Phillips sing. To fix the concept I shall employ only one example, drawn from the era in which rhythm and blues was born, marking a new stage in the mutation and internationalisation of African-American culture. It appears in the work of Percy Mayfield, a little-known songwriter and performer recognised, if at all, for penning "Hit the Road Jack" for Ray Charles in 1960[38] and for writing the standards "Strange Things Are Happening" and "Please Send Me Someone to Love." Mayfield conveyed something of the density of his craft in an interview where he commented on the fact that "Please Send Me Someone to Love" (his favourite song) was often mistaken for a love song when in fact it was a sacred one:

> . . . it's a prayer. I wrote it as a prayer for peace. See, let me explain something to you. You see a lot of people thought I was saying please send me a woman. When the mere average man sing it, he's impressing that he need a woman. When a woman sing it, she's tryin' to impress up on you that she need a man. But I was prayin' see. I was talkin' for the world. I wasn't talkin' about a mere woman . . . I was prayin' "Heaven please send to all mankind . . ." Martin Luther King, he came through and preached it. Love is the master of hate, you know what I mean? But he was walkin' the streets and all of a sudden he died. It was a prayer disguised by a blues melody. Which I was still prayin', you know what I mean? The Old Man came here in disguise didn't He? Born of a virgin woman and all that, you know. And so I didn't look at the song being an awkward thing. I put a melody to it in order to reach the mass. You see, people out there playin' them jukeboxes all night long and them hustlers, they could hear it because it sounds like I'm singin' the blues.[39]

Mayfield is hardly mentioned in the more orthodox histories of rhythm and blues music, but his work offers an especially refined version of the melancholia that typifies the negativity, dissonance, and stress of being in pain.[40] One song in particular, "The River's Invitation," lends itself to the argument here for several reasons. It announces its profane character through a precise and provocative inversion of the imagery of baptism and immersion in water. It expresses what is clearly an African ecology and cosmology in the way that nature interacts with the protagonist, and the song also contains echoes of the tales of slave suicide by drowning that appear intermittently in both African-American and Caribbean folklore.[41] The protagonist's fruitless search for his estranged lover proceeds in harmony with his performances as a wandering musician. Lost and alone, he encounters a river and engages it in a metaphysical dialogue. It invites him to find solace in the death its waters offer.

> I spoke to the river
> and the river spoke back to me
> and it said
> "you look so lonely,
> you look full of misery
> and if you can't find your baby
> come and make your home with me."[42]

He rejects the offer but we are told that this rejection is only temporary. He will return to take it up once his estranged lover can be found and induced by unspecified means to share his enthusiasm for a "home among the tide."

Children of Israel or Children of the Pharaohs?

It is often forgotten that the term "diaspora" comes into the vocabulary of black studies and the practice of pan-Africanist politics from Jewish thought. It is used in the Bible[43] but begins to acquire something like its looser contemporary usage during the late nineteenth century—the period which saw the birth of modern Zionism and of the forms of black nationalist thought which share many of its aspirations and some of its rhetoric. The themes of escape and suffering, tradition, temporality, and the social organisation of memory have a special significance in the history of Jewish responses to modernity. From this source they flow into the work of several generations of Jewish cultural and religious historians, literary critics, and philosophers who have delved into the relationship between modernity and anti-Semitism and into the roles of rationalism and irrationalism in the development of European racist thought.[44] In these settings, the same themes are associated with the ideas of dispersal, exile, and slavery. They also help to frame the problem of simultaneous intra- and intercultural change which has engaged Jewish thinkers in Europe from the eighteenth century onwards.

Some of these discussions, particularly the contributions from writers whose relationship to Jewish lore and law was remote or ambivalent, have been a rich resource for me in thinking about the problems of identity and difference in the black Atlantic diaspora.[45] In the preparation of this book I have been repeatedly drawn to the work of Jewish thinkers in order to

find both inspiration and resources with which to map the ambivalent experiences of blacks inside and outside modernity. I want to acknowledge
these debts openly in the hope that in some small way the link they reveal
might contribute to a better political relationship between Jews and blacks
at some distant future point. Many writers have been struck by some of the
correspondences between the histories of these groups, but thinkers from
both communities are not always prepared to admit them, let alone explore
any possible connections in an uninhibited way. As Ella Shohat[46] has recently demonstrated in her discussion of the relationship between Ashken-
azi and Sephardic Jews, there are important reasons to be cautious about
trying to suggest simplistic connections between traditions that are themselves complex and internally heterogeneous. On both sides, for example,
the lines that divide those who have been prepared to attempt to assimilate
from those who have not have been the site of some bitter intra-ethnic
conflicts. The uneven appeal of Zionism as a political project is a source of
further difficulties in using one strand of history as an analogical or allegorical means to explore others. However, noting the longevity of the overt
and covert conversations between black and Jewish thinkers and focusing,
where possible, on their impact upon the intellectuals of the black Atlantic
world remains a worthwhile though difficult project. It is also necessary to
proceed cautiously here because the significance of Jewishness for figures
like Lukács, Adorno, Benjamin, Kafka, and others whose work has influenced the production of this book is an obscure and hotly debated question which haunts the great radical movements of the twentieth century.
Fredric Jameson is acute in his observation that fruitful links between the
experiences of oppression encountered by these particular groups can be
deduced not from the formal and aesthetic stress on pain and suffering, on
dissonance and the negative, which is the most obvious cultural motif they
hold in common, but from

> a more primary experience, namely that of fear and of vulnerability—
> the primal fact, for Adorno and Horkheimer, of human history itself
> and of that "dialectic of Enlightenment," that scientific domination of
> nature and the self, which constitutes the infernal machine of western
> civilisation. But this experience of fear in all its radicality, which cuts
> across class and gender to the point of touching the bourgeois in the
> very isolation of his town houses or sumptuous apartments, is surely
> the very "moment of truth" of ghetto life itself, as the Jews and so
> many other ethnic groups have had to live it: the helplessness of the
> village community before the perpetual and unpredictable imminence
> of the lynching or the pogrom, the race riot.[47]

The black theologist James Cone states the obvious when he notes that "a significant number of black people were confident that the God of Israel was involved in black history, liberating them from slavery and oppression."[48] This consciousness which derives from the Old Testament was enhanced by other biblical tales of co-operation between blacks and Jews as well as by the sense that there were close parallels between the historical experiences of the two groups during particular periods. The story of Solomon and the Queen of Sheba has, for example, been endlessly remarked upon by slaves and their descendants, and its effects have been consistently complicated by the emergence of ethnological and historical data linking the populations together. Many other biblical tales could be used to bring this argument into focus. But it was Exodus which provided the primary semantic resource in the elaboration of slave identity, slave historicity, and a distinctive sense of time. Albert Raboteau, the historian of African-American religion, describes this: "The appropriation of the Exodus story was for the slaves a way of articulating their sense of historical identity as a people . . . The Christian slaves applied the Exodus story, whose end they knew, to their own experience of slavery, which had not ended . . . Exodus functioned as an archetypal event for slaves."[49] The heroic figure of Moses proved especially resonant[50] for slaves and their descendants. Martin Luther King, Jr., and Marcus Garvey are only two of the most obvious modern leaders who drew on the power of Old Testament patriarchy to cement their own political authority. Yet this identification with the Exodus narrative and with the history of the chosen people and their departure from Egypt seems to be waning. Blacks today appear to identify far more readily with the glamourous pharaohs than with the abject plight of those they held in bondage. This change betrays a profound transformation in the moral basis of black Atlantic political culture. Michael Jackson's repeated question "Do you remember the time?" (of the Nile Valley civilisations) has, for example, recently supplanted Burning Spear's dread enquiry into whether the days of slavery were being remembered at all.

In the shadow of these decisive shifts, I want to suggest that the concept of diaspora can itself provide an underutilised device with which to explore the fragmentary relationship between blacks and Jews and the difficult political questions to which it plays host: the status of ethnic identity, the power of cultural nationalism, and the manner in which carefully preserved social histories of ethnocidal suffering can function to supply ethical and political legitimacy.[51] These issues are inherent in both the Israeli political situation and the practices of the Africentric movement. The discussion of Delany in Chapter 1 provided an example of the political ambitions equivalent to Zionism that were a regular feature of black political ideologies in the eighteenth and nineteenth centuries. The practical aim of returning to Africa was not merely discussed but implemented on several different occasions. The proposal to build an independent black nation state somewhere elsewhere in the world was also extensively canvassed. These episodes contributed to the foundations on which the appropriation of the term "diaspora" by historians of Africa and new world racial slavery would take place during the 1950s and 60s.

There are other more evasive and mythical ideas which link the mentalities of these differently dispersed peoples. The notion of a return to the point of origin is the first of these. The slaves' dreams of return to Africa in death predate any formal organisation around this goal and fit in with what at the end of Chapter 2 I called their turn towards death. The condition of exile, forced separation from the homeland, provides a second linking theme, though black political culture does not attempt to distinguish between its different forms—willing and reluctant—or between forced bondage and the more stable forms of community that grow up outside an ancestral homeland, particularly when a transplanted people lose their desire to return there. In these circumstances, the memory of slavery becomes an open secret and dominates the post-slave experiences that are interpreted as its covert continuation. It is significant that for blacks the turn towards an African home which may also be a turn towards death is most vividly figured in the stories of slave suicide that appear intermittently in black literature, from William Wells Brown's association of death and freedom onwards.[52] The disentanglement and interpretation of these themes is an important process that can be used to delineate the boundaries that separate tradition from custom and invariant repetition from legitimate adaptation. The idea that the suffering of both blacks and Jews has a special redemptive power, not for themselves alone but for humanity as a whole, is a third common theme that has had some interesting consequences for modern black political thought.

There are many reasons why Edward Wilmot Blyden is an especially important figure in the history of the black Atlantic and its dissident intellectuals. His role in clarifying the connections—and the differences—between blacks and Jews makes it necessary to introduce him here. Born on St. Thomas, a Danish possession in the Caribbean, in 1832, Blyden was one of the very few black thinkers "to make a significant impact on the English-speaking literary and scholastic world in the nineteenth century."[53] He was, for example, one of the first black authors from the Americas to make authoritative interventions in early African history. He visited Egypt in 1866 and defended both the idea that civilisation had begun in Africa and the still controversial argument that the Nile Valley civilisations had been produced by Negroes. Denied the chance to acquire an education in

the United States, Blyden emigrated to Liberia in 1850 and spent the next
fifty-five years closely involved in the development of the Liberian state,
particularly in its educational institutions. His famous account of the feelings aroused within him by the sight of the Pyramids conveys a hint of the
flavour of his beliefs, which were to provide strong foundations for later
versions of Pan-Africanism:

> I felt that I had a peculiar "heritage in the Great Pyramid"—built
> before the tribes of man had been so generally scattered, and therefore
> before they had acquired their different geographical characteristics
> but built by that branch of the descendants of Noah, the enterprising
> sons of Ham, from which I descended. The blood seemed to flow
> faster through my veins. I seemed to hear the echo of those illustrious
> Africans. I seemed to feel the impulse of those stirring characters who
> sent civilisation to Greece—the teachers of the fathers of poetry, his-
> tory and mathematics—Homer, Herodotus and Euclid . . . I felt
> lifted out of the commonplace grandeur of modern times . . .[54]

Blyden is known less these days for carving his name and the word Liberia on the pyramid of Cheops than for his interest in theories of racial personality and his role as an important progenitor of Pan-African ideology.
He has also been recognised as a profound influence on African nationalist
thinking inside Africa.[55] His serious, sympathetic, and well-developed interest in the Jewish Question that he regarded as "the question of questions"[56] and in particular in "that marvellous movement called Zionism"[57]
can be used here briefly to indicate something of the significance of these
histories for the development of nineteenth-century black nationalism.[58] I
am not suggesting any simple causal relationship between Blyden's interest
in Jewish history, religion, language, and culture and his own nationalist
outlook, but his biographer Hollis Lynch points to a number of possible
continuities and it seems important to consider how analogies derived
from Jewish thought may have affected his thinking about the formation
and transmission of what he called racial personality. Literate and cosmopolitan in his intellectual interests, Blyden was also influenced by the cultural nationalism of Herder and Fichte, as well as the political nationalism
of contemporary figures like Mazzini and Dostoevsky.[59] For the present
discussion, it seems especially relevant that he was extremely concerned
about the issue of racial purity in the project of nation building in Africa.
He argued, for example, that the "unimpaired race instincts" that
equipped settlers to bear the burdens of the colonisation process were not
to be found among mulattoes, and he queried the logic which assigned
these weak, immoral, decadent, and hybrid people to the Negro race in
the first place.[60] This tone expresses more than the conflict between "Ne-

groes" and "Mulattoes" in Liberian politics. It illuminates the inner ambiguities of the model of racial identity that Blyden constructed from an analogy provided by the biblical history of the chosen people and developed through his sense of its utility for his emergent Pan-Africanism.

Blyden had been born into a predominantly Jewish community in Charlotte Amalie, the capital of St. Thomas, at a time when this community had produced an unusual crop of internationally renowned figures including the painter Camille Pissarro. Jewish culture and institutions held a special fascination for him from an early age:

> For years, the next door neighbors of my parents were Jews. I played with Jewish boys, and looked forward as eagerly as they did to the annual festivals and fasts of their church. I always went to the Synagogue on the solemn Day of Atonement—not inside. I took up an outside position from which I could witness the proceedings of the worshippers, hear the prayers and the reading, the singing and the sermon. The Synagogue stood on the side of a hill; and, from a terrace immediately above it, we Christian boys who were interested could look down upon the mysterious assembly, which we did in breathless silence, with an awe and a reverence which have followed me all the days of my life.[61]

Blyden became a close associate of David Cardoze, a young Jewish intellectual, who would become the rabbi of that community, and began his study of Hebrew under Cardoze's tutelage. From this education he started to develop a sense of the affinity between Jews and blacks based around the axes provided by suffering and servitude:

> The Negro is found in all parts of the world. He has gone across Arabia, Persia, and India to China. He has crossed the Atlantic to the western hemisphere, and here he has laboured in the new and in the old settlements of America . . . He is everywhere a familiar object, and he is, everywhere out of Africa the servant of others . . . Africa is distinguished as having served and suffered. In this, her lot is not unlike that of God's ancient people, the Hebrews, who were known among the Egyptians as the servants of all; and among the Romans, in later times, they were numbered by Cicero with the nations "born to servitudes," and were protected, in the midst of a haughty population only "by the contempt which they inspired."[62]

For Blyden, blacks and Jews were linked by a shared history in which Africa had fostered the development of civilisation among Jews and by a common contemporary mission to act as "the spiritual saviours or regenerators of humanity."[63]

The precise genealogy of the diaspora concept in black cultural history remains obscure, but George Shepperson,[64] who comes closest to providing it, has pointed to the fundamental impact of Blyden's Pan-African formulations on legitimising the importation of the term and to the significance of the *Présence Africaine* project in making it credible. The link between these phases of modern black Atlantic political culture is supplied by Negritude, something that Léopold Sédar Senghor, one of its founders, has also connected to Blyden's influence:

> During the 1930s when we launched the Negritude movement from Paris, we drew our inspiration especially—and paradoxically—from "Negro Americans" in the general sense of the word: from the Harlem Renaissance movement, but also from the "indigenist" movement in Haiti . . . all the themes which were to be developed by the Negritude movement were already treated by Blyden in the middle of the nineteenth century, both the virtues of Negritude and the proper mode of illustrating those virtues.[65]

Acknowledging the intercultural history of the diaspora concept and its transcoding by historians of the black dispersal into the western hemisphere remains politically important not just in North America, where the story of its borrowing could be used to open up the long and complicated relationship between blacks and Jews in radical politics, but in Europe too, where Ethiopianism and Africentricity have exhibited both Zionist and anti-Semitic features. I have already drawn attention to the central place of the metaphors of journey and exile in both political cultures. The pronounced eschatological character of many varieties of Ethiopianism strengthens the case that these convergences are significant. The spiritual commentary on black suffering and its profane equivalent, the condition of being in pain, are of course sharply divided by the line that separates those who look for redemption to take place in this world from others who are content to anticipate its effects in the next.[66] Here too the question of temporality enforces itself.

The manner in which modern Zionism provides an organisational and philosophical model for twentieth-century Pan-Africanism has been similarly neglected by squeamish cultural and political historians. Du Bois, whose role in the twentieth-century formalisation of Pan-Africanism is well known, was resident in Europe at the time of the Dreyfus trial and wrote about following its consequences as part of his own development.[67] He hinted at the impact of this episode in his autobiography and then puzzled

over the meaning of being mistaken for a Jew while travelling in Eastern
Europe: "Arriving one night in a town north of Slovenia, the driver of a
rickety cab whispered in my ear, 'Unter die Juden?'. I stared and then said
yes. I stayed in a little Jewish inn. I was a little frightened as in the gathering
twilight I traversed the foothills of the dark Tatras alone and on foot."[68]
Easy parallels are undermined by factors like the lack of religious unity
among new world blacks and the different ways that the different groups
formalise their imaginary, ritual returns to slavery and its terrors. Blacks in
the West lack the idea of descent from a common ancestor, and there are
also more recent political factors like the identification of blacks with the
Palestinian struggle for justice and democracy and the close relationship
between the states of Israel and South Africa which intervene in any attempts to develop a dialogue about the significance of these convergences.
But in spite of these obvious problems and differences it seems worth pur-
suing the connection a little further. This can be justified both by the elliptical relationship between the modern and the spiritual which these traditions construct, and more pragmatically by the gains involved in setting
the histories of blacks and Jews within modernity in some sort of mutual
relation. The issues of tradition and memory provide a key to bringing
them together in ways that do not invite a pointless and utterly immoral
wrangle over which communities have experienced the most ineffable
forms of degradation.

I want to proceed instead by asking the tradition of black expressive culture a series of questions derived from the standpoint Benjamin occupied
when he argued that social memory creates the chain of "ethnic" tradition.
How do black expressive cultures practice remembrance? How is their remembering socially organised? How is this active remembrance associated
with a distinctive and disjunctive temporality of the subordinated? How
are this temporality and historicity constructed and marked out publicly?
We might also pursue the line of enquiry suggested by Adorno's remarks
about the capacity of remembrance "to give flesh and blood to the notion
of utopia, without betraying it to empirical life."[69] The concept of Jubilee[70]
emerges in black Atlantic culture to mark a special break or rupture in the
conception of time defined and enforced by the regimes that sanctioned
bondage. This chapter now turns towards asking what part the memory of
the terrors and bondage that have been left behind plays in securing the
unity of the communities of sentiment and interpretation which black culture helps to reproduce. How do changes in the ways that these terrors are
summoned up illuminate the shifting, restless character of black political
culture?

Black Culture and Ineffable Terror

It is important to emphasise that any correspondences that can be identified between the histories of blacks and Jews take on a radically different significance after the Holocaust. I want to resist the idea that the Holocaust is merely another instance of genocide. I accept arguments for its uniqueness. However, I do not want the recognition of that uniqueness to be an obstacle to better understanding of the complicity of rationality and ethnocidal terror to which this book is dedicated. This is a difficult line on which to balance but it should be possible, and enriching, to discuss these histories together. This can be done without the development of an absurd and dangerous competition and without lapsing into a relativising mode that would inevitably be perceived as an insult.[71] There are a number of issues raised by literature on the Holocaust which have helped me to focus my own inquiries into the uncomfortable location of blacks within modernity. However, it seems appropriate to ask at this point why many blacks and Jews have been reluctant about initiating such a conversation. I want to argue that its absence weakens all our understanding of what modern racism is and undermines arguments for its constitutive power as a factor of social division in the modern world. The way that the history of scientific racism and eugenics in the Americas has been overlooked as a factor in the development of German racial science provides a striking example of this failure.[72] Black and Jewish writers have missed untold opportunities to develop this critical dialogue. Zygmunt Bauman, for example, whose work offers a wealth of insights into the complicity of rationality with racial terror and the advantages of marginality as a hermeneutic standpoint, discusses the relationship between racism and anti-Semitism without even mentioning the Americas let alone exploring the significant connections between what he calls the gardening state and the plantation state and the colonial state. Whether born of ignorance or disregard, his view of the Jews as "the *only* 'non national nation'"[73] (emphasis added) and the only group "caught in the most ferocious of historical conflicts: that between the premodern world and advancing modernity"[74] typifies a Eurocentrism that detracts from the richness of his intellectual legacy. Emmanuel Levinas's remarks about the qualitative uniqueness of the Holocaust suggest that he suffers from a similar blind spot[75] and that his understanding of the rational basis of these processes could not survive a serious encounter with the history of either slavery or colonial domination. These oversights are perhaps less surprising given that Stanley Elkins's misguided but extremely influential attempts to import the Holocaust as a comparative example into the literature on slave personality have also been comprehensively forgotten.

Bauman's indifference to or ignorance of the extent to which the Euro-centric conception of modernity forecloses on a sense of the relationship between anti-black racism in and after slavery and anti-Semitism in Europe supplies a depressing counterpart to the nullity and banality of similarly indifferent "Africentric" thinking in which themes like the involvement of Jews in the slave trade are invoked as simple eloquent facts without the need of interpretation. Bauman's rather cursory discussion of racism in *Modernity and the Holocaust* fits very neatly with his attempts elsewhere to lodge the dynamic interplay between modernity and ethnic particularity into the overloaded encounter between friends, enemies, and strangers and a model of the cultural politics of assimilation derived from their interaction. As I have tried to show in Chapter 2, the slaves stood opposed to their masters and mistresses as neither simply enemies nor strangers. Their relationships with those who owned them were governed by shifting modes of ambivalence and antipathy, intimacy and loathing, which engage Bauman so much in other settings, but his analysis comes nowhere near touching the complex dynamics of the master-mistress-slave relationship. It would seem that some of Simmel's heirs are less interested than they should be in the avenue of enquiry into modernity suggested by their inspiration's attendance at the First Universal Races Congress hosted in London in 1911.[76]

As in so many discussions of the scope and status of the concept of modernity, the issue of science becomes a pivotal matter, not least because it has such profound consequences for the final verdict upon rationality. Robert Proctor, Richard M. Lerner, and Benno Muller Hill[77] have been some of the very few voices prepared to speculate about the links between histories allocated to different academic specialisms and commanded by different political constituencies. Their work can be used to make a powerful case for showing that European eugenics developed closely in step with American racial science and received substantial encouragement from the development of colonial social relations.

It bears repetition that exploring these relationships need not in any way undermine the uniqueness of the Holocaust. It is therefore essential not to use that invocation of uniqueness to close down the possibility that a combined if not comparative discussion of its horrors and their patterns of legitimation might be fruitful in making sense of modern racisms. This may be an especially urgent task in Europe, where the lines of descent linking contemporary racisms with the Nazi movement are hard to overlook but have posed a series of insoluble questions for anti-racist political organisations. Perhaps amidst the forms of ethnic and racial jeopardy consequent upon the reactivation of European fascism it might be possible to ask whether that uniqueness might be more carefully specified? Primo Levi, whose thoughtful studies of the grey "zone of ambiguity which irradiates around regimes based on terror and obsequiousness"[78] have deepened our understanding of what racial slavery must have meant, can contribute something here. Levi speaks from a position that exemplifies the strengths of an understanding of the uniqueness of the Holocaust that is not prescriptive because it exists in a dialectical relationship with a sense of the ubiquity and normality of similar events. For example, he draws attention to the fact that a system of slave labour was one of the three core purposes of the concentration camps along with "the elimination of political adversaries and the extermination of the so-called inferior races." He links the issue of slavery to what he calls the useless violence of the camp experience but also to an argument about the ambiguous insertion of the camps into the normal economic structures of German society.[79] Levi's work can be used to specify other elements of the camp experience that might be used in a preliminary way to locate the parameters of a new approach to the history of those modern terrors that exhaust the capacity of language. His arguments about the nature of the journey to the camp and the condition of namelessness into which new inmates were inducted have the most ready equivalents in the literature and history of racial slavery in the new world. The value of combining these histories or at least of placing them relative to one another in the same conceptual scheme is a better indictment of the bourgeois humanist ideology which is clearly implicated in the suffering of both groups.[80] This is no trifling matter for, as Martin Bernal has recently demonstrated, anti-Semitism and racism are closely associated in nineteenth-century historiography and remain largely unacknowledged factors in the history of the human sciences.

The small world of black cultural and intellectual history is similarly populated by those who fear that the integrity of black particularity could be compromised by attempts to open a complex dialogue with other consciousnesses of affliction. Political urgency apart, some of the pivotal themes which make such a dialogue possible are the relationship between rationalities and racisms, the repudiation of the ideology of progress by the racially subordinated who have lubricated its wheels with their unfree labour, the similar patterns of social remembrance found among Jews and blacks and the effects of protracted familiarity with ineffable, sublime terror on the development of a political (anti)aesthetics. There are dangers for both blacks and Jews in accepting their historic and unsought association with sublimity. One has only to recall Nietzsche's attempts in *Dawn* to invest his hopes for the regeneration of mankind in the Jews to see the ambiguities inherent in this legacy.

This idea of a special redemptive power produced through suffering has its ready counterparts in the writings of black thinkers who have, at various times, identified similar relationships between the history of modern racial slavery and the redemption of both Africa and America. The capacity of blacks to redeem and transform the modern world through the truth and clarity of perception that emerge from their pain is, for example, a familiar element in the theology of Martin Luther King, Jr.,[81] which argues not only that black suffering has a meaning but that its meaning could be externalised and amplified so that it could be of benefit to the moral status of the whole world. Equally ambiguous is the use which some black thinkers have made of models of cultural struggle derived from a reading of the role that Jewish intellectuals have played in developing the political interests of their community. In this approach, the Jews supply a strategy which some black intellectuals try to emulate. They seek to follow the precedent established by Jewish thinkers who are thought to have been able to make the suffering of their people part of the ethical agenda of the West as a whole:

> The Jew's suffering is recognized as part of the moral history of the world and the Jew is recognized as a contributor to the world's history: this is not true for blacks. Jewish history, whether or not one can say it is honoured, is certainly known: the black history has been blasted, maligned, and despised. The Jew is a white man, and when white men rise up against oppression they are heroes: when black men rise they have reverted to their native savagery. The uprising in the Warsaw ghetto was not described as a riot, nor were the participants maligned as hoodlums: the boys and girls in Watts and Harlem are thoroughly aware of this, and it certainly contributes to their attitudes toward the Jews.[82]

These are James Baldwin's words. Baldwin is important to this aspect of black Atlantic political culture because he has been identified by both Harold Cruse[83] and Stanley Crouch as the progenitor of a strategy for black expression in which victims are first blessed and then required to play a special role in illuminating and transforming the world. Cruse deals harshly with Baldwin, but both of them end up enamoured of the role that Jewish intellectuals have played in consolidating the interests and self-consciousness of their communities through systematic cultural activism. Cruse sees this group as "propagandists" capable of supplying the Zionist cause with an "inner strength." He suggests that their activities point towards a black "cultural nationalism" equivalent to that which has made Jewish intellectuals a force to be reckoned with in America. Baldwin, on the other hand, sees "a genuinely candid confrontation between American Negroes and American Jews" as "of inestimable value"[84]—an essential pre-condition for the emancipation of American blacks. Baldwin's approach is doubly relevant here because he has also been identified by Crouch as the source of a political theory of black culture which has played a uniquely destructive role in the development of "racial letters." Crouch places Toni Morrison's novel *Beloved* in the shadow of this theory of art which is for him merely a theory of black martyrdom in which the downtrodden were canonised before their misery could be sifted for its special, moral magic. He attacks the novel as a list of atrocities rather than an explanation of "the mystery of human motive and behaviour."[85] His final, cruel charge against Morrison is that "*Beloved*, above all else, is a blackface holocaust novel." It is, he continues, a book that "seems to have been written in order to enter American slavery in the big-time martyr ratings contest." I do not accept that this is either Morrison's intention or the inevitable effect of her moving excursion into the relationship between terror and memory, sublimity and the impossible desire to forget the unforgettable. However, the argument I have tried to develop in this chapter prompts a restrained counter-question to Crouch's acid polemic which I shall use to focus my concluding pages. What would be the consequences if the book had tried to set the Holocaust of European Jews in a provocative relationship with the modern history of racial slavery and terror in the western hemisphere? Crouch dismisses without considering it the possibility that there might be something useful to be gained from setting these histories closer to each other not so as to compare them, but as precious resources from which we might learn something valuable about the way that modernity operates, about the scope and status of rational human conduct, about the claims of science, and perhaps most importantly about the ideologies of humanism with which these brutal histories can be shown to have been complicit.

These issues are perhaps of more immediate concern to Europe than to America. In Europe, the most active and violent proponents of racism focused by colour and phenotype openly draw their inspiration from fascist ideologies. Without wanting to ignore the important differences between anti-fascism and anti-racism, it is also vital to explore their practical articulation. It proved to be a major problem for the mass anti-racist movement of the 1970s and has created new difficulties with the reactivation of militant fascism in the period after the reunification of Germany and the collapse of "actually existing socialism" in which alliances between racial nationalists and ethnic purifiers of all hues are a real possibility.

In conclusion, I want to try to approach *Beloved* and some other parallel texts which share its interest in history and social memory in an experimental and openly politically spirit. I want to draw attention to the ways in which some black writers have already begun the vital work of enquiring into terrors that exhaust the resources of language amidst the debris of a catastrophe which prohibits the existence of their art at the same time as demanding its continuance. I want to repeat and extend the argument frequently stated above that even when these writers are black Americans their work should not be exclusively assimilated to the project of building an ethnically particular or nationalist cultural canon, because the logic of the great political movement in which these texts stand and to which they contribute operates at other levels than those marked by national boundaries. These texts belong also to the web of diaspora identities and concerns that I have labelled the black Atlantic.

In turning away from anti-textual, vernacular forms and towards literature, it is essential to appreciate that different genres in black expressive culture have responded to the aporetic status of post-emancipation black art in quite different ways. Scepticism about the value of trying to revisit the sites of ineffable terror in the imagination is probably most valid in relation to the novel—a precariously placed latecomer in the spaces of black vernacular culture, if it can be placed there at all. Benjamin's warning that "what draws the reader to the novel is the hope of warming his shivering life with a death he reads about"[86] should definitely be borne in mind when assessing the intermittent taste for fiction revealed by black Atlantic readerships from abolitionism onwards. However, this warning is principally an argument about the form of the novel and the different types of memory and remembrance which it solicits from its readers. The clutch of recent African-American novels which deal explicitly with history, historiography, slavery, and remembrance all exhibit an intense and ambivalent negotiation of the novel form that is associated with their various critiques of modernity and enlightenment. Charles Johnson's *Middle Passage,* which addresses these questions head on through the experiences of Rutherford Calhoun, an African-American crewman on a slaving voyage, has a neat intertextual relationship with Delany's *Blake* but, unlike its antecedent, presents itself in the guise of a journal. Sherley Anne Williams's *Dessa Rose* and David Bradley's *The Chaneysville Incident* both incorporate the antagonistic relationship between different kinds of inscription directly into their own structures, while Toni Morrison describes *Beloved* as "outside most of the formal constricts of the novel."[87] These remarks reveal a common degree of discomfort with the novel and a shared anxiety about its utility as a resource in the social processes that govern the remaking and conservation of historical memory. The source of these concerns may be equally located in the shift between oral and written culture and a response to the dominance of autobiographical writing within the vernacular mode of black literary production. Morrison describes these issues clearly:

> My sense of the novel is that it has always functioned for the class or group that wrote it. The history of the novel as a form began when there was a new class, a middle class, to read it; it was an art form that they needed. The lower classes didn't need novels at that time because they had an art form already: they had songs and dances, and ceremony and gossip and celebrations. The aristocracy didn't need it because they had the art that they had patronized, they had their own pictures painted, their own houses built, and they made sure their art separated them from the rest of the world . . . For a long time, the art form that was healing for black people was music. That music is no longer exclusively ours; we don't have exclusive rights to it. Other people sing and play it, it is the mode of contemporary music everywhere. So another form has to take its place, and it seems to me that the novel is needed . . . now in a way that it was not needed before.[88]

Beloved was being written at the time these words were recorded, and it is especially relevant to the overall argument of this book because it is partly a retelling of the Margaret Garner story discussed in Chapter 2. Black women's experiences, and in particular the meanings they attach to motherhood, are central themes in the book, which makes important arguments for congruence between the integrity of the racial group as a whole and the status of its female members. For Morrison, these issues cannot be divorced from a different contradiction, constituted by the tension between the racial self and the racial community. Speaking of the Garner story, she explained: "It occurred to me that the questions about community and individuality were certainly inherent in that incident as I imagined it. When you are the community, when you are your children, when that is your individuality, there is no division . . . Margaret Garner didn't do what Medea did and kill her children because of some guy. It was for me this classic example of a person determined to be responsible."[89] The Garner story illustrates more than just the indomitable power of slaves to assert their human agency in closely restricted circumstances. In Morrison's version, it encapsulates the confrontation between two opposed yet interdependent cultural and ideological systems and their attendant conceptions of reason, history, property, and kinship. One is the dilute product of Africa, the other is an antinomian expression of western modernity. Their meeting ground is the system of plantation slavery. It is thus the relationship between masters and slaves that supplies the key to comprehending the position of blacks in the modern world. The desire to return to slavery and to explore it in imaginative writing has offered Morrison and a number of other contemporary black writers a means to restage confrontations between rational, scientific, and enlightened Euro-American thought and the supposedly primitive outlook of prehistorical, cultureless, and bestial African slaves.

The desire to pit these cultural systems against one another arises from present conditions. In particular, it is formed by the need to indict those forms of rationality which have been rendered implausible by their racially exclusive character and further to explore the history of their complicity with terror systematically and rationally practised as a form of political and economic administration. Sherley Anne Williams offers a notable expression of these themes in her novel *Dessa Rose* where Dessa, a pregnant slave convicted of rebellion and awaiting the death that will follow the birth of her child, is intrusively interviewed by a white man preparing a scientific manual of slave husbandry: "The Roots of Rebellion in the Slave Population and Some Means of Eradicating Them."[90] Williams is primarily concerned with the differences between the marks inscribed on paper by Nehemiah's pen and the marks inscribed on or rather incorporated into Dessa's body by the brands and chains her slavery has required her to bear. Each supports a distinct system of meaning with its own characteristic forms of memory, rules, and racialised codes. They cross each other in Dessa herself. As a black writer looking backwards, over her shoulder, at slavery and making it both intelligible and legible, mediating terror by means of narrative, Williams is revealed to be the heir to both.

These imaginative attempts to revisit the slave experience and sift it for resources with which to bolster contemporary political aspirations do not point towards a simple disassociation (Africentric or otherwise) from the West and its distinctive understandings of being, thinking, and thinking about thinking and being. To be sure, the misguided association of slavery with antiquity and precapitalist systems of production and domination is broken, but the break indicates the opportunity to reconceptualise so that capitalist, racial slavery becomes internal to modernity and intrinsically modern. The same break is underscored in *Beloved* by Morrison's introduction of Schoolteacher, a slaveholder whose rational and scientific racism replaces the patrimonial and sentimental version of racial domination practiced at "Sweet Home" by his predecessor: "Schoolteacher was standing over one of them [his nephews] with one hand behind his back . . . when I heard him say No, no. That's not the way. I told you to put her human characteristics on the left; her animal ones on the right. And don't forget to line them up."[91]

In Charles Johnson's novels the tendency towards polarising two pure essences, African and European, is complicated by the insertion of African-American protagonists whose "creolised" double consciousnesses[92] belie the force of that fundamental dualism which Johnson fears might be "a bloody structure of the mind."[93] Andrew Hawkins, the picaresque hero of *Oxherding Tale,* is another ex-coloured man who can pass for white. He has been trained in metaphysics by a transcendentalist. In *Middle Passage* his successor, Calhoun, is morally compromised not just by his position as a crew member on a slaver but by his estrangement from his biological kin and by his conspicuous non-identity with the Allmuseri tribespeople who stand in both books as persuasive symbols of an Africa that remains stubbornly incompatible with the modern world.

These literary assertions of the emphatic modernness of western black experience in slavery and since are strikingly reminiscent of C. L. R. James's arguments in *The Black Jacobins*[94] and W. E. B. Du Bois's in *Black Reconstruction*.[95] It is being suggested that the concentrated intensity of the slave experience is something that marked out blacks as the first truly modern people, handling in the nineteenth century dilemmas and difficulties which would only become the substance of everyday life in Europe a century later. Morrison states this argument with special force:

> . . . modern life begins with slavery . . . From a women's point of view, in terms of confronting the problems of where the world is now, black women had to deal with post-modern problems in the nineteenth century and earlier. These things had to be addressed by black people a long time ago: certain kinds of dissolution, the loss of and the need to reconstruct certain kinds of stability. Certain kinds of madness, deliberately going mad in order, as one of the characters says in the book, "in order not to lose your mind." These strategies for survival made the truly modern person. They're a response to predatory western phenomena. You can call it an ideology and an economy, what it is is a pathology. Slavery broke the world in half, it broke it in every way. It broke Europe. It made them into something else, it made them slave masters, it made them crazy. You can't do that for hundreds of years and it not take a toll. They had to dehumanize, not just the slaves but themselves. They have had to reconstruct everything in order to make that system appear true. It made everything in world war two possible. It made world war one necessary. Racism is the word that we use to encompass all this.[96]

All these books, though especially *Beloved,* deal with the power of history on several levels: with the contending conceptions of time that make its enregisterment possible,[97] with the necessity of socialised historical

memory, and with the desire to forget the terrors of slavery and the simultaneous impossibility of forgetting. Morrison is once again acute: "The
struggle to forget which was important in order to survive is fruitless and
I wanted to make it fruitless."[98] These interlocking themes are rendered
with great force in David Bradley's *The Chaneysville Incident*,[99] where the
need for hermeneutic resources capable of unlocking the metaphysical
choices of modern slaves is posed through an enquiry into the meaning of
mass suicide by slaves cornered by the slave catchers. The protagonist here
is John Washington, an academic historian who has to first master and then
set aside his formal training in the discipline so that he can comprehend
the significance of the slaves' preference for death rather than continued
bondage.

In seeking to explain why she and other African-American novelists
made this decisive turn to history Morrison suggests an interesting motivation which accentuates the source of this desire in a present which places
little value on either history or historicity:

> It's got to be because we are responsible. I am very gratified by the
> fact that black writers are learning to grow in that area. We have aban-
> doned a lot of valuable material. We live in a land where the past is
> always erased and America is the innocent future in which immigrants
> can come and start over, where the slate is clean. The past is absent or
> it's romanticized. This culture doesn't encourage dwelling on, let
> alone coming to terms with, the truth about the past. That memory
> is much more in danger now than it was thirty years ago.[100]

Morrison's emphasis on the imaginative appropriation of history and concern with the cultural contours of distinctively modern experience make
her harsh on those who believe that being a black writer requires dogged
adherence to orthodox narrative structures and realist codes of writing.
Her work points to and celebrates some of the strategies for summoning
up the past devised by black writers whose minority modernism can be
defined precisely through its imaginative proximity to forms of terror that
surpass understanding and lead back from contemporary racial violence,
through lynching, towards the temporal and ontological rupture of the
middle passage. Here Morrison and the others are drawing upon and reconstructing the resources supplied to them by earlier generations of black
writers who allowed the confluence of racism, rationality, and systematic
terror to configure both their disenchantment with modernity and their
aspirations for its fulfilment.[101]

Their work accepts that the modern world represents a break with the
past, not in the sense that premodern, "traditional" Africanisms don't sur-

vive its institution, but because the significance and meaning of these survivals get irrevocably sundered from their origins. The history of slavery and the history of its imaginative recovery through expressive, vernacular cultures challenge us to delve into the specific dynamics of this severance.

The conclusion of this book is that this ought to be done not in order to recover hermetically sealed and culturally absolute racial traditions that would be content forever to invoke the premodern as the anti-modern. It is proposed here above all as a means to figure the inescapability and legitimate value of mutation, hybridity, and intermixture en route to better theories of racism and of black political culture than those so far offered by cultural absolutists of various phenotypical hues. The extreme circumstances out of which this obligation has grown only add to the urgency and the promise of this work. The history of blacks in the West and the social movements that have affirmed and rewritten that history can provide a lesson which is not restricted to blacks. They raise issues of more general significance that have been posed within black politics at a relatively early point. There is, for example, a potentially important contribution here towards the politics of a new century in which the central axis of conflict will no longer be the colour line but the challenge of just, sustainable development and the frontiers which will separate the overdeveloped parts of the world (at home and abroad) from the intractable poverty that already surrounds them. In these circumstances, it may be easier to appreciate the utility of a response to racism that doesn't reify the concept of race, and to prize the wisdom generated by developing a series of answers to the power of ethnic absolutism that doesn't try to fix ethnicity absolutely but sees it instead as an infinite process of identity construction. It merits repeating that this labour is valuable for itself and for the general strategy it can be shown to exemplify. At its most valuable, the history of contending racial identities affords a specific illustration of the general lessons involved in trying to keep the unstable, profane categories of black political culture open. Equally importantly, it can reveal a positive value in striving to incorporate the problems of coping with that openness into the practice of politics.

Notes

1. The Black Atlantic as a Counterculture of Modernity

1. Werner Sollors, *Beyond Ethnicity* (New York and Oxford: Oxford University Press, 1986).

2. "A unit of analysis for studying texts according to the ratio and nature of the temporal and spatial categories represented . . . The chronotope is an optic for reading texts as x-rays of the forces at work in the culture system from which they spring." M. M. Bakhtin, *The Dialogic Imagination,* ed. and trans. Michael Holquist (Austin: University of Texas Press, 1981), p. 426.

3. The concept of racialisation is developed by Frantz Fanon in his essay "On National Culture" in *The Wretched of the Earth* (Harmondsworth: Penguin, 1967), pp. 170–171. See also Robert Miles, *Racism* (New York and London: Routledge, 1989), pp. 73–77.

4. Mary Louise Pratt, *Imperial Eyes* (London and New York: Routledge, 1992).

5. Nancy Stepan, *The Idea of Race in Science: Great Britain, 1800–1960* (Basingstoke, Hampshire, and London: Macmillan, 1982); Michael Banton, *Racial Theories* (Cambridge: Cambridge University Press, 1987).

6. George Mosse, *Nationalism and Sexuality: Middle-Class Morality and Sexual Norms in Modern Europe* (Madison and London: University of Wisconsin Press, 1985). Reinhold Grimm and Jost Hermand, eds., *Blacks and German Culture* (Madison and London: University of Wisconsin Press, 1986).

7. Sander Gilman, *On Blackness without Blacks* (Boston: G. K. Hall, 1982).

8. See Henry Louis Gates, Jr., "The History and Theory of Afro-American Literary Criticism, 1773–1831: The Arts, Aesthetic Theory and the Nature of the African" (doctoral thesis, Clare College, Cambridge University, 1978); David Brion Davis, *The Problem of Slavery in Western Culture* (Ithaca, N.Y.: Cornell University Press, 1970) and *The Problem of Slavery in the Age of Revolution* (Ithaca, N.Y.: Cornell University Press, 1975); and Eva Beatrice Dykes, *The Negro in English Romantic Thought; or, A Study of Sympathy for the Oppressed* (Washington, D.C.: Associated Publishers, 1942).

9. Leon Poliakov, *The Aryan Myth* (London: Sussex University Press, 1974), ch. 8, and "Racism from the Enlightenment to the Age of Imperialism," in Robert Ross, ed., *Racism and Colonialism: Essays on Ideology and Social Structure* (The Hague: Martinus Nijhoff, 1982); Richard Popkin, "The Philosophical Basis of Eighteenth Century Racism," in *Studies in Eighteenth Century Culture,* vol. 3: *Racism in the Eighteenth Century* (Cleveland and London: Case Western Reserve

University Press, 1973); Harry Bracken, "Philosophy and Racism," *Philosophia* 8, nos. 2–3, November 1978. In some respects this pioneering work foreshadows the debates about Heidegger's fascism.

10. Hugh Honour's contribution to the DeMenil Foundation Project, *The Representation of the Black in Western Art* (London and Cambridge, Mass.: Harvard University Press, 1989), is a welcome exception to this amnesia.

11. W. Pietz, "The Problem of the Fetish, I," *Res,* 9 (Spring 1985).

12. Robin Blackburn, *The Overthrow of Colonial Slavery, 1776–1848* (London and New York: Verso, 1988).

13. Winthrop D. Jordan, *White over Black* (New York: W.W. Norton, 1977).

14. Edmund Burke, *A Philosophical Enquiry into the Origin of Our Ideas of the Sublime and the Beautiful,* ed. James T. Boulton (Oxford: Basil Blackwell, 1987).

15. Catherine Hall, *White, Male and Middle Class* (Cambridge: Polity Press, 1992).

16. Jenny Sharpe, "The Unspeakable Limits of Rape: Colonial Violence and Counter-Insurgency," *Genders,* no. 10 (Spring 1991): 25–46, and "Figures of Colonial Resistance," *Modern Fiction Studies* 35, no. 1 (Spring 1989).

17. Peter Linebaugh, "All the Atlantic Mountains Shook," *Labour/Le Travailleur* 10 (Autumn 1982): 87–121.

18. Peter Fryer, *Staying Power* (London: Pluto Press, 1980), p. 219.

19. *The Horrors of Slavery and Other Writings by Robert Wedderburn,* ed. Iain McCalman (Edinburgh: Edinburgh University Press, 1992).

20. Iain McCalman, "Anti-slavery and Ultra Radicalism in Early Nineteenth-Century England: The Case of Robert Wedderburn," *Slavery and Abolition* 7 (1986).

21. Fryer, *Staying Power,* p. 216. Public Records Office, London: PRO Ho 44/5/202, PRO Ho 42/199.

22. Their article "The Many Headed Hydra," *Journal of Historical Sociology* 3, no. 3 (September 1990): 225–253, gives a foretaste of these arguments.

23. John Adams quoted by Linebaugh in "Atlantic Mountains," p. 112.

24. Alfred N. Hunt, *Haiti's Influence on Antebellum America* (Baton Rouge and London: Louisiana State University Press, 1988), p. 119.

25. Douglass's own account of this is best set out in Frederick Douglass, *Life and Times of Frederick Douglass* (New York: Macmillan, 1962), p. 199. See also Philip M. Hamer, "Great Britain, the United States and the Negro Seamen's Acts" and "British Consuls and the Negro Seamen's Acts, 1850–1860," *Journal of Southern History* 1 (1935): 3–28, 138–168. Introduced after Denmark Vesey's rebellion, these interesting pieces of legislation required free black sailors to be jailed while their ships were in dock as a way of minimising the political contagion their presence in the ports was bound to transmit.

26. Linebaugh, "Atlantic Mountains," p. 119.

27. Paul Gilroy, "Art of Darkness, Black Art and the Problem of Belonging to England," *Third Text* 10 (1990). A very different interpretation of Turner's painting is given in Albert Boime's *The Art of Exclusion: Representing Blacks in the Nineteenth Century* (London: Thames and Hudson, 1990).

28. Patrick Wright, *On Living in an Old Country* (London: Verso, 1985).

29. Bernard Semmel, *Jamaican Blood and the Victorian Conscience* (Westport, Conn.: Greenwood Press, 1976). See also Gillian Workman, "Thomas Carlyle and the Governor Eyre Controversy," *Victorian Studies* 18, no. 1 (1974): 77–102.

30. Vol. 1, sec. 5, ch. 3, sec. 39. W. E. B. Du Bois reprinted this commentary while he was editor of *The Crisis;* see vol. 15 (1918): 239.

31. Eric Hobsbawm, "The Historians' Group of the Communist Party," in M. Cornforth, ed., *Essays in Honour of A. L. Morton* (Atlantic Highlands, N.J.: Humanities Press, 1979).

32. Linebaugh, "Atlantic Mountains." This is also the strategy pursued by Marcus Rediker in his brilliant book *Between the Devil and the Deep Blue Sea* (Cambridge: Cambridge University Press, 1987).

33. "A space exists when one takes into consideration vectors of direction, velocities, and time variables. Thus space is composed of intersections of mobile elements. It is in a sense articulated by the ensemble of movements deployed within it." Michel de Certeau, *The Practice of Everyday Life* (Berkeley and London: University of California Press, 1984), p. 117.

34. See Michael Cohn and Michael K. Platzer, *Black Men of the Sea* (New York: Dodd, Mead, 1978). I have been heavily reliant on George Francis Dow's anthology *Slave Ships and Slaving,* publication no. 15 of the Marine Research Society (1927; rpt. Cambridge, Md.: Cornell Maritime Press, 1968), which includes extracts from valuable eighteenth- and nineteenth-century material. On England, I have found the anonymously published study *Liverpool and Slavery* (Liverpool: A. Bowker and Sons, 1884) to be very valuable. Memoirs produced by black sea captains also point to a number of new intercultural and transcultural research problems. Captain Harry Dean's *The Pedro Gorino: The Adventures of a Negro Sea Captain in Africa and on the Seven Seas in His attempts to Found an Ethiopian Empire* (Boston and New York: Houghton Mifflin, 1929) contains interesting material on the practical politics of Pan-Africanism that go unrecorded elsewhere. Captain Hugh Mulzac's autobiography, *A Star to Steer By* (New York: International Publishers, 1963), includes valuable observations on the role of ships in the Garvey movement. Some pointers towards what a black Atlantic rereading of the history of Rastafari might involve are to be found in Robert A. Hill's important essay which accentuates complex post-slavery relations between Jamaica and Africa: "Dread History: Leonard P. Howell and Millenarian Visions in Early Rastafari Religions in Jamaica," *Epoché: Journal of the History of Religions at UCLA* 9 (1981): 30–71.

35. Stephen Greenblatt, *Marvellous Possessions* (Oxford: Oxford University Press, 1992). See also Pratt, *Imperial Eyes.*

36. James T. Clifford, "Travelling Cultures," in *Cultural Studies,* ed. Lawrence Grossberg et al. (New York and London: Routledge, 1992), and "Notes on Theory and Travel," *Inscriptions* 5 (1989).

37. *Manchester Weekly Advertiser,* July 21, 1860; *Punch,* July 28, 1860; *The Morning Star,* July 18, 1860; and F. A. Rollin, *Life and Public Services of Martin R. Delany* (Lee and Shepard: Boston, 1868), p. 102.

38. Peter Winzen, "Treitschke's Influence on the Rise of Imperialist and Anti-British Nationalism in Germany," in P. Kennedy and A. Nicholls, eds., *Nationalist and Racialist Movements in Britain and Germany before 1914* (Basingstoke: Macmillan, 1981).

39. Ida B. Wells quoted in Vron Ware, *Beyond the Pale: White Women, Racism, and History* (London and New York: Verso, 1992), p. 177.

40. Carolyn Ashbaugh, *Lucy Parsons: American Revolutionary* (Chicago: Charles H. Kerr, 1976). I must thank Tommy Lott for this reference.

41. Frank Hooker, *Black Revolutionary: George Padmore's Path from Commu-*

nism to Pan-Africanism (London: Pall Mall Library of African Affairs, 1967).

42. William S. McFeely, *Frederick Douglass* (New York: W.W. Norton, 1991), p. 329.

43. Michel Fabre, *Black American Writers in France, 1840–1980* (Urbana and Chicago: University of Illinois Press, 1991).

44. Ursula Broschke Davis, *Paris without Regret* (Iowa City: University of Iowa Press, 1986), p. 102 .

45. I challenge this view in Chapter 5.

46. Some of the problems associated with this strategy have been discussed by Cornel West in "Minority Discourse and the Pitfalls of Canon Formation," *Yale Journal of Criticism* 1, no. 1 (Fall 1987): 193–201.

47. Molefi Kete Asante, *Kemet, Afrocentricity and Knowledge* (Trenton, N.J.: Africa World Press, 1990), p. 112.

48. Martin R. Delany, *Principia of Ethnology: The Races and Color, with an Ar-cheological Compendium of Ethiopian and Egyptian Civilisation from Years of Care-ful Examination and Enquiry* (Philadelphia: Harper and Brother, 1879), p. 95.

49. See Delany's opposition to the proposal to nominate a black vice-presidential candidate, *New York Tribune,* August 6, 1867, p. 1.

50. R. Blackett, "In Search of International Support for African Colonisation: Martin R. Delany's Visit to England, 1860" *Canadian Journal of History* 10, no. 3 (1975).

51. A taste of Delany in this mode is provided by his "Comets," *Anglo-African Magazine* 1, no. 2 (February 1859): 59–60.

52. Thomas Szasz, "The Sane Slave: An Historical Note on the Use of Medical Diagnosis as Justificatory Rhetoric," *American Journal of Psychotherapy* 25 (1971): 228–239; J. D. Guillory, "The Pro-slavery Arguments of S. A. Cartwright," *Louisiana History* 9 (1968): 209–227.

53. Ann Dally, *Women under the Knife* (London: Radius, 1991).

54. Dorothy Sterling, *The Making of an Afro-American: Martin Robison Delany, 1812–1885* (New York: Doubleday, 1971), p. 139.

55. Nell Irvin Painter, "Martin R. Delany," in L. Litwak and A. Meier, eds., *Black Leaders of the Nineteenth Century* (Urbana and London: University of Illinois Press, 1988).

56. W. Montague Cobb, "Martin Robison Delany," *Journal of the National Medical Association* 44 (May 1952).

57. See the material on Delany at the Countway Library of the Harvard Medical School. Records of the Medical Faculty of Harvard University, vol. 2, minutes of meetings on November 4 and 23, 1850. Students submitted petitions against the presence of the black students on December 10 and 11. Delany's experiences at Harvard contrast very unfavourably with the pleasant situation of three coloured young men observed by William Wells Brown during his 1851 visit to the Medical School in Edinburgh. See his *Places and People Abroad* (New York: Sheldon, Lamport and Blakeman, 1855), p. 265.

58. *The Condition, Elevation, Emigration and Destiny of the Colored People of the United States Politically Considered* (Philadelphia: Published by the Author, 1852), pp. 12–13.

59. "Central and South America, are evidently the ultimate destination and future home of the colored race on this continent," ibid., ch. 21 and 22 passim.

60. Ibid., pp. 168–169.

61. C. Peter Ripley, ed., *The Black Abolitionist Papers,* vol. 2: *Canada, 1830–1865* (Chapel Hill and London: University of North Carolina Press, 1986).

62. *Official Report of the Niger Valley Exploring Party,* republished as *Search for a Place: Black Separatism and Africa, 1860,* intro. by Howard H. Bell (Ann Arbor: University of Michigan Press, 1969).

63. Ibid., p. 64.

64. Ibid., pp. 101–106.

65. Delany, *The Condition,* p. 215.

66. Ibid., p. 196.

67. Delany, *Report of the Niger Valley Exploring Party,* pp. 110–111.

68. William W. Austin, *"Susanna," "Jeanie" and "The Old Folks at Home": The Songs of Stephen C. Foster from His Time to Ours* (Urbana and Chicago: University of Illinois Press, 1987).

69. Giles Deleuze and Felix Guattari, "Rhizome," *Ideology and Consciousness* 8 (1980), and *A Thousand Plateaus* (London: Athlone Press, 1988), pp. 3–25.

70. Martin Delany, *Blake; or, The Huts of America,* pt. II, ch. 61 (Boston: Beacon Press, 1970).

71. This phrase is taken from Wright's novel *The Outsider* (New York: Harper and Row, 1953), p. 129. In his book of essays, *White Man Listen!* (Garden City, N.Y.: Anchor Books, 1964), he employs the phrase "dual existence" to map the same terrain. See Chapter 5 below.

72. Edouard Glissant, *Le discours antillais* (Paris: Editions du Seuil, 1981).

73. Stuart Hall, "New Ethnicities," in K. Mercer, ed., *Black Film: British Cinema* (London: ICA Documents 7, 1988), p. 28.

74. See *Ten.8* 2, no. 3 (1992), issue entitled *The Critical Decade.*

75. Etienne Balibar and Immanuel Wallerstein, *Race, Nation, Class* (London and New York: Verso, 1991).

76. Nelson George, *The Death of Rhythm and Blues* (London: Omnibus, 1988).

77. I should emphasise that it is the assimilation of these cultural forms to an unthinking notion of nationality which is the object of my critique here. Of course, certain cultural forms become articulated with sets of social and political forces over long periods of time. These forms may be played with and lived with as though they were natural emblems of racial and ethnic particularity. This may even be an essential defensive attribute of the interpretive communities involved. However, the notion of nationality cannot be borrowed as a ready-made means to make sense of the special dynamics of this process.

78. W. E. B. Du Bois, *Dusk of Dawn,* in *Dubois Writings* (New York: Library of America, 1986), p. 577.

79. Zygmunt Bauman, "The Left As the Counterculture of Modernity," *Telos* 70 (Winter 1986–87): 81–93.

80. Anthony Jackson's dazzling exposition of James Jamerson's bass style is, in my view, indicative of the type of detailed critical work which needs to be done on the form and dynamics of black musical creativity. His remarks on Jamerson's use of harmonic and rhythmic ambiguity and selective employment of dissonance were especially helpful. To say that the book from which it is taken has been geared to the needs of the performing musician rather than the cultural historian is to indict the current state of cultural history rather than the work of Jackson and his collabo-

rator Dr. Licks. See "An Appreciation of the Style," in Dr. Licks, ed., *Standing in the Shadows of Motown* (Detroit: Hal Leonard, 1989).

81. I am thinking here both of Wright's tantalising discussion of the Dozens in the essay on the "Literary Tradition of the Negro in the United States" in *White Man Listen!* and also of Levinas's remarks on useless suffering in another context: "useless and unjustifiable suffering [are] exposed and displayed . . . without any shadow of a consoling theodicy." See "Useless Suffering," in R. Bernasconi and D. Wood, eds., *The Provocation of Levinas* (London: Routledge, 1988). Jon Michael Spencer's thoughtful but fervently Christian discussion of what he calls the Theodicy of the Blues is also relevant here. See *The Theology of American Popular Music*, a special issue of *Black Sacred Music* 3, no. 2 (Durham, N.C.: Duke University Press, Fall 1989). I do not have space to develop my critique of Spencer here.

82. *There Ain't No Black in the Union Jack: The Cultural Politics of Race and Nation* (London: Hutchinson, 1987), ch. 5.

83. Cedric Robinson, *Black Marxism* (London: Zed Press, 1982).

84. This concept and its pairing with the politics of transfiguration have been adapted from their deployment in Seyla Benhabib's inspiring book *Critique, Norm and Utopia* (New York: Columbia University Press, 1987).

85. T. W. Adorno, *Aesthetic Theory* (London: Routledge, 1984), p. 196.

86. Salman Rushdie, *Is Nothing Sacred?* The Herbert Read Memorial Lecture 1990 (Cambridge: Granta, 1990), p. 16.

2. Masters, Mistresses, Slaves, and the Antinomies of Modernity

1. Edward Said, "Representing the Colonised," *Critical Inquiry* 15, no. 2 (Winter 1989): 222.

2. Jean-François Lyotard, "Defining the Postmodern," in L. Appignanesi, ed., *Postmodernism* (London: ICA documents 4, 1986).

3. There are other possibilities signalled in Edward Said's pathbreaking work *Orientalism* (Harmondsworth: Penguin, 1985) and in the work of other critics and cultural historians who have followed the Foucauldian path in other directions. See Peter Hulme, *Colonial Encounters* (London: Methuen, 1986), and V. Y. Mudimbe, *The Invention of Africa* (Bloomington and Indianapolis: Indiana University Press, 1988).

4. Jürgen Habermas, "Modernity: An Incomplete Project," in Hal Foster, ed., *Postmodern Culture* (London: Pluto Press, 1983).

5. Marshall Berman, *All That Is Solid Melts into Air* (London: Verso, 1983); Peter Dews, ed., *Habermas: Autonomy and Solidarity* (London: Verso, 1986); Zygmunt Bauman, *Legislators and Interpreters* (Cambridge: Polity Press, 1987); Andreas Huyssen, *After the Great Divide* (Bloomington and Indianapolis: Indiana University Press, 1986); David White, *The Recent Work of Jürgen Habermas: Reason, Justice and Modernity* (Cambridge: Cambridge University Press, 1988); David Ingram, *Habermas and the Dialectic of Reason* (New Haven and London: Yale University Press, 1987); Cornel West, "Fredric Jameson's Marxist Hermeneutic," in Jonathan Arac, ed., *Postmodernism and Politics* (Manchester: Manchester University Press, 1986); Alice A. Jardine, *Gynesis: Configurations of Women and Modernity* (Ithaca and London: Cornell University Press, 1985); David Kolb, *The Critique of Pure Modernity* (Chicago and London: Chicago University Press, 1986); John

McGowan, *Postmodernism and Its Critics* (Ithaca and London: Cornell University Press, 1991); William E. Connolly, *Political Theory and Modernity* (Oxford: Basil Blackwell, 1988).

6. Bauman, *Legislators and Interpreters*. The specific attributes and locations of black intellectuals, who have rarely also been academics, has been usefully discussed by bell hooks and Cornel West in their collaboration *Breaking Bread* (Boston: South End Press, 1991).

7. Montesquieu, *Persian Letters* (Harmondsworth: Penguin, 1986), p. 83.

8. *Patterns of Dissonance* (Cambridge: Polity Press, 1991), p. 193.

9. Berman, *All That Is Solid Melts into Air*, p. 132.

10. Ibid., p. 15.

11. *The Politics of Authenticity: Radical Individualism and the Emergence of Modern Society* (London: George Allen and Unwin, 1971), p. 317.

12. Ibid.

13. "The Signs in the Street: A Response to Perry Anderson," *New Left Review* 144 (1984).

14. "Urbicide," *Village Voice* 29 no. 36 (September 4, 1984).

15. Manuel Moreno Fraginals, *The Sugar Mill: The Socioeconomic Complex of Sugar in Cuba* (New York: Monthly Review Press, 1976).

16. Berman, "Urbicide," p. 25.

17. Ibid., p. 17.

18. Studies of cultural syncretism in terms of day-to-day experiences have begun to appear: Mechal Sobel's *The World They Made Together: Black and White Values in Eighteenth-Century Virginia* (Princeton, N.J.: Princeton University Press, 1987) seems to me to be an exemplary text of this type.

19. The work of David Brion Davis is an important exception here, but he is an American and a historian.

20. Jurgen Habermas, *The Philosophical Discourse of Modernity* (Cambridge: Polity Press, 1987), p. 28.

21. Ibid., p. 43.

22. David Brion Davis, *The Problem of Slavery in the Age of Revolution, 1770–1823* (Ithaca and London: Cornell University Press, 1975).

23. A. Kojève, *Introduction to the Reading of Hegel* (New York: Basic Books, 1969); Hussein A. Bulhan, *Frantz Fanon and the Psychology of Oppression* (New York: Plenum Press, 1985). The division between those who, like Deleuze, argue that Hegel says the future belongs to the slave and those who interpret his words as pointing to a world beyond the master/slave relationship remains a deep one. See Deleuze, *Nietzsche and Philosophy* (London: Athlone Press, 1983).

24. Sandra Harding, *The Science Question in Feminism* (Milton Keynes: Open University Press, 1986), p. 158; Nancy Hartsock, *Money, Sex and Power* (Boston: Northeastern University Press, 1983), p. 240.

25. Hill Collins's emphasis on the outsider within could for example be readily assimilated to the notions of "double consciousness," "double vision," and "dreadful objectivity" discussed elsewhere in this book. It is interesting that she does not attempt to link this theme in her own work with the history of these ideas in African-American political culture. See Patricia Hill Collins, "Learning from the Outsider Within: The Sociological Significance of Black Feminist Thought," *Social Problems* 33, no. 6 (1986): 14–32.

26. Patricia Hill Collins, *Black Feminist Thought: Knowledge, Consciousness and the Politics of Empowerment* (New York and London: Routledge, 1991), p. 27. The deconstructive zeal with which Hill Collins urges her readers to take traditional epistemological assumptions apart is exhausted after tackling "woman" and "intellectual." It runs out long before she reaches the key words "black" and "Afrocentric," which appear to be immune to this critical operation (see p. 17).

27. Ibid., p. 40.

28. Ibid., pp. 32–33.

29. Ibid., p. 23.

30. Jane Flax, *Thinking Fragments* (Berkeley and Oxford: University of California Press, 1990).

31. Trans. J. B. Baillie (New York: Harper and Row, 1967), ch. 4.

32. Cornel West, "The Religious Foundations of the Thought of Martin Luther King, Jr.," in *We Shall Overcome: Martin Luther King and the Black Freedom Struggle,* ed. Peter J. Albert and Ronald Hoffman (New York: Pantheon, 1990).

33. Quoted by Kimberley Benston in *Baraka* (New Haven: Yale University Press, 1976), p. 90. For a discussion of the relationship between Baraka and Hegel see Esther M. Jackson, "LeRoi Jones (Imamu Amiri Baraka): Form and the Progression of Consciousness," in Kimberly W. Benston, ed., *Imamu Amiri Baraka (LeRoi Jones): Twentieth Century Views* (Englewood Cliffs, N.J.: Prentice Hall, 1978).

34. *Being and Nothingness* (London: Methuen 1969), bk. 1, pp. 157–158.

35. Eric Foner, *Nothing but Freedom* (Baton Rouge and London: Louisiana State University Press, 1983), p. 1.

36. Walter Benjamin, "Paris: The Capital of the Nineteenth Century," in *Charles Baudelaire: A Lyric Poet in the Era of High Capitalism* (London: Verso, 1976), p. 159. See also Richard Wolin, *Walter Benjamin: An Aesthetic of Redemption* (New York: Columbia University Press, 1982).

37. Andrew Benjamin, "Tradition and Experience," in Andrew Benjamin, ed., *The Problems of Modernity* (London: Routledge, 1989).

38. See Orlando Patterson's discussion of Hegel in *Slavery and Social Death* (Cambridge, Mass.: Harvard University Press, 1982), pp. 97–101.

39. Dominique Lecourt, "On Marxism as a Critique of Sociological Theories," in M. O'Callaghan, ed., *Sociological Theories: Race and Colonialism* (Paris: UNESCO, 1980), p. 267.

40. ". . . somewhere between men and cattle God had created a tertium quid, and called it Negro,—a clownish, simple creature, at times lovable within its limitations, but straitly foreordained to walk within the Veil." *The Souls of Black Folk* (1903; New York: Bantam, 1989), p. 63.

41. For a critique of these appeals see Joan Wallach Scott, "The Evidence of Experience," *Critical Inquiry* 17 (Summer 1991): 773–797.

42. Michel Foucault, "What Is Enlightenment?" in *The Foucault Reader,* ed. Paul Rabinow (Harmondsworth: Peregrine, 1986), p. 50.

43. George Shepperson, "Frederick Douglass and Scotland," *Journal of Negro History* 38, no. 3 (1953): 307–321.

44. Waldo E. Martin, *The Mind of Frederick Douglass* (Durham and London: University of North Carolina Press, 1984); L. Litwack and A. Meier, *Black Leaders of the Nineteenth Century* (Urbana and Chicago: University of Illinois Press, 1988);

William S. McFeely, *Frederick Douglass* (New York: W. W. Norton, 1991).

45. *The Life and Times of Frederick Douglass* (New York: Macmillan, 1962); *My Bondage and My Freedom* (New York and Auburn: Miller, Orton and Mulligan, 1855); and *Narrative of the Life of Frederick Douglass, An American Slave, Written by Himself* (Cambridge, Mass.: Harvard University Press, 1960). All quotations below are taken from these editions.

46. Douglass, *My Bondage and My Freedom,* p. 49.

47. Ibid., p. 50.

48. Ibid., p. 198. The anti-religious theme is shared by a number of other narratives for example Henry Bibb's caustic comments on the complicity of Christianity with the institution of slavery. See also the remarks of Mr. Listwell in Douglass's novella *The Heroic Slave* in Ronald Takaki, ed., *Violence in the Black Imagination: Essays and Documents* (New York: G. P. Putnam's Sons, 1972); and Robert B. Stepto, "Sharing the Thunder: The Literary Exchanges of Harriet Beecher Stowe, Henry Bibb and Frederick Douglass," in Eric Sundquist, ed., *New Essays on Uncle Tom's Cabin* (Cambridge: Cambridge University Press, 1986).

49. *The Life and Writings of Frederick Douglass,* ed. Philip S. Foner, vol. 2 (New York: International Publishers, 1950), pp. 289–309.

50. Stephen Jay Gould, *The Mismeasure of Man* (Harmondsworth: Pelican, 1984), ch. 2.

51. *Black Athena: The Afroasiatic Roots of Classical Civilization,* vol. 1: *The Fabrication of Ancient Greece, 1785–1985* (London: Free Association Books, 1987).

52. Martin, *The Mind of Frederick Douglass,* ch. 9.

53. George James, *Stolen Legacy: The Greeks Were Not the Authors of Greek Philosophy, but the People of North Africa, Commonly Called the Egyptians* (San Francisco: Julian Richardson, 1976).

54. McFeely, *Frederick Douglass,* p. 263.

55. Douglass, *My Bondage,* p. 170.

56. Ibid., p. 184.

57. Ibid., p. 185.

58. Ibid. The confrontation with Covey is a pivotal moment in all three versions of Douglass's autobiography.

59. Ibid., p. 187.

60. Ibid., p. 190.

61. Jacques Lacan, *Écrits: A Selection* (London: Tavistock, 1977), p. 308.

62. Patterson, *Slavery and Social Death.*

63. I am thinking in particular of the spectacular suicide of Clotel/Isabella (the tragic slave daughter of Thomas Jefferson) in the icy waters of the Potomac that can be found in William Wells Brown's novels *Clotel; or, The President's Daughter, A Narrative of Slave Life in the United States* (1853; rpt. New York: Collier Books, 1970) and *Clotelle: A Tale of the Southern States* (Boston: Redpath, 1864). Ch. 16 of *Clotelle* is entitled "Death Is Freedom."

64. See also Ronald Takaki's discussion of this theme in the work of William Wells Brown and Martin Delaney in *Violence in the Black Imagination;* and L. F. Goldstein, "Violence as an Instrument of Social Change: The Views of Frederick Douglass (1817–1895)," *Journal of Negro History* 61, pt. 1 (1976).

65. *Darkwater Voices from within the Veil* (New York: Harcourt Brace and Co., 1921), p. 176.

66. Toni Morrison's version of the story seems to have been prompted by a contemporary account reproduced in Harris Middleton et al., eds., *The Black Book* (New York: Random House, 1974), p. 10. Morrison would have been responsible for editing this volume during her employment at Random House.

67. *Annual Report Presented to the American Anti-Slavery Society,* New York, May 1856, pp. 44–47. Levi Coffin, *Reminiscences of Levi Coffin, the Reputed President of the Underground Railroad* (Cincinnati, 1876, rpt. New York: Augustus Kelley, 1968), p. 560. Most of the references to newspapers are given by Julius Yanuck in "The Garner Fugitive Slave Case," *Mississippi Valley Historical Review* 40 (June 1953): 47–66. See also Herbert Aptheker, "The Negro Woman," *Masses and Mainstream* 2 (February 1949): 10–17.

68. *Reminscences of Levi Coffin,* p. 562.

69. Stanley W. Campbell, *The Slave Catchers: Enforcement of the Fugitive Slave Law, 1850–1860* (Chapel Hill: University of North Carolina Press, 1968).

70. *Reminiscences of Levi Coffin,* p. 560.

71. *New York Daily Times,* February 16, 1856.

72. This version is reprinted in *The Black Book.*

73. *Annual Report Presented to the American Anti-Slavery Society,* p. 45.

74. *New York Daily Times,* February 2, 1856; see also *Cincinnati Commercial,* January 30, 1856.

75. *Cincinnati Daily Gazette,* January 29, 1856.

76. Alice Stone Blackwell, *Lucy Stone: Pioneer of Women's Rights* (Boston: Little, Brown, 1930), pp. 183–184.

77. Coffin claims to have been in the court when these words were spoken. This report is taken from his account. A further version of this episode is given by Alice Stone Blackwell in *Lucy Stone,* p. 184: "While visiting Margaret Garner in prison, Mrs. Stone asked her, in case she should be taken back into slavery, if she had a knife. In court, Mrs. Stone was asked if it was true that she had offered Margaret a knife. She answered, 'I did ask her if she had a knife. If I were a slave, as she is a slave, with the law against me, and the church against me, and with no death dealing weapon at hand, I would with my own teeth tear open my veins, and send my soul back to God who gave it.'"

78. *Reminiscences of Levi Coffin,* p. 565; *Cincinnati Daily Gazette,* February 14, 1856.

79. "A Coloured Lady Lecturer," *Englishwoman's Review* 7 (June 1861): 269–275; Mathew Davenport Hill, ed., *Our Exemplars, Poor and Rich* (London: Peter Cassell and Co., 1861), pp. 276–286 (I am grateful to Clare Midgeley for this reference); Ruth Bogin, "Sarah Parker Remond: Black Abolitionist from Salem," *Essex Institute Historical Collections* 110 (April 1974): 120–150; Dorothy Porter, "Sarah Parker Remond, Abolitionist and Physician," *Journal of Negro History* 20 (July 1935): 287–293.

80. *Journals of Charlotte Forten Grimké,* ed. B. Stephenson (New York and Oxford: Oxford University Press, 1988), pp. 116–117 (entry for December 17, 1854). Partly because of their common vocation as physicians, Remond's odyssey from New England to Rome marks an interesting counterpoint to the life of Martin Delany discussed in Chapter 1.

81. *Warrington Times,* January 29, 1859; see also C. Peter Ripley, ed., *The Black Abolitionist Papers,* vol. 1 (Chapel Hill and London: University of North Carolina Press, 1985), pp. 437–438.

82. Douglass, *Narrative*, p. 49.

83. William L. Andrews, *To Tell a Free Story* (Urbana and Chicago: University of Illinois Press, 1986).

84. H. L. Gates, Jr., *Figures in Black: Words, Signs, and the "Racial" Self* (Oxford and New York: Oxford University Press, 1986).

85. Andrews, *To Tell a Free Story*, p. 103.

86. Douglass, *Narrative*, p. 56.

87. W. E. B Du Bois, *Black Reconstruction in America* (New York: Atheneum, 1977), p. 703.

3. "Jewels Brought from Bondage": Black Music and the Politics of Authenticity

1. Andrew Bowie, *Aesthetics and Subjectivity* (Manchester: Manchester University Press, 1990), p. 68.

2. These views are echoed by Richard Wright's insistence on the blues as merely the sensualisation of suffering.

3. "The threshold between Classicism and modernity . . . had been definitely crossed when words ceased to intersect with representations and to provide a spontaneous grid for the knowledge of things." Michel Foucault, *The Order of Things* (London: Tavistock, 1974), p. 304.

4. Frederick Douglass, *Narrative of the Life of Frederick Douglass, an American Slave, Written by Himself* (Cambridge, Mass.: Harvard University Press, 1960), p. 46.

5. St. Clair Drake, *Black Folks Here and There*, Afro-American Culture and Society Monograph Series no. 7 (Los Angeles: University of California, 1987).

6. Edouard Glissant, *Caribbean Discourse*, trans. J. Michael Dash (Charlottesville: University of Virginia Press, 1989), p. 248; John Baugh, *Black Street Speech* (Austin: University of Texas Press, 1983).

7. Robert Farris Thompson, *Flash of the Spirit* (New York: Vantage Press, 1983) and "Kongo Influences on African-American Artistic Culture," in J. E. Holloway, ed., *Africanisms in American Culture* (Bloomington and Indianapolis: Indiana University Press, 1990).

8. bell hooks and Cornel West, *Breaking Bread* (Boston: South End Press, 1991).

9. We may follow Kristeva too into the idea that the condition of exile which partially defines the experience of these artists also compounds their experience of dissidence. "A New Type of Intellectual: The Dissident," in Toril Moi, ed., *The Kristeva Reader* (Oxford: Basil Blackwell, 1986).

10. Robert Proctor, *Value-Free Science? Purity and Power in Modern Knowledge* (Cambridge, Mass.: Harvard University Press, 1991); Donna Haraway, "Manifesto For Cyborgs," in Linda Nicholson, ed., *Feminism/Postmodernism* (New York and London: Routledge, 1990).

11. Paul Gilroy, "Living Memory: An Interview with Toni Morrison," in Paul Gilroy, *Small Acts* (London: Serpent's Tail, 1993), pp. 175–182.

12. Ralph Ellison, *Shadow and Act* (New York: Random House, 1964), p. 234.

13. C. L. R. James, *Notes on Dialectics* (London: Allison and Busby, 1980).

14. C. L. R. James, "The Mighty Sparrow," in *The Future in the Present* (London: Allison and Busby, 1978); Kathy Ogren, " 'Jazz Isn't Just Me': Jazz Autobiog-

raphies as Performance Personas," in Reginald T. Buckner et al., eds., *Jazz in Mind: Essays on the History and Meanings of Jazz* (Detroit: Wayne State University Press, 1991).

15. Kobena Mercer, "Black Art and the Burden of Representation," *Third Text* 10 (Spring 1990), and "Looking for Trouble," *Transition* 51 (1991).

16. This concept is suggestively explored by Glissant in *Caribbean Discourse* and by St. Clair Drake in his two-volume study *Black Folk Here and There* (1987 and 1990).

17. Judith Butler, *Gender Trouble* (New York and London: Routledge, 1990); Jane Flax, *Thinking Fragments* (Berkeley and Oxford: University of California Press, 1990); E. Spelman, *Inessential Woman* (Boston: Beacon Press, 1988); Sandra Harding, "The Instability of Analytical Categories in Feminist Theory," in S. Harding and J. O'Barr, eds., *Sex and Scientific Enquiry* (Chicago: University of Chicago Press, 1988).

18. These processes have been examined in Gurinder Chudha's film *I'm British But* (British Film Institute, 1988).

19. On Apache Indian see John Masouri, "Wild Apache," *Echoes,* February 1, 1992, p. 11; Laura Connelly, "Big Bhangra Theory," *Time Out,* February 19–26, 1992, p. 18; and Vaughan Allen, "Bhangramuffin," *The Face* 44 (May 1992): 104–107.

20. For example Malkit Singh, *Golden Star (U.K.),* "Ragga Muffin Mix 1991," remixed by Bally Sagoo, Star Cassette SC 5120. Thanks to Chila Kumari Burman for this reference.

21. I am thinking here of the way in which the street funk experiments of the Los Angelino band War paved the way for modernist reggae experiments. Play War's "Slippin' into Darkness" back to back with the Wailers' "Get Up Stand Up" and you will see what I mean.

22. Dennis Wepman et al., *The Life: The Lore and Folk Poetry of the Black Hustler* (Philadelphia: University of Pennsylvania Press, 1976).

23. Henry Louis Gates, Jr., "Rap Music: Don't Knock It If You're Not onto Its 'Lies,'" *New York Herald Tribune,* June 20, 1990.

24. Eric Berman, "A Few Words with Eric B. and Rakim," *Crossroads Magazine* 1, no. 4 (December 1990): 10.

25. Cornel West, "Black Culture and Postmodernism," in B. Kruger and P. Mariani, eds., *Re-Making History* (Seattle: Bay Press, 1989).

26. Trey Ellis's piece "The New Black Aesthetic (N.B.A.)," *Callaloo* 12, no. 1 (Winter 1989): 233–247, exemplified the perils of casual, "anything goes" postmodernism for black cultural production. It was striking how, for example, profound questions of class antagonism *within* the black communities were conjured out of sight. Apart from his conflation of forms which are not merely different but actively oppose one another, Ellis did not seriously consider the notion that the N.B.A. might have a very particular and highly class-specific articulation within a small and isolated segment of the black middle class which has struggled with its dependency on the cultural lifeblood of the black poor.

27. Edward Said, "Travelling Theory," in *The World, the Text and the Critic* (Cambridge, Mass.: Harvard University Press, 1983).

28. I am thinking of fractal geometry as an analogy here because it allows for the possibility that a line of infinite length can enclose a finite area. The opposition

between totality and infinity is thus recast in a striking image of the scope for agency in restricted conditions.

29. Peter Linebaugh has recently discussed the etymology of the word "jubilee" and some of the political discourses that surround it in "Jubilating," *Midnight Notes,* Fall 1990. Reviews of the Singers' performances in England can be found in *East Anglian Daily Times,* November 21, 1874, and the *Surrey Advertiser,* December 5, 1874.

30. John M. MacKenzie, ed., *Imperialism and Popular Culture* (Manchester: Manchester University Press, 1986).

31. Joel Boskin, *Sambo: The Rise and Demise of an American Jester* (New York and Oxford: Oxford University Press, 1986); R. C. Toll, *Blacking Up: The Minstrel Show in Nineteenth-Century America* (New York and Oxford: Oxford University Press, 1974).

32. L. D. Silveri, "The Singing Tours of the Fisk Jubilee Singers: 1871–1874," in G. R. Keck and S. V. Martin, eds., *Feel the Spirit: Studies in Nineteenth-Century Afro-American Music* (Westport, Conn.: Greenwood Press, 1989).

33. D. Scroff, "The Original Fisk Jubilee Singers and the Spiritual Tradition," pt. 1, *Keskidee* 2 (1990): 4.

34. J. B. T. Marsh, *The Story of the Jubilee Singers with Their Songs* (London: Hodder and Staughton, 1875), p. 69.

35. Sam Dennison, *Scandalize My Name: Black Imagery in American Popular Music* (New York and London: Garland Press, 1982). See also William Wells Brown, comp., *The Anti-Slavery Harp: A Collection of Songs for Anti-Slavery Meetings, Compiled by William W. Brown, a Fugitive Slave* (Boston: Bela Marsh, 1848).

36. Marsh, *The Jubilee Singers,* p. 36.

37. Seroff's research lists more than twenty choirs in the period between 1871 and 1878.

38. Gareth Stedman Jones, "Working-Class Culture and Working-Class Politics in London, 1870–1900: Notes on the Remaking of a Working Class," in Gareth Stedman Jones, *Languages of Class* (Cambridge: Cambridge University Press, 1983).

39. An "Eva Gets Well" version of Uncle Tom's Cabin was doing excellent business on the London stage in 1878. See also Toll, *Blacking Up;* Barry Anthony, "Early Nigger Minstrel Acts in Britain," *Music Hall* 12 (April 1980); and Josephine Wright, "Orpheus Myron McAdoo," *Black Perspective in Music* 4, no. 3 (Fall 1976).

40. These events are described in Gladstone's diaries for 14 and 29 July 1873. Apart from the Singers' own text, there is a lengthy description of these events in the New York *Independent,* August 21, 1873. See also Ella Sheppard Moore, "Historical Sketch of the Jubilee Singers," *Fisk University News* (October 1911): 42.

41. W. E. B. Du Bois, *The Souls of Black Folk* (New York: Bantam, 1989), p. 179.

42. In his essay on the Fisk Singers in Britain, Doug Seroff cites the example of the East London Jubilee Singers of Hackney Juvenile Mission, a "Ragged School" formed after an inspirational visit by the Fisk Singers to Hackney in June 1873. John Newman, the manager of the Mission, "felt that such singing from the soul should not be forgotten, and speedily set to work to teach the children of the Mission the songs the Jubilee singers had sung." See R. Lotz and I. Pegg, eds., *Under*

the Imperial Carpet: Essays in Black History, 1780–1950 (Crawley: Rabbit Press, 1986).

43. H. L. Gates, Jr., "The Trope of the New Negro and the Reconstruction of the Image of the Black," *Representations* 24 (1988): 129–156.

44. Alain Locke, ed. *The New Negro* (1925; rpt. New York: Atheneum, 1968), p. 199.

45. Hazel Carby, "The Politics of Fiction, Anthropology and the Folk: Zora Neale Hurston," in Michael Awkward, ed., *New Essays on Their Eyes Were Watching God* (Cambridge: Cambridge University Press, 1990).

46. Zora Neale Hurston, "Spirituals and Neo-Spirituals," in Nancy Cunard, ed., *Negro* (1933; rpt. New York: Ungar Press, 1970), p. 224.

47. Zora Neale Hurston, "The Characteristics of Negro Expression," in Cunard, *Negro,* p. 31.

48. Various drafts of this unpublished script as well as the reader's report on it by Emily Brown, the Hollywood script editor who rejected it in 1944, are held in the James Welson Johnson Collection at the Beinecke Archive, Yale University. Brown felt that the script lacked the simplicity and dignity that its theme deserved. See "Jubilee" JWJ Wright 219.

49. "Noel and Mitch would sometimes use racial slurs when they talked. They would use 'nigger' and 'coon' in banter." David Henderson, *'Scuse Me While I Kiss the Sky: The Life of Jimi Hendrix* (New York: Bantam, 1981), p. 92. For the banterers' side of all this cheerful chat see Noel Redding and Carol Appleby, *Are You Experienced: The Inside Story of the Jimi Hendrix Experience* (London: Fourth Estate, 1990); and Mitch Mitchell with John Platt, *Jimi Hendrix: Inside the Experience* (New York: Harmony, 1990). See also Harry Shapiro and Caesar Glebbeek, *Jimi Hendrix: Electric Gypsy* (London: Heinemann, 1990).

50. Charles Shaar Murray, *Crosstown Traffic* (London: Faber, 1989), p. 68.

51. Marshall Berman discusses the form that this relationship took during the Enlightenment in *The Politics of Authenticity* (London: George Allen and Unwin, 1971).

52. Nelson George, *The Death of Rhythm and Blues* (London: Omnibus Press, 1988), p. 109.

53. Henderson, *'Scuse Me,* p. 92.

54. The phenomenon of Jamaican male vocal trios is discussed by Randall Grass, "Iron Sharpen Iron: The Great Jamaican Harmony Trios," in P. Simon, ed., *Reggae International* (London: Thames and Hudson, 1983). Key exponents of this particular art would be the Heptones, the Paragons, the Gaylads, the Meditations, the Itals, Carlton and the Shoes, Justin Hines and the Dominoes, Toots and the Maytals, Yabby Yu and the Prophets, the Gladiators, the Melodians, the Ethiopians, the Cables, the Tamlins, the Congoes, the Mighty Diamonds, the Abyssinians, Black Uhuru, Israel Vibration, and of course the Wailers, whose Neville O'Reilly/Bunny Livingstone/Bunny Wailer does the best Curtis Mayfield impersonation of the lot.

55. Nelson Mandela, speech in Detroit, June 29, 1990. I am grateful to Suzy Smith of Yale University for this reference.

56. George, *The Death of Rhythm and Blues,* book jacket.

57. Nick Kent, "Miles Davis Interview," *The Face* 78 (1986): 22–23. "They got Wynton playing some old dead European music . . . Wynton's playing their dead shit, the kind of stuff anybody can do. All you've got to do is practice, practice,

practice. I told him I wouldn't bow down to that music, that they should be glad someone as talented as he is is playing that tired-ass shit." Miles Davis with Quincy Troupe, *Miles: The Autobiography* (New York: Simon and Schuster, 1989), pp. 360–361.

58. These issues are discussed in a different context by John Hutchinson in *The Dynamics of Cultural Nationalism: The Gaelic Revival and the Creation of the Irish Nation State* (London: Allen and Unwin, 1987).

59. Alexander Crummell, *Africa and America* (Springfield, Mass.: Willey and Co., 1891), p. 46.

60. Du Bois, *The Souls of Black Folk*, p. 139.

61. Houston A. Baker, Jr., *Modernism and the Harlem Renaissance* (Chicago: University of Chicago Press, 1987), pp. 105–106.

62. Kobena Mercer, "Monster Metaphors: Notes on Michael Jackson's 'Thriller,'" *Screen* 27, no. 1 (1986).

63. A similar argument has been made in the context of feminist political theory by Judith Butler in *Gender Trouble* (New York and London: Routledge, 1990).

64. Michel Foucault, *Discipline and Punish* (London: Penguin, 1979), p. 29.

65. Michel de Certeau, *The Practice of Everyday Life* (Berkeley and London: University of California Press, 1988), p. xvii.

66. T. W. Adorno, "On The Fetish Character in Music and the Regression of Listening," in A. Arato and E. Gebhardt, eds., *The Essential Frankfurt School Reader* (Oxford: Basil Blackwell, 1978).

67. Ronnie Laws, *Identity* (Hype Mix), A. T. A. Records LSNCD 30011, 1990.

68. ". . . we must consider the rendition of a song not as a final thing, but as a mood. It won't be the same thing next Sunday." Hurston, "Spirituals and Neo Spirituals," p. 224.

69. Jean Baudrillard, *Fatal Strategies* (New York and London: Semiotext(e), 1990), p. 118.

70. LL Cool J, *Round the Way Girl*, Def Jam 4473610 12".

71. Raymond Horricks, *Quincy Jones* (London: Spellmount Ltd./Hippocrene Books Inc.), 1985.

72. Quincy Jones, *Listen Up*, Qwest 926322–2 compact disc.

73. Jones made these remarks in an interview for British Channel 4 TV's Media Show item "Black Prime Time," directed by Mandy Rose and shown in October 1990.

74. Quincy Jones, *Back on The Block*, Qwest LP 26020–1.

75. Quincy Jones, *Listen Up: The Many Lives of Quincy Jones* (New York: Warner Books, 1990), p. 167.

4. "Cheer the Weary Traveller": W. E. B. Du Bois, Germany, and the Politics of (Dis)placement

1. Immanuel Geiss, *The Pan-African Movement* (London: Methuen, 1974).

2. W. E. B. Du Bois, *The Souls of Black Folk* (New York: Bantam, 1989), p. 154.

3. W. E. B. Dubois, *Dusk of Dawn* (New York: Library of America, 1986), p. 590.

4. Frederick Douglass, "The Negro Exodus from the Gulf States," *Journal of Social Science* 11 (May 1880): 1–21.

5. Arnold Rampersad, *The Art and Imagination of W. E. B. Du Bois* (New York: Schocken Books, 1990).

6. W. E .B. Du Bois, *The Autobiography of W. E. B. Du Bois* (New York: International Publishers, 1968), p. 122.

7. Ibid., p. 108.

8. Dubois, *Dusk of Dawn*, p. 627.

9. Rampersad discovers the "Jacksonian affinities" in Du Bois's thought in *The Art and Imagination of W. E. B. Dubois*, p. 217. In his biography *W. E. B. Dubois: Black Radical Democrat* (Boston: G. K. Hall, 1986), Manning Marable sees Du Bois in rather more radical terms.

10. Du Bois, *The Souls*, p. 114.

11. Ibid., pp. 62–63.

12. On the political struggles against lynching in this period see Ida B. Wells, "Southern Horrors: Lynch Law in All Its Phases," in Trudier Harris, ed., *The Selected Works of Ida B. Wells Barnett* (New York and Oxford: Oxford University Press, 1991). For a more general overview see Herbert Shapiro, *White Violence and Black Response: From Reconstruction to Montgomery* (Amherst: University of Massachusetts Press, 1988). The significance of this episode for Du Bois is discussed most interestingly despite inaccurate detail by Allison Davis in his pyschological study *Leadership, Love, and Aggression* (New York: Harcourt Brace Jovanovich, 1983). Du Bois's own accounts of the significance of this event are set down in the *Autobiography*, p. 222, and *Dusk of Dawn*, pp. 602–603. Du Bois is reported to have told Herbert Aptheker, the editor of his collected work, that "something within me died that day"; see Aptheker's introduction to the Kraus Thompson reprint of *Dark Princess* (Millwood, N.Y.: Kraus Thomson, 1974), p. 17.

13. Du Bois, *Dusk of Dawn*, p. 738.

14. Du Bois, *The Souls*, p. 79.

15. Ibid., p. 76.

16. Ibid., p. 59.

17. Cedric Robinson, *Black Marxism* (London: Zed Press, 1981).

18. Du Bois, *The Souls*, p. 145.

19. This, after all, is why young people wear pendants in the shape of Africa around their necks.

20. Houston A. Baker, Jr., *Modernism and the Harlem Renaissance* (Chicago: University of Chicago Press, 1987).

21. There is a single citation from the Bible. The final essay, on the "sorrow songs," employs a fragment from one of the songs being discussed.

22. H. L. Gates, Jr., makes this point in his valuable introduction to the Bantam edition; Houston Baker sees the text this way in *Long Black Song* (Charlottesville: University Press of Virginia, 1990); as does Robert Stepto in *From Behind the Veil* (Urbana and Chicago: University of Illinois Press, 1979), where he identifies the three parts as stasis, immersion, and ascent. Arnold Rampersad, whose understanding of the structure of the book is closest to my own, differs in that he sees the final block of the work as being defined and unified by its concern with black spirituality.

23. Du Bois, *Dusk of Dawn*, pp. 639–670.

24. *The Negro* (New York: Henry Holt, 1915); *Black Folk: Then and Now* (New York: Henry Holt, 1939); *The World and Africa* (New York: International Publishers, 1965).

25. Du Bois, *The Souls,* p. 29.

26. Ibid., p. 21.

27. Ibid., p. 47.

28. Ibid., p. 57.

29. Ibid., p. 136.

30. Ibid., p. 134.

31. Ibid., p. 52.

32. Ibid., p. 186.

33. James Weldon Johnson, *Along This Way: The Autobiography of James Weldon Johnson* (Harmondsworth: Penguin, 1990), p. 203.

34. *The Autobiography of an Ex-Coloured Man* (New York: Vintage Press, 1989), p. 168.

35. Stepto, *From Behind the Veil,* pp. 52–127.

36. Johnson, *Ex-Coloured Man,* p. 153.

37. Ibid., p. 181.

38. Ibid., p. 186. On the significance of these brutal rituals see Mick Taussig, *Shamanism, Colonialism and The Wildman: A Study in Terror and Healing* (Chicago: University of Chicago Press, 1987), pt. 1, "Terror."

39. Johnson, *Ex-Coloured Man,* pp. 189–190.

40. Ibid., p. 142.

41. Adrienne Rich, "Notes towards a Politics of Location," in *Bread, Blood, and Poetry* (London: Virago, 1987); James Clifford, "Travelling Cultures," in Lawrence Grossberg et al., eds., *Cultural Studies* (New York and London: Routledge, 1992), and "Notes on Theory and Travel," *Inscriptions* 5 (1989): 177–185; bell hooks, "Whiteness in the Black Imagination," also in *Cultural Studies* and rpt. in *Black Looks* (Boston: South End Press, 1992); Dennis Porter, *Haunted Journeys: Desire and Transgression in European Travel Writing* (Princeton, N.J.: Princeton University Press, 1991); Mary Louise Pratt, *Imperial Eyes* (London and New York: Routledge, 1992).

42. See Brailsford R. Brazeal, *The Brotherhood of Sleeping Car Porters* (New York: Harper and Brothers, 1946). Ch. 1 includes a discussion of the background to George Pullman's decision to employ blacks in this role.

43. André Gorz, *The Critique of Economic Reason* (London: Verso, 1990), ch. 11.

44. Joel Williamson, *The Crucible of Race* (New York and Oxford: Oxford University Press, 1984), pp. 399–409; Francis Broderick, "German Influence on the Scholarship of W. E. B. Dubois," *Phylon* 11 (Winter 1958): 367–371.

45. Du Bois, *Dusk of Dawn,* p. 626.

46. Du Bois, *The Souls,* p. 3.

47. G. W. F. Hegel, *The Philosophy of History* (London: Dover Publications, 1956), p. 99.

48. *The Autobiography of W. E. B. Du Bois,* pp. 108–109.

49. *The Crisis* 27, no. 6 (April 1924): 273.

50. W. E. B. Du Bois, *Black Reconstruction in America* (1938; New York: Atheneum, 1977), pp. 124–125.

51. Cornel West, *The American Evasion of Philosophy* (London: Macmillan, 1989), p. 147.

52. This point, so germane to West's discussion of Du Bois, is recognised by

Richard Rorty in an insightful review of West's book where he describes its author as "patriotic, religious and romantic." *Transition* 52 (1991): 70–80.

53. Stepto, *From Behind the Veil.*

54. A critical response to this position might begin from the analysis developed in a different historical setting by Marilyn Strathern in *After Nature: English Kinship in the Late Twentieth Century* (Cambridge: Cambridge University Press, 1992).

55. Victor Turner, *Dramas, Fields and Metaphors: Symbolic Action in Human Society* (Ithaca: Cornell University Press, 1974).

56. Du Bois, *The Souls,* p. 150.

57. Wilson J. Moses, *Alexander Crummell: A Study of Civilization and Discontent* (New York and Oxford: Oxford University Press, 1989); Gregory Rigsby, *Alexander Crummell: Pioneer in Nineteenth Century Pan-African Thought* (Westport, Conn.: Greenwood Press, 1987).

58. Du Bois, *The Souls,* p. 188.

59. Wyndham Lewis, *Paleface; or, The Philosophy of the Melting Pot* (London: Chatto and Windus, 1929), pp. 28–51. This exchange has been completely overlooked in scholarly and critical writing about Lewis. Sarat Maharaj discusses it briefly in his "The Congo Is Flooding the Acropolis," *Third Text* 15 (Summer 1991).

60. Francis L. Broderick, *W. E. B. Du Bois: Negro Leader in a Time of Crisis* (Stanford: Stanford University Press, 1959), p. 154.

61. Rampersad, *The Art and Imagination of W. E. B. Dubois,* p. 204.

62. Du Bois, *Dark Princess,* p. 19.

63. Ibid., p. 26.

64. Ibid., p. 46.

65. Ibid., p. 147.

66. Ibid., p. 220.

67. Ibid., p. 307.

68. *Chicago Bee,* August 4, 1928.

5. "Without the Consolation of Tears": Richard Wright, France, and the Ambivalence of Community

1. One of his biographers mentions that Wright kept leather-bound volumes of his books that had been translated into Braille and into Hebrew, Japanese, and Bengali as well as a variety of European languages. Constance Webb, *Richard Wright: A Biography* (New York: G. P. Putnam's Sons, 1968), p. 386.

2. *Uncle Tom's Children* was sold for the low price of 49 cents.

3. Richard Wright, "The American Problem: Its Negro Phase," in D. Ray, R. M. Farnsworth, and C. T. Davis, eds., *Richard Wright: Impressions and Perspectives* (Ann Arbor: University of Michigan Press, 1974), pp. 11–12.

4. "In *Uncle Tom's Children,* in *Native Son,* and above all in *Black Boy,* I found expressed, for the first time in my life, the sorrow, the rage and the murderous bitterness which was eating up my life and the lives of those around me." James Baldwin, "Alas Poor Richard," in *Nobody Knows My Name* (London: Corgi, 1969), p. 152.

5. Kent's absorbing book of this title was published in 1972 and has been plagia-

rised in debates of African-American culture ever since. *Blackness and the Adventure of Western Culture* (Chicago: Third World Press, 1972).

6. Wright uses this term in both *Pagan Spain* (New York: Harper and Brothers, 1957) and *The Colour Curtain* (London: Dobson, 1956).

7. *The Outsider* (New York: Harper and Row, 1965), p. 27.

8. Michel Fabre, *The Unfinished Quest of Richard Wright* (New York: Morrow, 1973), p. 387.

9. Wright, *Colour Curtain*, p. 150.

10. Richard Wright, *White Man Listen!* (New York: Anchor Books, 1964), p. 72.

11. Ibid., p. 80.

12. Richard Wright, *Twelve Million Black Voices* (London: Lindsay Drummond Ltd., 1947), p. 30.

13. Fabre, *Unfinished Quest*, p. 415.

14. Kent, *The Adventure*, p. 83.

15. Ralph Ellison, *Going to the Territory* (New York: Random House, 1986), p. 198.

16. Ibid., p. 212.

17. Wright, *The Outsider*, p. 198.

18. On the book jacket of the first edition of *Native Son*, Edward Weeks, editor of the *Atlantic Monthly*, described the book's impact: "It has us all by the ears. It is certainly a performance of great talent—powerful, disturbing, unquestionably authentic."

19. Allison Davis, *Leadership, Love and Aggression* (New York: Harcourt Brace Jovanovich, 1983), p. 155.

20. St. Clair Drake and Horace Cayton, *Black Metropolis: A Study of Negro Life in a Northern City*, with an introduction by Richard Wright (New York: Harcourt, Brace, 1945).

21. H. L. Gates, Jr., "Writing, 'Race,' and the Difference It Makes," in *Loose Canons* (New York and Oxford: Oxford University Press, 1992), pp. 51–55.

22. "How Bigger Was Born" published as the introduction to the Penguin edition of *Native Son* (Harmondsworth, 1979), p. 31.

23. Addison Gayle, *Ordeal of a Native Son* (Garden City, N.Y.: Anchor Press, 1980).

24. 24 Other members of the Chicago club during Wright's tenure were Nelson Algren, Jackson Pollock, and Ben Shahn. Wright became an editor of Left Front, the journal of the clubs in the midwest.

25. Wright's own account of these events is set down in the second part of his autobiography, which was separated by its publisher from the first section, *Black Boy*, and published years later as *American Hunger* (London: Gollancz, 1978), and in Anthony Crosland's anthology *The God That Failed* (New York: Harper, 1949) as "I Tried to Be a Communist."

26. The discussion of this text in Houston Baker's *Workings of the Spirit* (Chicago: University of Chicago Press, 1991) is a notable exception.

27. Arnold Rampersad, Foreword to *Lawd Today* (Boston: Northeastern University Press, 1986).

28. "In its secular form, black chauvinism derives, ironically enough from European racial theory. Like the concept of civilization, racial chauvinism can be traced back to the writings of Hegel, Guizot, Gobineau and other continental racial theo-

rists of the nineteenth century. Indeed it was the German, Herder, who in the eighteenth century, developed theories of organic collectivism upon which Blyden and Crummell later built their own brand of ethnic chauvinism." Wilson Moses, *The Golden Age of Black Nationalism, 1850–1925* (New York and Oxford: Oxford University Press, 1988), p. 25.

29. Bernard W. Bell, *The Folk Roots of Contemporary Afro-American Poetry* (Detroit: Broadside Press, 1974).

30. Ellison, *Going to the Territory*, p. 208.

31. "Red Clay Blues," a collaboration with Langston Hughes, was published in the *New Masses*, August 1, 1939. The collaboration with Basie and Robeson was recorded in 1941 and released on Okeh (6475); see Fabre, *Unfinished Quest*, p. 236.

32. London: Collier Books, 1963, pp. 7–12.

33. *White Man Listen!*, pp. 90–91.

34. Paul Oliver, *The Meaning of the Blues* (New York: Collier Books, 1963), p. 9.

35. Wright, "How Bigger Was Born," p. 15.

36. Wright, *The Outsider*, p. 140.

37. Ibid., p. 88.

38. Ibid., p. 140.

39. "The Man Who Lived Underground," in *Eight Men* (New York: Pyramid Books, 1969), pp. 54–55.

40. C. L. R. James, "Black Studies and the Contemporary Student," in *At the Rendezvous of Victory* (London: Allison and Busby, 1984), p. 196.

41. Fabre, *Unfinished Quest*, p. 333; Webb, *A Biography*, p. 326.

42. Richard Wright, Foreword to George Padmore, *Pan-Africanism or Communism* (London: Dobson, 1956), pp. 11–14.

43. Wright, *White Man Listen!*, p. 6.

44. See Wright, *The Outsider*, p. 129: "Negroes as they enter our culture, are going to inherit the problems we have but with a difference. They are outsiders and they are going to *know* that they have these problems. They are going to be self-conscious; they are going to be gifted with a double vision, for, being Negroes, they are going to be both *inside* and *outside* of our culture at the same time. Every emotional and cultural convulsion that ever shook the heart and soul of Western man will shake them. Negroes will develop unique and specially defined psychological types. They will become psychological men, like the Jews . . . They will not be Americans or Negroes; they will be centers of *knowing*, so to speak . . ."

45. *White Man Listen!*, p. 2.

46. Ibid., p. 53.

47. *Pagan Spain*, p. 192.

48. Wright, Foreword to Drake and Cayton, *Black Metropolis*, p. xx.

49. *The Outsider*, p. 423.

50. Ibid., p. 384.

51. Ibid., p. 377.

52. Wright interviewed by William Gardner Smith, *Ebony* 8 (July 1953): 40.

53. *The Outsider*, p. 366.

54. Ibid., p. 364.

55. Ibid., pp. 366–367.

56. *White Man Listen!*, p. 73.

57. *The Outsider*, p. 366.

58. Wright, "The Voiceless Ones," *Saturday Review*, April 16, 1960, p. 22.

59. Wilson Record, *The Negro and the Communist Party* (New York: Atheneum, 1971); Mark Naison, *Communists in Harlem during the Depression* (Urbana and London: University of Illinois Press, 1983).

60. Wright, "Blueprint for Negro Writing," *New Challenge* (Fall 1937), rpt. in *Race and Class* 21, no. 4 (Spring 1980): 403–412.

61. Ibid., pp. 404–405.

62. Ibid., p. 405.

63. Ibid., p. 409.

64. "Psychiatry Comes to Harlem," *Freeworld*, no. 12 (September 1946): 49–51.

65. Octave Mannoni, *Prospero and Caliban: The Psychology of Colonization* (Ann Arbor: Ann Arbor Paperbacks, 1990); Jock McCulloch, *Black Soul, White Artifact: Fanon's Clinical Psychology and Social Theory* (Cambridge: Cambridge University Press, 1983), p. 17. McCulloch is correct to emphasise that Fanon's relationship to Mannoni was complex and changed between his early and later works. The critique of Mannoni in *Black Skin, White Masks* (London: Pluto, 1986), pp. 83–108, is misleading for this reason, and Fanon gets closer to his arguments in *Wretched of the Earth* (Harmondsworth: Penguin, 1977), pp. 200–250. On the relationship of Wright and Fanon see the 1953 letter from Fanon to Wright reprinted in Ray, Farnsworth, and Davis, *Richard Wright: Impressions and Perspectives*, p. 150.

66. *The Outsider*, p. 135.

67. Ibid., p. 425.

68. "Your Nietzsche, your Hegel, your Jaspers, your Heidegger, your Husserl, your Kierkegaard, and your Dostoevski were the clues . . . I said to myself that we were dealing with a man who had wallowed in guilty thought." Ibid., p. 421.

69. Ibid., p. 140.

70. Ibid., p. 372.

71. Ibid., p. 422.

72. Fabre, *Unfinished Quest*; Amiri Baraka, *Daggers and Javelins* (New York: Quill, 1984), pp. 145–147 and p. 181; Charles T. Davis, *Black Is the Color of the Cosmos* (New York and London: Garland, 1982), p. 275.

73. The account of bullfighting in *Pagan Spain* seems to bear the mark of Bataille's influence.

74. Baldwin, "Alas Poor Richard," p. 148.

75. Miriam DeCosta-Willis, "Avenging Angels and Mute Mothers: Black Southern Women in Wright's Fictional World," *Callaloo* 28, vol. 9, no. 3 (Summer 1986): 540–551; Maria K. Mootry, "Bitches, Whores and Woman Haters: Archetypes and Topologics in the Art of Richard Wright," in R. Macksey and F. E. Moorer, eds., *Richard Wright: A Collection of Critical Essays* (Englewood Cliffs, N.J.: Prentice Hall, 1984); Sylvia H. Keady, "Richard Wright's Women Characters and Inequality," *Black American Literature Forum* (Winter 1976): 124–128; Diane Long Hoeveler, "Oedipus Agonistes: Mothers and Sons in Richard Wright's Fiction," *Black American Literature Forum* (Summer 1978): 65–68.

76. Ellison, *Shadow and Act*, pp. 85–86.

77. Baldwin, "Alas Poor Richard," p. 151.

78. Margaret Walker, *Richard Wright: Daemonic Genius* (New York: Warner Books, 1988).

79. For example, *Pagan Spain*'s foregrounding of women's experiences under fascism would seem to be an anomaly in need of some explanation.

80. *Présence Africaine*, no. 8–9–10 (June–November 1956): 348.

81. Henry Louis Gates, Jr., "A Negro Way of Saying," *New York Times Book Review*, April 21, 1985; Barbara Johnson, *A World of Difference* (Baltimore: Johns Hopkins University Press, 1987). June Jordan escapes this polarisation in her classic essay "Towards a Black Balancing of Love and Hate," in *Civil Wars* (Boston: Beacon Press, 1981).

82. Richard Wright, "Between Laughter and Tears," *New Masses*, October 5, 1937.

83. David Bradley, Foreword to the American reissue of *Eight Men* (New York: Thunder's Mouth Press, 1987).

84. *Eight Men*, p. 189.

85. Ibid., p. 194.

86. Ibid., p. 198.

87. A final unpublished novel, "Island of Hallucination," is held in the Beinecke Library at Yale University.

88. Wright, *The Long Dream* (New York: Harper, 1987), p. 36; see also pp. 204–205.

89. Ibid., p. 131.

90. Ibid., p. 264.

91. Ibid., pp. 264–265.

92. Ibid., pp. 78–79.

93. Deidre Bair, *Simone de Beauvoir* (London: Cape, 1990), pp. 388–389; A. Madsen, *Hearts and Minds* (New York: Morrow, 1977), p. 134.

6. "Not a Story to Pass On": Living Memory and the Slave Sublime

1. "Africalogy is defined, therefore, as the Afrocentric study of phenomena, events, ideas and personalities related to Africa. The mere study of phenomena of Africa is not Africalogy but some other intellectual enterprise. The scholar who generates research questions based on the centrality of Africa is engaged in a very different research enquiry than one who imposes Western criteria on the phenomena . . . Afrocentric is perhaps the most important word in the above definition of Africalogy. Otherwise one could easily think that any study of African phenomena or people constitutes Africalogy." Molefi Kete Asante, *Kemet, Afrocentricity and Knowledge* (Trenton, N.J.: Africa World Press, 1990), p. 14.

2. Asante, *Afrocentricity*, rev. ed. (Trenton, N.J.: Africa World Press, 1989), p. viii. Asante suggests that Afrocentric psychological theories have close affinities with the work of Jung; see *Kemet*, pp. 180–183.

3. Rebel MC, "Soul Rebel," Desire Records, London, 1991.

4. Asante, *Kemet*, p. 15.

5. Frances Cress Welsing, *The Isis Papers: The Keys to the Colors* (Chicago: Third World Press, 1990); Richard King, *African Origin of Biological Psychiatry* (New

York: Seymour Smith, 1990); Michael Eric Dyson, "A Struggle for the Black Mind: Melanin Madness," *Emerge* 3, no. 4 (February 1992).

6. Asante, *Afrocentricity*, pp. 106–107.

7. Ibid., p. 104.

8. I have found Julia Kristeva's remarks on different temporalities in "Women's Time" very helpful in framing this argument. Her essay appears in *Feminist Theory: A Critique of Ideology*, ed. Nannerl O. Keohane et al. (Brighton: Harvester Press, 1981), pp. 31–54. See also Homi K. Bhabha's adaptation of Kristeva's work to the post-colonial predicament in *Nation and Narration* (London: Routledge, 1990).

9. Asante's assertion that Fanon wrote "in the tradition established by Garvey and Du Bois" is one example of this; *Kemet*, p. 179. He also puzzles over the fact that black Americans are only 47 percent of new world blacks. All the "essential grounds" of his theory of Afrocentricity are drawn from African-American history; see *Afrocentricity*, pp. 1–30.

10. Kwame Anthony Appiah, *In My Father's House* (London: Methuen, 1992).

11. I attempt this in "It's a Family Affair," in Gina C. Dent, ed., *Black Popular Culture* (Seattle: Bay Press, 1992).

12. Richard Wright, *Black Power: A Record of Reactions in a Land of Pathos* (New York: Harper and Brothers, 1954), pp. 346–347.

13. "A Dialogue with Karenga," *Emerge* 3, no. 3 (January 1992), p. 11.

14. Shahrazad Ali, *The Blackman's Guide to Understanding the Blackwoman* (Philadelphia: Civilized Publications, 1989), p. 40.

15. This evasive possibility was recently signified by its absence in the narratives of Clarence Thomas and Anita Hill, Mike Tyson and Desiree Washington.

16. "How Black Men Are Responding to the Black Male Crisis," *Ebony Man* (September 1991): 36.

17. "America, in the eighties was essentially about taking black men's jobs, lives—and souls. In fact, it was really a war about money and how it was used, a war about lies and how those lies were deployed to cover the strategy and tactics of the war makers." William Strickland, "Taking Our Souls," *Essence* 22, no. 7, 10th Annual Men's Issue (November 1991): 48.

18. The first congress had been held in the Amphitheatre Descartes at the Sorbonne in 1956.

19. *Présence Africaine*, no. 24–25 (February–May 1959).

20. Ibid., pp. 45–54.

21. Jürgen Habermas, *The Philosophical Discourse of Modernity* (Cambridge: Polity Press, 1987), pp. 1–22.

22. *Postmodernism; or, The Cultural Logic of Late Capitalism* (Durham: Duke University Press, 1991), p. 154.

23. Freud makes this point when discussing the significance of gramophone records on memory in *Civilisation and Its Discontents* (London: Hogarth Press, 1975), p. 28: "In the photographic camera he [man] has created an instrument which retains the fleeting visual impressions, just as a gramophone disc retains the equally fleeting auditory ones; both are at bottom materializations of the power he possesses of recollection, his memory."

24. James Brown with Bruce Tucker, *James Brown: The Godfather of Soul* (New York: Macmillan, 1986), p. 221.

25. Fred Zindi, *Roots: Rocking in Zimbabwe* (Gweru: Mambo Press, 1985).

26. Veit Erlmann, *African Stars: Studies in Black South African Performance* (Chicago: University of Chicago Press, 1991), ch. 2.

27. P. D. Cole, "Lagos Society in the Nineteenth Century," in A. B. Aderibigbe, ed., *Lagos: The Development of an African City* (Lagos: Longman, 1975); and M. Echeruo, *Victorian Lagos* (London: Macmillan, 1976).

28. I am thinking here of Sterling Stuckey's work on ring rituals, *Slave Culture: Nationalist Theory and the Foundations of Black America* (New York and Oxford: Oxford University Press, 1987), ch. 1.

29. Walter Benjamin, "The Storyteller," *Illuminations* (London: Fontana, 1973), p. 91.

30. See my book *There Ain't No Black in the Union Jack* (London: Hutchinson, 1987), ch. 5, where I suggest that an anti-capitalist political stance is constructed from three discernible elements: a politics around work and its overcoming, a politics around law and its disassociation from racial domination, and a folk historicism that sets special store by the recovery of historical sensibility.

31. Charles Keil, *Urban Blues* (Chicago: University of Chicago Press, 1970), p. 152.

32. "I think Bootsy learned a lot from me. When I met him he was playing a lot of bass—the ifs, the ands, and the buts. I got him to see the importance of the *one* in funk—the downbeat at the beginning of every bar. I got him to key in on the dynamic parts of the one instead of playing all around it. Then he could do all his other stuff in the right places—*after* the one." Brown with Tucker, *Godfather of Soul,* pp. 218–219.

33. Ellison, *Invisible Man* (Harmondsworth: Penguin, 1976), p. 11.

34. Gilroy, *There Ain't No Black in the Union Jack,* ch. 5.

35. I am thinking, for example, of Charles Mingus's autobiographical volume *Beneath the Underdog* (Harmondsworth: Penguin, 1975).

36. James Baldwin, "Of the Sorrow Songs: The Cross of Redemption," *Views on Black American Music,* no. 2 (1984–85): 12.

37. Wright, *White Man Listen!* (New York: Anchor Books, 1964), p. 79.

38. Ray Charles with David Ritz, *Brother Ray* (New York: Dial Press, 1978), p. 190.

39. Percy Mayfield interviewed by Dick Shurman in *Living Blues* (March 1981): 24.

40. It may illuminate his work to say that Mayfield is the closest that the world of rhythm and blues gets to the cosmic pessimism of Giacomo Leopardi.

41. See for example *Drums and Shadows: Survival Studies among the Georgia Coastal Negroes,* by the Savannah Unit of the Georgia Writers' Project (Athens: University of Georgia Press, 1940).

42. Percy Mayfield, "The River's Invitation," on *The Incredible Percy Mayfield,* Specialty Records, SNTF 5010, 1972.

43. Deuteronomy 28: 25.

44. A. Hertzberg, *The French Enlightenment and the Jews* (New York: Columbia University Press, 1990); L. Poliakov, *The History of Anti-Semitism,* vol. 1 (Oxford: Oxford University Press, 1985); Zygmunt Bauman, *Modernity and the Holocaust* (Cambridge: Polity, 1988), and *Intimations of Postmodernity* (London: Routledge, 1991); Leon Poliakov, *The Aryan Myth* (London: Sussex University Press, 1974);

Gershom Scholem, *From Berlin to Jerusalem: Memories of My Youth,* trans. Harry Zohn (New York: Schocken Books, 1980), and *The Messianic Idea in Judaism and Other Essays on Jewish Spirituality* (New York: Schocken, 1971); George Mosse, *Nationalism and Sexuality* (Madison: University of Wisconsin Press, 1985); Paul Lawrence Rose, *Revolutionary Anti-Semitism in Germany from Kant to Wagner* (Princeton, N.J.: Princeton University Press, 1990).

45. Robert Alter, *Necessary Angels: Tradition and Modernity in Kafka, Benjamin, and Scholem* (Cambridge, Mass.: Harvard University Press, 1991), ch. 2, "On Not Knowing Hebrew."

46. Ella Shohat, "Sephardim in Israel: Zionism from the Standpoint of Its Jewish Victims," *Social Text* 19/20 (Fall 1988).

47. Fredric Jameson, "History and Class Consciousness as an Unfinished Project," *Rethinking Marxism* 1, no. 1 (Spring 1988): 70. See also Marianna Torgovnick's discussion of Lévi-Strauss's *Tristes Tropiques:* "he is motivated by his sense of danger as a Jew, and besieges the visa offices . . . he saw himself 'as potential fodder for the concentration camp.' This tiny private moment in the text moves me: it captures a sense of the doubleness and duplicity of the self (so typical of modernity in general)." *Savage Intellects, Modern Lives* (Chicago: University of Chicago Press, 1990), p. 211.

48. James Cone, *The Spirituals and the Blues: An Interpretation* (Westport, Conn.: Greenwood Press, 1980), p. 108.

49. Albert Raboteau, *Slave Religion* (New York and Oxford: Oxford University Press, 1980), p. 311.

50. Among the other black figures who have been compared to Moses are Harriet Tubman, conductor on the Underground Railroad, and the soul singer Isaac Hayes, who made elaborate use of the Moses myth during the early 1970s.

51. Ben Halpern, "Exile: Abstract Condition and Concrete Community," in "Negating the Diaspora: A Symposium," *Jewish Frontier* 47, no. 10 (December 1979): 9; Elliott P. Skinner, "The Dialectic between Diasporas and Homelands," in J. E. Harris, ed., *Global Dimensions of the African Diaspora* (Washington, D.C.: Howard University Press, 1982).

52. See for example Julius Lester's *Long Journey Home* (London: Longman, 1972); it is also a good example of the process of ritual tale telling as a political practice.

53. Hollis R. Lynch, *Edward Wilmot Blyden, 1832–1912: Pan Negro Patriot* (Oxford and New York: Oxford University Press, 1967), p. 54.

54. Blyden, *From West Africa to Palestine* (Freetown, 1873), p. 112.

55. See V. Y. Mudimbe, *The Invention of Africa* (Bloomington and Indianapolis: University of Indiana Press, 1988), ch. 4; and Léopold Senghor, "Edward Wilmot Blyden: Precursor of Negritude," Foreword to Hollis R. Lynch, ed., *Selected Letters of Edward Wilmot Blyden* (Millwood, N.J.: Kraus Thomson International, 1976), pp. xix–xx.

56. Edward Wilmot Blyden, *The Jewish Question* (Liverpool: Lionel Hart, 1989), p. 5. "The Jews, as witnesses of the Supreme Being, are an indispensable element— if at present a suppressed element—in the spiritual culture and regeneration of humanity. I have for many years—indeed since my childhood—been an earnest student of the history of God's chosen people. I do not refer merely to the general teaching which every child brought up in the Christian religion receives in Old

Testament history . . . but also to that special teaching outside of books, which comes from contact with living illustrations."

57. Ibid., p. 7.

58. Hollis R. Lynch, "A Black Nineteenth-Century Response to Jews and Zionism: The Case of Edward Wilmot Blyden," in Joseph R. Washington, Jr., ed., *Jews in Black Perspectives: A Dialogue* (Lanham, Md. and London: University Press of America, 1989). Blyden's pamphlet *The Jewish Question* sets out his own account of this relationship.

59. H. Kohn, *Prophets and Peoples: Studies in Nineteenth-Century Nationalism* (London: Macmillan, 1946).

60. E. W. Blyden, "Africa and the Africans," *Fraser's Magazine* 18 (August 1878): 188. See also his "Mixed Races in Liberia," *Annual Report of the Board of Regents of the Smithsonian Institution* (Washington, D.C.: 1871), pp. 386–388.

61. *The Jewish Question*, p. 5.

62. E. W. Blyden, *Christianity, Islam and the Negro Race* (1887; rpt. Edinburgh: Edinburgh University Press, 1967), p. 120.

63. *The Jewish Question*, p. 11.

64. George Shepperson, "African Diaspora: Concept and Context," in Joseph E. Harris, ed., *Global Dimensions of the African Diaspora*, pp. 46–53.

65. Senghor, "Blyden: Precursor of Negritude," pp. xix–xx.

66. See Paul Gilroy, "Steppin' out of Babylon: Race, Class and Community," in *The Empire Strikes Back* (London: CCCS/Hutchinson, 1982).

67. W. E. B. Du Bois, *The Autobiography of W. E. B. Du Bois* (New York: International Publishers, 1968), p. 122.

68. Ibid., p. 175.

69. T.W. Adorno, *Aesthetic Theory* (London: Routledge, 1984), p. 192.

70. Peter Linebaugh, "Jubilating; or, How the Atlantic Working Class Used the Biblical Jubilee against Capitalism with Some Success," *New Enclosures: Midnight Notes* 10 (Fall 1990).

71. This charge is made by Michael Burleigh and Wolfgang Wippermann in *The Racial State: Germany, 1933–1945* (Cambridge: Cambridge University Press, 1991).

72. Robert Proctor's book *Racial Hygiene: Medicine under the Nazis* (Cambridge, Mass.: Harvard University Press, 1988) is a rare and valuable exception to this rule.

73. Zygmunt Bauman, *Intimations of Postmodernity* (London: Routledge, 1991), p. 225.

74. Zygmunt Bauman, *Modernity and the Holocaust* (Cambridge: Polity Press, 1989), p. 45.

75. "Yes, it was not a question of the number of people, it was the way, the way . . . Well the number, there were plenty of numbers as well: but the flesh . . . of the murdered people transported on lorries . . . it was referred to in neutral terms— die Scheiss—they weren't human bodies. That was what was exceptional. It was murder carried out in contempt, more than in hatred . . ." Raoul Mortley, ed., *French Philosophers in Conversation* (London: Routledge, 1991), p. 21.

76. Gustav Spiller, ed., *Papers on Inter-Racial Problems: Universal Races Congress* (London: P. S. King and Son, 1911); E. M. Rudwick, "W. E. B. Dubois and the Universal Races Congress of 1911," *Phylon* 20, no. 4 (1959): 372–378; and

"Report of the First Universal Races Congress," *African Times and Orient Review* 1, no. 1 (July 1912): 27–30.

77. Richard M. Lerner, *Final Solutions: Biology, Prejudice and Genocide* (University Park: Pennsylvania State University Press, 1992); Benno Muller Hill, *Murderous Science: Elimination by Scientific Selection of Jews, Gypsies and Others, Germany, 1933–1945* (Oxford: Oxford University Press, 1988). Bauman discusses this work and the work of Robert Proctor in ch. 1 of his *Modernity and Ambivalence* (Ithaca: Cornell University Press, 1991).

78. Primo Levi, *The Drowned and the Saved* (London: Abacus, 1988), p. 41.

79. Ibid., p. 100.

80. Jean-François Lyotard, *The Inhuman* (Cambridge: Polity, 1992).

81. Keith D. Miller, *Voice of Deliverance: The Language of Martin Luther King and Its Sources* (New York: Free Press, 1992); Cornel West, "The Religious Foundations of the Thought of Martin Luther King, Jr.," in Peter J. Albert and Ronald Hoffman, eds., *We Shall Overcome: Martin Luther King and the Black Freedom Struggle* (New York: Pantheon, 1990). See also James H. Cone, *For My People: Black Theology and the Black Church* (Braamfontein: Skotaville Publishers, 1985).

82. James Baldwin, "Negroes Are Anti-Semitic Because They Are Anti-White," in *The Price of the Ticket* (London: Michael Joseph, 1985), p. 428.

83. Harold Cruse, "Negroes and Jews: The Two Nationalisms and the Bloc(ked) Plurality," in *The Crisis of the Negro Intellectual* (New York: Quill, 1984).

84. Baldwin, *The Price*, p. 430.

85. Stanley Crouch, "Aunt Medea," in *Notes of a Hanging Judge* (New York: Oxford University Press, 1990), p. 205.

86. Walter Benjamin, *Illuminations* (London: Fontana, 1973), p. 101.

87. Interview with Morrison, published as "Living Memory: Meeting Toni Morrison," in Paul Gilroy, *Small Acts* (London: Serpent's Tail, 1993), pp. 175–182.

88. Mari Evans, ed., *Black Women Writers: Arguments and Interviews* (London: Pluto Press, 1983), p. 340.

89. Gilroy, "Living Memory."

90. *Dessa Rose* (London: Futura, 1988), p. 23. A useful exploration of the nineteenth-century American literature on slave management is provided by James O. Breeden, ed., *Advice among Masters: The Ideal in Slave Management in the Old South* (Westport, Conn.: Greenwood Press, 1980).

91. Morrison, *Beloved* (London: Cape, 1988), p. 193.

92. "The 'I' that I was, was a mosaic of many countries, a patchwork of others and objects stretching backwards to perhaps the beginning of time. What I felt, seeing this, was indebtedness. What I felt, plainly, was a transmission to those on deck of all I had pilfered, as though I was but a conduit or window through which my pillage and booty of 'experience' passed." Charles Johnson, *Middle Passage* (New York: Atheneum, 1990), p. 162.

93. "Dualism is a bloody structure of the mind. Subject and object, perceiver and perceived, self and other—these ancient twins are built into mind like the stem piece of a merchantman." Ibid., p. 98.

94. "When three centuries ago the slaves came to the West Indies, they entered directly into the large-scale agriculture of the sugar plantation, which was a modern system. It further required that the slaves live together in a social relation far closer

than any proletariat of the time. The cane when reaped had to be rapidly transported to what was factory production. Even the cloth the slaves wore and the food they ate was imported. The Negroes, therefore, from the very start lived a life that was in its essence a modern life. That is their history—as far as I have been able to discover, a unique history." James, *The Black Jacobins* (London: Allison and Busby, 1980), appendix, p. 392.

95. "Negro slaves in America represented the worst and lowest conditions among *modern* labourers. One estimate is that the maintenance of a slave in the South cost the master $19 a year, which means that they were among the poorest paid labourers in the *modern* world" (emphasis added). W. E. B. Du Bois, *Black Reconstruction in America* (New York: Atheneum, 1977), p. 9.

96. "Living Memory."

97. Homi Bhabha, "Post-colonial Authority and Post-modern Guilt," in ed. L. Grossberg et al., eds., *Cultural Studies* (New York: Routledge, 1992).

98. "Living Memory."

99. David Bradley, *The Chaneysville Incident* (London: Serpent's Tail, 1986).

100. "Living Memory."

101. Charles Chesnutt's *The Marrow of Tradition* (Boston and New York: Houghton, Mifflin, 1901) and Arna Bontemps's *Black Thunder* (New York: Macmillan, 1936) are two older books that come to mind here, the former through its treatment of lynching, the latter through its reconstruction of a slave rebellion.

Acknowledgements

A kind of fragile community can be composed of people who disagree with one another, constituted by the fruitful mode of disagreement that grows with discipline and mutual respect. With that possibility in mind I would like to thank the people who have argued with me over the contents of this book during the years it has taken me to write it. I have had detailed comments on parts of it from Stuart Hall, Barnor Hesse, Hedda Ekerwald, Isaac Julien, Dick Hebdige, Iain Chambers, bell hooks, Roland François Lack, Angela McRobbie, Cora Kaplan, and Eddie Glaude. It is much better than it would have been as a result of these stimulating conversations. Though he did not look at this manuscript, my discussions and disagreements with Kobena Mercer also helped me to clarify my thoughts.

Sections of the book were presented as academic papers and talks at Duke University; Essex University; the University of Pennsylvania, Trinity College in Hartford; New York University; Claremont Colleges; Oberlin College; the University of California, Santa Barbara, Santa Cruz, and Davis; Stockholm University; University College, Birkbeck College, and Goldsmiths' College, all of the University of London; Cheltenham and Gloucester College of Education; St. Anthony's College, Oxford; and the Istituto Universitario Orientale in Naples. I would like to thank the people who arranged these visits and everybody who bothered to come and re spond to my lectures.

I should also thank the former colleagues who helped me out in various ways: Laurence Marlow, Tony Woodiwiss, Mary Girling, Brenda Corti, Peter Hulme, and Elaine Jordan.

Other people have encouraged and supported me in London. Thanks under this heading to Mandy Rose, David A. Bailey, Karen Alexander, Cynthia Rose, Pratibha Parmar, Patrick Wright, and Beryl Gilroy.

Friends in the United States have also helped in different ways. I thank Hazel Carby and Mike Denning above all for their assistance with books and other obscure library demands; Professor Ed Gordon for making it possible for me to visit Yale; James Clifford for the stimulating discussions we had while commuting and a great deal more; Gloria Watkins for seeing things no-one else can see; Manthia Diawara for his sceptical view of African American particularity; and Professor Houston A. Baker, Jr., for helping me to get "There Ain't No Black in the Union Jack" into print on acid-free paper with the University of Chicago Press. Mick Taussig's encouragement was appreciated, as was Dana Seman's occasional provision of a home from home.

A different type of gratitude is due to Bill French of the University Place Bookstore in Manhattan; Pete Webb of Compendium Books in Camden Town; Integrity in Music in Weatherfield, Connecticut; and Honest John's in Portobello Road. Thanks to Mark Ainley especially for 24 Karat Black and to Kellie Jones for sharing my fatal enthusiasm for vinyl. One day the complete works of Rudy Ray Moore will be ours.

My initial exposure to the Fisk Jubilee Singers resulted from Pat Preston's thoughtfulness. I would like to thank her now for that generous gift from the library of her late husband. The trail it opened up led me to the black Atlantic via the Archive Bookstore in Bell Street and a signed first edition. I am grateful to Val Wilmer for the loan of several rare items from her own collection. Along with Yvonne Occampo, Peter Linebaugh, and Flemming Røgilds, she is appreciated here for the example she sets and various forms of practical help.

Robert Reid Pharr, Sandhya Shukla, and Anne-Marie Fortier challenged me in dialogues that grew out of their own research projects.

Anthony Jackson, the greatest bass player on the planet, whose quirky, elemental genius is something I strive to emulate, is thanked here for the pleasure his dissonant work has given me while writing and thinking about black culture.

Finally, but also firstly, I have an unquantifiable debt to Vron Ware, my co-parent, ideal reader, and sternest, most constructive critic.

Index